the National Wildflower Research Center's

WILDFLOWER
handbook

the National Wildflower Research Center's
WILDFLOWER
handbook

The National Wildflower Research Center is a nonprofit organization dedicated to researching and promoting wildflowers to further their economic, environmental, and aesthetic use in North America.

Members of the Wildflower Center receive subscriptions to *Wildflower*, the newsletter and *Wildflower, Journal of the National Wildflower Research Center*, 10 percent discount on unique Center products from a colorful catalog, special advance notice of and discounts to Center seminars, a membership card, and other privileges from the Clearinghouse.

National Wildflower Research Center
2600 FM 973 North
Austin, Texas 78725-4201
(512) 929-3600

★
TexasMonthlyPress

Texas Monthly Press
P.O. Box 1569
Austin, Texas 78767

A   B   C   D   E   F   G   H

Library of Congress Cataloging-in-Publication Data

The National Wildflower Research Centers wildflower handbook.

Bibliography: p.
1. Wild flower gardening—United States—
handbooks, manuals, etc.   2. Native plant
gardening—United States—Handbooks, manuals,
etc.   3. Wild flowers—United States—Handbooks,
manuals, etc.   4. Native plants for cultivation—
United States—Handbooks, manuals, etc.
I. National Wildflower Research Center (U.S.)
SB439.N38   1989   635.9'676   89-4346
ISBN 0-87719-167-0

Book design and illustrations by Rosario Baxter

ACKNOWLEDGMENTS

Editor:	Annie Paulson
Staff contributors:	Beth Anderson
	Elinor Crank
	Katy Kramer-McKinney
	David K. Northington
	Annie Paulson
Assistant editor:	Candace Kiene
Volunteer support:	Beth Blair
	David Dunlap
	John Gleason
	Fiona Otten
	Christine Wotkyns
Additional contributors:	Christina Allday-Bondy
	Mae Daniller

Special thanks to members of the
National Wildflower Research Center's Board of Trustees
who serve on the Publications Committee:

Nash Castro
Marie Schwartz
Marybeth Weston-Bergman

TABLE OF CONTENTS

Rudbeckia hirta

INTRODUCTION The National Wildflower Research

Center is an organization dedicated to the study of wildflowers, native grasses, shrubs and trees, and to encouraging their propagation and use in planned landscapes.

We are a proponent of conservation efforts to protect as much of our native flora as possible and to reestablish components of that flora. Specifically, we strongly encourage the use of *propagated, indigenous natives* in planned landscapes. Though we do not feel that removal of naturalized species is realistic, control of invasive species is needed, and the introduction of foreign species to our native flora is unwise and unnecessary.

There is no reliable method of predicting the outcome when a species from another country or even a different habitat within our continent is introduced. It may naturalize successfully, become invasively aggressive, or not adapt and fail to establish. The best possible outcome is successful naturalization, and even that is not desirable because of the effect on existing native species.

Our efforts to carry this message to the public include publication of our newsletter, our journal, information fact sheets from our Clearinghouse, and popular and technical articles in newspapers, magazines, and newsletters; sponsorship of local and regional seminars, workshops, and conferences; participation in programs of related organizations; and now, the publication of this resource book.

The intent of this publication is to provide a single source for basic information needed by the general public, and by professionals in a broad range of disciplines. The network of interested audiences includes landscape architects, botanists, ecologists, resource managers, conservationists, landscape contractors, grounds maintenance staff, vegetation managers, land planners, home owners, developers, taxonomists, native plant societies, seed producers, restorationists and others.

The increased propagation and reestablishment of native plant species provides regional aesthetic beauty, allows for sound economic management of water and other resources, and helps replenish the native flora upon which the ecological stability of each region depends.

Only humans, our domesticated animals, and our cultivated crops and plants exist outside of Earth's naturally balanced ecosystems. Our conversion of natural habitats to pastures and cropland, housing developments and other manmade habitats has been extensive. The result has been the loss of habitats where native flora and fauna can thrive and reproduce.

The continued loss of native species, and their replacement with nonnative, ornamental species that do not fit easily into existing ecosystems, are threatening the ecological balance that is necessary for all living organisms to survive—including humans.

We use plants in residential and commercial landscapes to provide shade and decrease reflective light, and to reduce heat in homes and offices. Plants stabilize our hillsides, preventing erosion and mudslides. And importantly, plants provide us with a psychologically pleasing setting, which experts tell us is essential to stress reduction and relaxation.

Learning how to increase our use of hardy, drought-resistant, indigenous native plant species will allow us to have the best of all worlds. We can enjoy our landscaped areas; we can protect our water supply; we can increase ecological stability; and we can preserve the genetic information essential to native plants' continued existence and our future utilization of them.

As a basic guide to terms used throughout this publication, the following definitions are offered:

1. *Wildflowers.* Flowering plants, native to a specific geographical area or habitat, capable of growing in unimproved habitats without the assistance of humans; normally assumed to have attractive, showy flowers. Wildflowers can include naturalized species that coexist with the other plants in the same habitat, but are not aggressively competitive or invasive.

2. *Native plants.* Grasses, shrubs, vines, trees, and herbaceous wildflowers that exist in a given region (e.g. North America) through nonhuman introduction.

3. *Naturalized plants.* Plants that have been introduced by humans and have escaped cultivation. They have successfully existed in the wild for a sufficient period to have survived normal climatic fluctuations for the area.

4. *Indigenous.* Wildflowers and native plants found in a specific geographical area or habitat type; a species indigenous to the piedmont soils of the Southeast, for example.

5. *Weed.* A plant growing where you do not want it. The term implies an aggressive and probably unsightly plant that is difficult to remove, and is often found in disturbed or cultivated habitats. A weedy species that is displacing native and successfully naturalized plants is termed an invasive weed.

6. *Exotic.* A plant that has been introduced from another area, often a thoroughly different kind of habitat in another part of the world. Exotics are used as ornamentals in landscaping, and many of them have been horticulturally selected or bred for improved flower size, new colors, or lush vegetation.

7. *Conservation.* Protection of our native plants and their natural habitats through wise land management; the establishment of wilderness areas, preserves, and natural areas; and careful development in unprotected areas to save as much of the native flora as possible.

8. *Planned landscape.* An area that has been planted with a desired result in mind. The term implies a landscaped area as opposed to a natural area; however, an area that has purposefully been managed as a natural area or natural-looking landscape also fits the description.

9. *Propagated.* Reproduced either sexually, by seed; or vegeta-

tively, by cuttings from stems, roots, or buds. Container-grown plants are usually propagated in a soil-free medium in a controlled environment.

I hope the information contained in this resource book both encourages you to become involved in the propagation and establishment of wildflowers and native grasses, shrubs and trees, and assists you in the success of those efforts. There is still much to learn. Many years of research and work are needed to answer questions and solve problems that arise in landscaping with native plants. This accumulation of materials and resources, however, should provide the needed impetus for many to begin or expand their efforts in each region of the country.

David K. Northington, Ph.D.
Executive Director
National Wildflower Research Center

Oenothera speciosa

WHAT YOU SHOULD KNOW ABOUT WILDFLOWER MEADOW MIXES

Wildflower meadow seed mixes have become one of the hottest items at garden centers. Seed catalogs entice consumers with colorful photographs of wildflower fields, while nurseries stock their shelves with attractively labeled meadow mixes. Newspapers and magazines are filled with articles touting the low-maintenance advantages of meadow gardening. Purchasers of wildflower mixes are often misled by these advertisements and, unfortunately, expect spectacular results within a year with as little effort as casting a few seeds from a can.

The concept of creating a wildflower meadow is often misunderstood. Wildflower mixes are marketed through promises of instant wildflowers without the inconvenience of maintaining a lawn. Wildflowers can deliver low-maintenance advantages in time, but only if they are established correctly, and modeled after surrounding natural plant communities. Do not expect instant beauty with no work or maintenance! Remember that it has taken Mother Nature thousands of years and billions of seeds to produce her seasonal displays.

DEFINITION OF TERMS

What exactly is a wildflower? The National Wildflower Research Center defines a wildflower as a flowering native plant, indigenous to a specific geographical area or habitat (e.g., a plant indigenous to the piedmont soils of the Southeast) and capable of growing in unimproved habitats. The Wildflower Center encourages the public to plant only species native (indigenous) to their regions. Seed for many species is not currently produced or collected on a large scale. However, many large wildflower seed companies grow seed on contract or collect seed locally, and may be able to supply seed of indigenous species.

The definition of a *meadow* can vary. Some define a meadow as a grassland occurring in areas of high rainfall. Others define a meadow as a *prairie*, an area of low rainfall. Generally, a meadow is a mixture of grasses and flowers growing in a sunny, open area, often in a forested region. Natural meadows are found in areas where environmental factors limit growth of woody species and prevent stages of natural succession from occurring, e.g., alpine meadows or prairies. Most meadows, however, are a transitional stage, and will eventually be invaded and replaced by shrubs and trees.

Meadow gardeners usually try to improve on Mother Nature. Instead of being content with a field of grass with scattered wildflowers, they strive for a field of wildflowers with occasional clumps of grass. Grasses are an essential component of wildflower meadows, and most natural resource managers recommend a 50 to 80 percent component of native grasses in a meadow planting. People are often less familiar with grasses than they are with wildflowers. It is vital to learn to recognize valuable native grasses, and to discourage the growth of sod-forming, cold-season grasses and weedy aggressive grasses such as *Sorghum halepense* (Johnson grass).

Researchers at the Wildflower Center have tested many wildflower seed mixes available commercially. The Center has found that the wildflower seed industry follows two basic philosophies in developing mixes: the *shotgun* approach and the *regional* mix approach. The Wildflower Center has developed findings into general recommendations rather than endorsement of specific products.

SHOTGUN APPROACH

The shotgun approach to designing a mix is to attempt to cover a wide geographical area. These mixes contain seed for 20 to 30 species. Do not expect results from all species, however. The mixes have been developed to cover an extensive area — something will work somewhere. Some of the species that are guaranteed to be successful in the first year are wildflowers from other continents, wildflowers from elsewhere in this continent, or horticultural varieties.

Sometimes it is difficult to determine the amount of seed for each species that has been included in the mix. Percent-by-volume figures are not always on the labels, and because of the wide range of seed sizes, such a measurement is not particularly useful. Shotgun mixes may also include inexpensive, bulky filler seed, such as commonly cultivated flowers (not wildflowers), or cool-season grasses such as fescue. Often this filler seed is present in such large amounts as to crowd out most of the native species that germinate.

Many mixes create spectacular displays of exotic annual flowers the first year (e.g., bachelor's buttons or poppies), which fail to reseed and reappear the next season. Undesirable weed species may appear the following year, and the few perennials and native annuals that may be in the mix must struggle against them.

This scenario requires replanting the area each fall in order to produce a color display similar to the first year's. One publicized advantage of wildflower plantings, that they reseed each year, is lost if gardeners set their hearts on having a dramatic display of nonindigenous annuals each year.

REGIONAL MIX APPROACH

The regional mix approach to developing wildflower seed mixes is followed for the most part by small, local wildflower seed companies, which often obtain seed through local field-collection. Consequently, the mixes contain a high percentage of species native to the area for which they are marketed. The advantage of these mixes is that species they contain have a much greater chance for successful long-term establishment if planted in the appropriate area. By buying a mix that contains species that thrive in your area, you are investing your money wisely. Among the disadvantages of using regional mixes are limited supplies and variable seed quality.

Many larger seed companies are now producing regional wildflower seed mixes, composed partially of species native to the region being served and partially of species native to other areas with similar climatic conditions. In addition, the inclusion of nonnative, showy annual flowers is a common occurrence; as a result these are not true regional mixes. These mixes are commonly categorized and sold by geographical regions such as Southeast, Midwest, Southwest, and Northeast. While this is a step in the right direction, the key to both first-year and long-term planting success is to buy seed of indigenous species!

HOW TO BUY A WILDFLOWER MIX

As a consumer, you have control over the quality of what you purchase. Ideally, you should answer the following questions:

• *What wildflower species are included in the mix and which of these are indigenous to your area? Are nonnatives included?*

• *What percentage of the total mix does each species comprise? Is inexpensive bulk seed included as a high percentage of the mix?* Some producers of wildflower mixes will vary the composition depending upon availability of seeds. Often, mixtures contain an abundance of annuals, which provide a splash of color the first year. But a high percentage of nonnative annuals does not reseed the second year.

• *What percentage of the material in the package is seed, and what percentage is inert material such as chaff, other plant parts or other seeds?*

• *What are the germination test results for each species?* A lower germination rate indicates that more seed for that species needs to be included for a reasonable chance of producing a strong stand of flowers. Tests should have been conducted on the same seed lot and within the past six months.

• *What is the blooming season?* The mix should offer species that bloom successively, for a long-lasting display.

HOW TO CUSTOM MIX

There are many more questions than answers on the subject of mixing wildflower seed. That is why it is best to start small. Learn about meadow gardening in a small area, and add to your knowledge each year. This learn-as-you-go method enables you to experiment while investing only a small amount of money, time, and labor. Once you learn what grows well in your area, you can increase the size of your wildflower planting.

Many people prefer to purchase single species in bulk, and then customize their mixes. This process is called *mixture formulation*. Presently, few guidelines are available for designing your own wildflower mixes that both maximize color display and minimize seed cost. Any method of combining species should take the following factors into account:

• *flower architecture.* How many flowers does each species display and what size are they?

• *germination time of each species.* Late fall, early spring, other times?

• *bloom time.* Does the species provide several weeks of color or only a short-term display?

• *seed size.* Species with small seeds contain more seed per pound than species with large seeds, and thus yield more individual plants. They usually have a lower seeding rate as well.

The Wildflower Center is conducting field research and obtaining information from individuals in the seed business to better understand the process of putting a wildflower mix together. Jack B. Bodger, general manager of Environmental Seed Producers, Inc. in California, provided valuable input in this research. Until research is complete, the Wildflower Center recommends the following guidelines for determining the seeding rates (quantity of seed that needs to be planted in a given area) for a customized mix:

1. Calculate seeding rates based on density (number of seed per unit weight) rather than weight (usually measured in pounds or ounces). First, calculate the number of seed that you should plant per acre for each species *as if you were planting only that species*, using the following formula:

$A \times B = C$

A = commercially recommended seeding rate per acre (This is a weight-based figure usually available on the seed packet.)

B = number of seed per pound (See seed packet or the chart in the following chapter.)

C = number of seed to be planted per acre for one species

2. Add together the numbers of seed per acre for each species (this total will be a large number).

3. Divide the total obtained in step 2 by the total number of species in the mix. This will determine the total number of seed that should be planted per acre for this mixture. The result is a constant number that you can use to determine the number of seed that goes in the mix for each species.

4. Decide what proportion of each species you wish to plant, and multiply the total number of seed per acre (obtained in step 3) by the desired proportion. For example, if you want 25 percent *Oenothera speciosa*, multiply the total number of seed per acre by .25.

5. For each species, convert the number of seed to be planted per acre (obtained in step 4) to pounds of seed to be planted per acre. This is your seeding rate for each species in the mix. Use this formula:

C / B = seeding rate for a species in the mix

C = number of seed to be planted per acre for the species (step 4)

B = number of seed per pound for the species

The following example combines *Oenothera speciosa* (pink evening primrose), *Phlox drummondii* (Drummond's phlox), and *Verbena tenuisecta* (moss verbena).

1. Multiply the commercially recommended seeding rate per acre by the number of seed per pound to derive the number of seed that you should plant per acre for each species. Remember that these are single species seeding rates, which means that these rates would be used if you were planting only this species at your site:

Oenothera speciosa = .5 pounds per acre x 3,280,000 seed per pound = 1,640,000 seed per acre

Phlox drummondii = 10 pounds per acre x 234,000 seed per pound = 2,340,000 seed per acre

Verbena tenuisecta = 6 pounds per acre x 473,600 seed per pound = 2,841,600 seed per acre

2. Add together the number of seed to be planted per acre for all three species:

Oenothera speciosa	=	1,640,000
Phlox drummondii	=	2,340,000
Verbena tenuisecta	=	2,841,600
		6,821,600

3. Divide the total obtained in step 2 by the number of species included in the mix (in this case three species) to obtain the adjusted seeding rate for the mix:

$$\frac{6,821,600 \text{ (total obtained in step 2)}}{3 \text{ (number of species in the mix)}} = 2,273,867 \text{ seed per acre}$$

4. Use the resulting number (2,273,867 seed per acre) as the constant for the total number of seed that should be planted per acre. The number of seed to include in the mix for each species can be determined by multiplying this constant by the proportions you want the mix to have. In this case, we want the mix to have the following proportions:

20% - *Oenothera speciosa*
40% - *Phlox drummondii*
40% - *Verbena tenuisecta*

Oenothera speciosa: 2,273,867 x .20 = 454,773 seed per acre

Phlox drummondii: 2,273,867 x .40 = 909,547 seed per acre

Verbena tenuisecta: 2,273,867 x .40 = 909,547 seed per acre

5. For each species, convert the number of seed per acre (obtained in step 4) to pounds per acre. This is your seeding rate for each species in the mix.

Oenothera speciosa:

$$\frac{454{,}773 \text{ (number of seed per acre)}}{3{,}280{,}000 \text{ (seed per pound)}} = .14 \text{ pounds per acre}$$

Phlox drummondii:

$$\frac{909{,}547 \text{ (number of seed per acre)}}{234{,}000 \text{ (seed per pound)}} = 3.9 \text{ pounds per acre}$$

Verbena tenuisecta:

$$\frac{909{,}547 \text{ (number of seed per acre)}}{473{,}600 \text{ (seed per pound)}} = 1.9 \text{ pounds per acre}$$

$$= 5.9 \text{ pounds per acre}$$

The overall seeding rate for this mix is 5.9 pounds per acre.

Formulating a wildflower mix may be more of an art than a science. The above example combines species in which the size and weight of the seeds and the seeding rates differ very little. If seed size and weight and seeding rates vary tremendously, complex adjustments requiring specialized knowledge may be necessary.

There are less scientific approaches to formulating mixes. For landscapes that are to be observed from close range, such as residential meadow plantings, a seeding rate of six to ten seeds per square foot is usually sufficient. For a landscape that will be observed at a distance, such as a roadside planting, a seeding rate of four to five seeds per square foot is usually adequate. These rates can be adjusted, taking into consideration the mature size of the plants and the visual effect you desire.

Phlox drummondii

WILDFLOWERS CONTAINED IN REGIONAL SEED MIXES

HOW TO USE THIS CHART

Since the National Wildflower Research Center is a nonprofit organization, the Center's policy is to refrain from endorsing any company or product over another. However, since Center staff members have conducted field tests for most readily available mixes, the Center does have some general recommendations to make based on the results.

The Center suggests buying seed mixes that contain the highest percentage of wildflower species indigenous to the specific area to be planted. When selecting a seed mix, obtain a species list from the company that produces the mix. The list should include the proportions in which individual species occur in the total volume of the mix. Note how the species listed compare to species that are native to your area. The following chart lists the species that are usually included in regional seed mixes, and can serve as a quick *cross reference* in these comparisons.

Botanical name	Common name	Origin	Life cycle	Exposure	Site preference
Achillea filipendulina	Gold Yarrow	Eurasia	Perennial	Sun	Wide variety of soils
Achillea millefolium	White Yarrow	Eurasia	Perennial	Sun - part sun	Wide variety of soils
Alyssum "white"	Carpet of Snow	Hybrid	Annual		
Alyssum maritimum	Sweet Alyssum	Europe	Perennial	Sun - part sun	Wasteland, disturbed sites
Alyssum saxatile	Basket of Gold	Southern & central Europe, Turkey	Perennial	Sun	Rock gardens
Ammi majus	Bishop's Flower	North Africa, Eurasia	Annual	Sun	
Anagallis arvensis var. caerulea	Poor Man's Weather Glass	Europe	Annual	Sun - part shade	Moist areas in prairies & flatlands
Aquilegia caerulea	Columbine	Northwest, Rocky Mountains	Perennial	Sun - full shade	Rocky to sandy loam; thrives on rock slides & outcrops; also in shade
Asclepias tuberosa	Butterfly Weed	Great Plains, Midwest, TX Mid-Atlantic, Southeast	Perennial	Sun - part sun	Dry or moist prairies & upland woods; especially sandy soils
Aster novae-angliae	New England Aster	Northeast	Perennial	Sun - part shade	Moist, open or sometimes wooded sites
Aster tanacetifolius	Prairie Aster	North TX, north to eastern MT; scattered east to central KS	Annual	Sun	Sandy soils
Baileya multiradiata	Desert Marigold	Southern CA, UT, TX	Annual	Sun	Desert areas & mesas; sandy soils
Calendula officinalis	Pot Marigold	Eurasia, North Africa	Annual	Sun	

Comments	# of seed/lb	Seeding rate/acre	Seeding rate/1000 sq ft
Naturalized throughout U.S.	8,192,000	1/2 lb / acre	.2 oz / 1000 sq ft
Naturalized throughout U.S.	2,770,000	1 lb / acre	.4 oz / 1000 sq ft
Common escape from gardens in waste places & along roads; also called Lobularia maritima	1,100,000	4 lb / acre	1.6 oz / 1000 sq ft
Proper name probably Aurinia saxatilis	461,000	4 lb / acre	1.6 oz / 1000 sq ft
Naturalized in U.S.; widely cultivated for cut-flower trade	867,000	2 lb / acre	.8 oz / 1000 sq ft
Common weed at low elevations	544,000	4 lb / acre	1.6 oz / 1000 sq ft
	368,400	7 lb / acre	2.8 oz / 1000 sq ft
Do not expect flowering until the 2nd or 3rd yr., but once established it will persist	102,400	24 lb / acre	9.6 oz / 1000 sq ft
	1,216,000	2 lb / acre	.8 oz / 1000 sq ft
Name changed to Machaeranthera tanacetifolia	496,000	5 lb / acre	2 oz / 1000 sq ft
Highly toxic to livestock	1,060,000	2 lb / acre	.8 oz / 1000 sq ft
Occasionally escapes from gardens in CA; common garden annual	73,000	25 lb / acre	10 oz / 1000 sq ft

Botanical name	Common name	Origin	Life cycle	Exposure	Site preference
Castilleja indivisa	Indian Paintbrush	Eastern 1/2 of TX, southeastern OK	Annual	Sun	Sandy loam soils
Centaurea cyanus	Bachelor's Button	Europe	Annual	Sun	Light, neutral soils
Cerastium bierbersteinii	Snow in Summer	Crimea	Perennial	Sun - part sun	
Cheiranthus allionii	Wallflower	Europe	Annual	Sun	
Cheiranthus cheiri	Wallflower	Southern Europe, Asia	Perennial	Sun	
Chrysanthemum carinatum	Painted Daisy	Morocco	Annual	Sun	
Chrysanthemum coronarium	Garland Chrysanthemum	Mediterranean	Annual	Sun	
Chrysanthemum leucanthemum	Ox-eyed Daisy	Eurasia	Perennial	Sun	Fields, roadsides, waste places
Clarkia amoena	Farewell-to-Spring	Pacific NW & northern CA	Annual	Sun - part sun	Open or wooded, dry & usually grassy areas, blossoming as grass dries
Clarkia concinna	Red Ribbons	CA; coastal ranges & Sierran foothills	Annual	Sun - part sun	Dry, loose soil below 4,000 ft., mixed evergreen and oak woods
Clarkia unguiculata	Clarkia	Northwest coastal ranges; Sierra foothills	Annual	Sun - shade	Dry slopes below 5,000 ft.
Collinsia heterophylla	Chinese Houses	Cismontane areas of CA; Humboldt & Shasta Co. to No. CA	Annual	Shade	Shaded places below 2500 ft.; sandy, moist areas
Coreopsis lanceolata	Lance-leaved Coreopsis	Midwest, High Plains, east TX & Southeast	Perennial	Sun - part sun	Grasslands; dry, often sandy soils

Comments	# of seed/lb	Seeding rate/acre	Seeding rate/1000 sq ft
	4,000,000	.25 lb / acre	.1 oz / 1000 sq ft
Escaped cultivar throughout U.S.	96,000	4 lb / acre	1.6 oz / 1000 sq ft
Aggressive growth rate as a mat-forming perennial.			
Plants known by this name probably belong to Erysimum hieraciifolium	340,000	6 lb / acre	2.4 oz / 1000 sq ft
	235,000	8 lb / acre	3.2 oz / 1000 sq ft
Occasionally naturalizes in CA	288,000	5 lb / acre	2 oz / 1000 sq ft
Naturalized throughout U.S.	432,000	5 lb / acre	2 oz / 1000 sq ft
Escaped cultivar throughout the U.S.	1,790,000	2 lb / acre	.8 oz / 1000 sq ft
	1,600,000	2 lb / acre	.8 oz / 1000 sq ft
	1,660,000	2 lb / acre	.8 oz / 1000 sq ft
	410,000	6 lb / acre	2.4 oz / 1000 sq ft
	221,000	10 lb /acre	4 oz / 1000 sq ft

Botanical name	Common name	Origin	Life cycle	Exposure	Site preference
Coreopsis tinctoria	Plains Coreopsis	Central & southern Great Plains, TX, east to AR & LA	Annual	Sun	Seasonally moist sites, roadsides & disturbed areas; sandy soils
Cosmos sulphureus	Sulphur Cosmos	Mexico	Annual	Sun	
Cynoglossum amabile	Chinese Forget-Me-Not	Eastern Asia	Biennial		
Daucus carota	Queen Anne's Lace	Europe	Biennial	Sun - part shade	
Delphinium ajacis	Rocket larkspur	Europe	Annual	Sun - part sun	Grasslands & shrublands
Delphinium cardinale	Scarlet Larkspur	CA	Perennial	Sun - part sun	Dry openings in brush & woods below 5,000 ft.
Dianthus barbatus	Sweet William	Europe	Annual	Sun - part sun	
Dianthus deltoides	Pink	Europe	Perennial	Sun - part sun	
Digitalis purpurea	Foxglove	Europe	Biennial	Part - full shade	Wooded areas
Dimorphotheca aurantiaca	African Daisy	South Africa	Annual	Sun - part sun	Improved soils
Dimorphotheca pluvialis	White African Daisy	South Africa	Annual	Sun	
Dimorphotheca sinuata	African Daisy	South Africa	Annual	Sun	Improved soils, warm sunny locations
Echinacea purpurea	Purple Coneflower	Midwest, Southeast	Perennial	Sun	Prairies & open dry woods; sandy soils

Comments	# of seed/lb	Seeding rate/acre	Seeding rate/1000 sq ft
Widely cultivated; escapes & is irregularly established elsewhere	1,400,000	2 lb / acre	.8 oz / 1000 sq ft
Escaped from cultivation in south TX; this is the commonly cultivated Cosmos	63,000	15 lb / acre	6 oz / 1000 sq ft
Often grown in flower gardens; sometimes rather weedy			
Naturalized, especially in Southern California			
	320,000	8 lb / acre	3.2 oz / 1000 sq ft
Naturalized & widely cultivated; escaped	150,000	10 lb / acre	4 oz / 1000 sq ft
Escaped from cultivation; naturalized throughout U.S.			
Cultivated & escapes locally into wasteplaces	2,480,000	1 lb / acre	.4 oz / 1000 sq ft
Commonly cultivated	4,360,000	.5 lb / acre	.2 oz / 1000 sq ft
Naturalized in U.S. & Europe			
	67,000	15 lb / acre	6 oz / 1000 sq ft
Naturalized in U.S. & Europe	251,000	9 lb / acre	3.6 oz / 1000 sq ft
	117,000	12 lb / acre	4.8 oz / 1000 sq ft

Botanical name	Common name	Origin	Life cycle	Exposure	Site preference
Eschscholzia caespitosa	Dwarf California Poppy	CA	Annual	Sun	Grasslands and chaparral
Eschscholzia californica	California Poppy	Cismontane areas of CA; west to Mojave Desert	Annual	Sun	Open, grassy areas
Gaillardia aristata	Blanketflower	Great Plains, Midwest	Perennial	Sun	Plains, meadows & other open places
Gaillardia pulchella	Firewheel, Indian Blanket	Midwest, Great Plains, TX & Southeast	Annual	Sun	Ranges from clay to sandy soils; grasslands & shrublands
Gilia capitata	Globe Gilia	Saskatchewan west to B.C., south to AZ & NM	Annual	Sun	Open areas
Gilia leptantha sp. purpusii	Showy Blue Gilia	CA	Annual	Part sun	Sandy & gravelly places at 5000 to 7700 ft.; mostly yellow pine forest
Gilia tricolor	Bird's Eyes	Various CA grasslands & coastal ranges	Annual	Sun	Open, grassy plains or slopes; dry, sandy soil
Gypsophila elegans	Baby's Breath	Ukraine, eastern Turkey & northern Iran	Annual	Sun	
Gypsophila muralis	Baby's Breath	Europe	Annual	Sun	
Hesperis matronalis	Dame's Rocket	Eurasia	Perennial	Sun	Moist woodlands, shrublands & grasslands
Iberis gibraltarica	Gibraltar Candy-tuft	Gibraltar & Morocco	Perennial	Sun	
Iberis umbellata	Candytuft	Mediterranean	Annual	Sun	Alkaline soils
Ipomopsis rubra	Standing Cypress	Central or east TX; Southeast, Midwest & Mid-Altanic	Biennial	Sun	Dry, sandy or rocky soils; grasslands & shrublands

Comments	# of seed/lb	Seeding rate/acre	Seeding rate/1000 sq ft
	512,000	5 lb / acre	2 oz / 1000 sq ft
Exceedingly variable with over 50 spp. proposed	293,000	8 lb / acre	3.2 oz / 1000 sq ft
Occasionally introduced or escapes from cultivation	132,000	10 lb / acre	4 oz / 1000 sq ft
State flower of Oklahoma	153,000	10 lb / acre	4 oz / 1000 sq ft
	1,020,000	2 lb / acre	.8 oz / 1000 sq ft
	492,000	5 lb / acre	2 oz / 1000 sq ft
	1,020,000	2 lb / acre	.8 oz / 1000 sq ft
Naturalized	174,000	10 lb / acre	4 oz / 1000 sq ft
Naturalized in eastern North America	174,000	5 lb / acre	2 oz / 1000 sq ft
Naturalized	296,000	8 lb / acre	3.2 oz / 1000 sq ft
Often used as an ornamental	288,000	8 lb / acre	3.2 oz / 1000 sq ft
	341,000	6 lb / acre	2.4 oz / 1000 sq ft

Botanical name	Common name	Origin	Life cycle	Exposure	Site preference
Iris missouriensis	Western Blue Flag	CO, WY, ND and NE	Perennial	Part - full shade	Marshes, seepy meadows & along streams in open woods
Lasthenia glabrata	Goldfields	CA	Annual	Sun	Heavy soils, vernal pools, low alkaline fields & hillsides
Lavatera trimestris	Tree Mallow	Mediterranean	Annual	Sun - part sun	Sandy loam; grasslands & shrublands
Layia platyglossa	Tidy Tips	Grassy areas below 300 ft in coastal CA	Annual	Sun	Sandy, open grassy areas
Liatris pycnostachya	Gayfeather, Blazing Star	East and southeast TX; IN to SD, south to LA & TX	Perennial	Sun	Open, sandy areas
Liatris spicata	Gayfeather, Blazing Star	Southeast, north to Mid-Altantic, Great Plains, Midwest	Perennial	Sun	Sandy & rocky soil; open areas of grasslands
Linanthus grandiflorus	Mountain Phlox	CA	Annual	Sun - part sun	Open woods & sandy places below 3,500 ft.
Linaria maroccana	Toadflax	Morocco	Annual	Sun	
Linaria vulgaris	Butter & Eggs	Europe	Perennial	Sun	Disturbed sites
Linum grandiflorum var. rubrum	Scarlet Flax	North Africa	Annual	Sun	Sandy, grassy areas
Linum lewisii	Blue flax	West & Southwest	Perennial	Sun	Dry slopes & ridges, mostly 4,000 - 11,000 ft.
Lobularia maritima	Sweet Alyssum	Mediterranean	Perennial	Sun	
Lupinus bicolor	Pigmy-leaved lupine	Central AZ, CA	Annual	Sun	Sandy places

Comments	# of seed/lb	Seeding rate/acre	Seeding rate/1000 sq ft
	21,000	12 lb / acre	4.8 oz / 1000 sq ft
Not indigenous to Southwestern desert			
Naturalized in eastern half of U.S., Rocky Mts. & coastal WA & OR	7,000	30 lb / acre	12 oz / 1000 sq ft
	350,000	6 lb / acre	2.4 oz / 1000 sq ft
	128,000	12 lb / acre	4.8 oz / 1000 sq ft
	138,000	12 lb / acre	4.8 oz / 1000 sq ft
	907,000	2 lb / acre	.8 oz / 1000 sq ft
Naturalized in the Northeast	6,850,000	.5 lb / acre	.2 oz / 1000 sq ft
Considered a weed throughout the U. S.	4,096,000	.75 lb / acre	.3 oz / 1000 sq ft
Naturalized, occasionally escapes from cultivation	122,000	15 lb / acre	6 oz / 1000 sq ft
	293,000	8 lb / acre	3.2 oz / 1000 sq ft
Naturalized throughout U.S.; commonly escapes from gardens	1,270,000	2 lb / acre	.8 oz / 1000 sq ft

Botanical name	Common name	Origin	Life cycle	Exposure	Site preference
Lupinus densiflorus var. aureus	Golden Lupine	Coastal ranges in CA	Annual	Sun	Grassy, open fields & hillsides below 2000 ft.
Lupinus perennis	Perennial Lupine	Southeast, Northeast, West to the Midwest	Perennial	Sun	Sandy soils, open woods, shrubland, & grassland
Lupinus polyphyllus	Russell Lupine	B.C. to CA, from coast into mountains	Perennial	Sun - part sun	Along streams or in fairly moist soils
Lupinus succulentus	Arroyo Lupine	Coastal ranges of CA	Annual	Sun	Heavy soils in grassy flats & slopes; below 2000 ft.
Lupinus texensis	Texas Bluebonnet	TX	Annual	Sun	Well drained calcareous soils
Lupinus vallicola	Valley Lupine	Northern CA	Annual	Sun - Part sun	Grasslands & yellow pine forests
Machaeranthera tanacetifolia	Prairie Aster, Tahoka Daisy	Eastern MT to North TX; scattered east to central KS	Annual	Sun	Sandy disturbed sites
Machaeranthera xanacetifolius	Prairie Aster, Tahoka Daisy	TX; High Plains & Trans-Pecos, east to the Edwards Plateau	Annual	Sun	Sandy soils
Mentzelia lindleyi	Blazing Star	Desert areas in central CA	Annual	Sun	Rocky slopes below 2,500 ft.
Mimulus puniceus	Mission Red Monkey Flower	CA	Perennial	Sun	Dry slopes & mesas below 2,500 ft.
Mirabilis jalapa	Four O'clock	Tropical America	Perennial	Sun	Sandy, open areas
Monarda citriodora	Lemon Mint, Horsemint	Southeast, TX, OK, north to KS & MO	Annual	Sun	Sandy loams or rocky soils on slopes, or in prairies & meadows
Myosotis sylvatica	Forget-Me-Not	Eurasia	Annual	Part shade	Moist conditions

Comments	# of seed/lb	Seeding rate/acre	Seeding rate/1000 sq ft
Most variable, about 24 varieties	12,800	35 lb / acre	14 oz / 1000 sq ft
	22,700	20 lb / acre	8 oz / 1000 sq ft
	15,600	20 lb / acre	8 oz / 1000 sq ft
State flower of Texas	16,000	20 lb / acre	8 oz / 1000 sq ft
	496,000	5 lb / acre	2 oz / 1000 sq ft
Sometimes listed as Aster tanacetifolius	496,000	5 lb / acre	2 oz / 1000 sq ft
Occasionally escapes from gardens	586,000	4 lb / acre	1.6 oz / 1000 sq ft
Small shrub			
Widely cultivated as an ornamental & escapes	8,000	25 lb / acre	10 oz / 1000 sq ft
	819,000	3 lb / acre	1.2 oz / 1000 sq ft
Naturalized			

Botanical name	Common name	Origin	Life cycle	Exposure	Site preference
Nemophila maculata	Five Spot	Various grasslands, foothills & forests of CA	Annual	Sun	Varies from grasslands, foothills and forests
Nemophila menziesii	Baby Blue Eyes	Europe	Annual	Sun	Sandy loam
Oenothera argillicola	Shale Evening Primrose	Appalachian mountains	Perennial	Sun	Grasslands & shrublands
Oenothera cheiranthifolia	Beach Evening Primrose	CA	Perennial	Sun - part sun	Coastal areas
Oenothera hookeri	Evening Primrose	TX, western U. S., CA	Perennial	Sun	Dry sites
Oenothera lamarckiana	Evening Primrose	Arose in cultivation, not established in cooler areas	Annual	Sun	
Oenothera missouriensis	Missouri Primrose	Western plains east to MO & AR, south to TX	Perennial	Sun	Limestone prairies & dry hillsides
Oenothera pallida	White Evening Primrose	West TX, UT & AZ, north to ID	Perennial	Sun	
Orthocarpus purpurascens	Owl's Clover	Forests of northern AZ & western NM, Rocky Mts; also in CA	Annual	Sun - part sun	
Papaver nudicaule	Iceland Poppy	Eurasia, arctic regions	Perennial	Sun	
Papaver rhoeas	Corn Poppy	Eurasia, north Africa	Annual	Sun	
Penstemon palmeri	Palmer Penstemon	CA, UT & AZ	Perennial	Sun - part sun	Dry, rocky gullies at 4000 to 6000 ft.
Penstemon strictus	Rocky Mt. Penstemon	Western U.S.	Perennial	Sun	Sandy or gravelly soil

Comments	# of seed/lb	Seeding rate/acre	Seeding rate/1000 sq ft
	87,000	20 lb / acre	8 oz / 1000 sq ft
Escaped cultivation in CA; widely used on coast & mts.	258,000	8 lb / acre	3.2 oz / 1000 sq ft
	1,020,000	2 lb / acre	.8 oz / 1000 sq ft
	4,090,000	.5 lb /acre	.2 oz / 1000 sq ft
	861,000	2 lb / acre	.8 oz / 1000 sq ft
Sometimes called O. erythrosepala	864,000	2 lb / acre	.8 oz / 1000 sq ft
Name has been changed to O. macrocarpa	80,700	5 lb / acre	2 oz / 1000 sq ft
	512,000	5 lb / acre	2 oz / 1000 sq ft
Not native to the desert Southwest	900,000	4 lb / acre	1.6 oz / 1000 sq ft
Naturalized in Colorado	2,780,000	1 lb / acre	.4 oz / 1000 sq ft
	3,200,000	1 lb / acre	.4 oz / 1000 sq ft
	610,000	3 lb / acre	1.2 oz / 1000 sq ft
	592,000	4 lb / acre	1.6 oz / 1000 sq ft

Botanical name	Common name	Origin	Life cycle	Exposure	Site preference
Petalostemum purpureum	Purple Prairie Clover	Great Plains east to IL, south to LA	Perennial	Sun	Rocky prairies, roadsides & hillsides; open wooded areas
Phacelia campanularia	California Blue Bells	CA; western Colorado Desert	Annual	Sun	
Phacelia tanacetifolia	Lacey Phacelia	CA, AZ, NV	Annual	Sun	Open flats & slopes below 4,000 ft.
Phlox drummondii	Phlox	Endemic to TX, but escaped eastward	Annual	Sun	Open, well-drained soils
Ratibida columnaris	Mexican Hat	Midwest, western U.S., south to TX & OK	Perennial	Sun	Open, calcareous soils; grasslands, prairies & shrublands
Romneya coulteri	Matilija Poppy	CA	Perennial	Sun	Dry washes & canyons below 4,000 ft.; Santa Ana mountains to San Diego Co.
Rudbeckia amplexicaulis	Clasping Coneflower	Throughout coastal states in Southeast, eastern 2/3rd of TX	Annual	Sun	Moist areas
Rudbeckia hirta	Black-eyed Susan	Eastern 2/3rd of U.S.	Perennial	Sun	Sandy prairies & open woods
Salvia farinacea	Blue Sage	Central & West TX, NM	Perennial	Sun - part shade	Limestone soils in prairies, thickets, meadows & hillsides
Silene armeria	Catchfly, Sweet William	Mediterranean	Annual	Sun	
Sisyrinchium bellum	Blue-Eyed Grass	Northern CA	Perennial	Sun	Widely distributed; often in grassy coastal areas
Venidium fastuosum	Monarch Daisy	South Africa	Perennial		
Verbena gooddingii	Southwestern Verbena	Southwest	Perennial	Sun	Wide variety of soils
Verbena tenuisecta	Moss Verbena	South America	Perennial	Sun	Roadsides, fields & waste places

Comments	# of seed/lb	Seeding rate/acre	Seeding rate/1000 sq ft
	293,000	8 lb / acre	3.2 oz / 1000 sq ft
	856,000	3 lb / acre	1.2 oz / 1000 sq ft
	235,000	3 lb / acre	1.2 oz / 1000 sq ft
Naturalized in Southeast	234,000	10 lb / acre	4 oz / 1000 sq ft
Naturalized farther east	1,230,200	2 lb / acre	.8 oz / 1000 sq ft
Name was changed to Dracopis amplexicaulis	922,000	3 lb / acre	1.2 oz / 1000 sq ft
	1,710,000	2 lb /acre	.8 oz / 1000 sq ft
	368,000	6 lb / acre	2.4 oz / 1000 sq ft
Once popular in cultivation; often escapes as a weed	1,400,000	1 lb / acre	.4 oz / 1000 sq ft
Exceedingly variable	315,000	8 lb / acre	3.2 oz / 1000 sq ft
Occasionally escapes from cultivation	588,000	5 lb / acre	2 oz / 1000 sq ft
Naturalized in TX, LA, NC, GA, FL			
Isolated community in AZ	473,000	6 lb / acre	2.4 oz / 1000 sq ft

Castilleja indivisa

PLANTING WILDFLOWERS ON A LARGE SCALE

The word "wildflower" often conjures images of miraculously hardy plants that can survive against all odds. Although this is true in nature, reestablishing wildflowers so that they are able to survive on their own requires several years of effort.

Working with native plants, and restoring them in the patterns found in nature, will eventually create a landscape that exists in harmony with environmental conditions governing the site. Creating a naturalistic landscape requires learning as much as you can about the land, and the interrelationships of the native species that inhabit it. Whether you are planting wildflowers on a small or large scale, you should have a basic understanding of how natural forces work together, and why certain species grow together.

Establishing a wildflower area is *not* the same as sitting back and letting nature take its course. An area that is left uncut may begin to support a colorful variety of wild plants, but generally, the no-mow approach is undesirable. The first wild species to appear are likely to be plants that are associated with human disturbances in our ecosystem. Examples of these plants are *Agropyron repens* (quackgrass), *Sorghum halepense* (Johnson grass), and *Cirsium arvense* (Canadian thistle). Most of these species are from the agricultural fields of Europe and Asia, and in North America can justifiably be called weeds.

Establishing a low-maintenance wildflower area may require as much time and labor during the first three to five years as a clipped and cultivated lawn or garden. But unlike gardens where annual flowers are replanted each year to produce a luxuriant display, a seeded wildflower area, once established, can be maintained with minimal effort.

Following are guidelines for large-scale wildflower plantings in *open, sunny, well-drained areas*. Your overall planting plan should be developed before planting begins, and should include:

- *selection of appropriate species*
- *planting times*
- *ground preparation*
- *seeding methods*
- *wildflower site management*

SELECTION OF APPROPRIATE SPECIES

After selecting a site, the first step in establishing a wildflower area is to match appropriate species to that site. The National Wildflower Research Center recommends using indigenous species. An indigenous species is one that grows in a specific geographical area. It is important to understand that a plant will not grow in your backyard just because it is native to your state. Plants are adapted to environmental factors, such as soil type, moisture, and pH. Recognition of these specific field conditions is essential.

Before you start a planting project, study the natural areas in your locale, and do some background reading on planting wildflowers in your region. Since no single planting procedure is universally effective, it is important to learn from natural models. By looking closely at undisturbed or relatively undisturbed natural areas nearby, you can decide which species you like, and discover which are adapted to the conditions of your site. You can also note maximum size and bloom sequence, and where a particular wildflower occurs naturally, such as at the edge of a forest or in an open meadow. Observe wildflowers during all stages of growth before choosing the ones you wish to plant. It is important to determine which plants will grow at your site without your intervention.

What are the components of the surrounding native plant community? Are you surrounded by an oak-hickory forest, or do you live in a grassland area in the Midwest? What are some of the previous land use practices? Do you intend to plant an acre of an old field, or a quarter-acre lot that was landscaped but left untended? These factors will determine what you need to plant and how you need to manage your area.

Considerations in wildflower species selection also include:

• *height*. What is the maximum height of the mature plant?

• *bloom period*. When does the species flower? Selecting species with complementary flowering times provides color throughout the growing season.

• *life history*. A mix of perennials and self-seeding annuals and biennials is recommended. Annuals generally germinate and flower the first year. Biennials germinate and form a leafy rosette the first year, flowering the second year. Perennials often take two to three years to mature before flowering, expending most of their initial energy on development of a healthy root system.

• *seed availability*. Is seed commercially available?

• *noxious weed*. Is the species highly aggressive or competitive? Does it have the potential to become invasive? When an alien species is introduced to a region, you never can predict how it will react. It may naturalize, as European *Achillea millefolium* (yarrow) did, or aggressively take over a habitat. Many of our common weeds, such as *Cichorium intybus* (chicory), *Pueraria lobata* (kudzu), and *Daucus carota* (Queen Anne's lace) were introduced from Europe or Asia. *Lythrum salicaria* (purple loosestrife), for instance, is still imported from Europe as an ornamental plant, and its seed can be found in some wildflower seed mixes. This plant, which disturbs wetland habitats profoundly, is listed as a noxious weed in many areas of the country.

A wildflower area is a complex interactive plant community, not just a compartmentalized collection of species. One approach to selecting seed for a wildflower planting is to choose a seed mixture of native species which, over a period of time, will naturally sort themselves out. In other words, the species best adapted to the site will be the ones that thrive after the first few years. A more efficient, scientific approach is to inventory the site and its microhabitats, such as wet, low-lying areas, shady areas, or open fields, and then determine the species best suited to these site conditions.

Shop for commercial wildflower seed mixes carefully. Although some suppliers offer seed mixes formulated for specific regions, more often the mixes are designed for a broad geographical area, and may contain species that are not well-adapted to conditions in your location. Try to learn as much as possible about a wildflower seed mix before buying it. The best value is a mix containing primarily indigenous species. If a mix includes nonnative species, which is often the case, they should not comprise a large percentage of the mix. Many seed companies provide a species list as part of their packaging. As a consumer, you are the best agent of quality control. Ideally, you should obtain a species list for the seed mix you are considering, and determine if the mix is appropriate for your site.

Native warm-season grasses are an essential element in wildflower plantings. Most people who manage meadows and prairies recommend that native grasses comprise 50 to 80 percent of the mix. Grasses have five major functions:

- *providing support and protection for tall flowers*
- *forming a dense cover that resists penetration by introduced weeds*
- *lending color and texture to the landscape, especially in the fall when vegetation changes color*
- *preventing soil erosion*
- *providing an important food source for wildlife*

Grasses are either mat-forming or bunch-forming. These different growth characteristics help stabilize the soil. Many native grasses such as *Schizachyrium scoparium* (little bluestem) and *Sorghastrum nutans* (Indian grass), are bunch-forming, and permit space for other herbaceous plants, such as wildflowers, to grow.

Turf grasses are often too tightly woven in their root structure to allow space for other plants to become established. Many turf grasses are also cool-season grasses, such as the commonly used fescues. Cool-season perennial grasses renew their growth in early spring, and maximum development occurs from late March to early June. These grasses reach maturity and produce seed in late spring or early summer. They become semidormant during the summer, but growth usually resumes during the cool months of fall and the grasses remain green despite frost. Cool-season grasses pose competition problems for wildflowers, since their growth periods occur at the same time.

Warm-season grasses renew their growth in late spring and continue growing until early fall, producing much foliage in midsummer. Growth periods for warm-season grasses do not coincide with periods of wildflower seed germination and seedling establishment.

WHEN TO PLANT

A recognized problem with some wildflower species is getting the seed to germinate. Dormancy occurs more often in native plants than in seed from cultivated plants listed in nursery seed catalogs. The seed from cultivated species offered by general seed companies is harvested from plants that have been bred through many generations to produce a high proportion of viable seed free of germination barriers. Mechanical and chemical barriers often prevent germination in freshly harvested seeds of many native plants, sometimes for up to two years. These barriers are evolutionary adaptations which ensure survival of species by preventing germination until favorable conditions, usually in temperature and moisture, exist. Each successive season, some of the residual seed will germinate.

The cool, wet months of fall are the optimum time to plant seed for next spring's wildflowers for two reasons. Some species germinate in the fall, especially in southern states. This adaptation allows the seedling time to establish a root system, and grow into a leafy rosette of vegetation before overwintering in a protective, ground-hugging state. Other species may require stratification (a cold, moist period) to break seed dormancy, or scarification (abrasive action) to wear down hard seed coats. Germination is then induced by a warm, wet spring. Mechanisms for breaking dormancy vary from species to species and may fall into other categories, as well.

Although many species will germinate if seeded in the spring, including them with species planted in the fall does not decrease the potential for success. Seeding in the fall is the most economical approach to establishing both spring and early summer wildflowers.

All plants require water to germinate! If rain is insufficient, water your planting if possible. In southern states, where many annuals germinate in the fall and overwinter as seedlings, watering is recommended if fall rainfall is below average. Water your planting thoroughly once, and then lightly each week until the first freeze. Frequency is more important than quantity during the first three weeks after planting. It is the number of waterings, rather than the amount of water that ensures germination and seedling survival. As a rule of thumb, keep the soil surface damp. During dry winters, water a few times in December and January. This provides moisture to the roots of the seedlings, and helps insulate them from extremely cold temperatures. It is also an effective cold-wet treatment for breaking dormancy of some spring-germinating seeds. In spring, if rainfall is light or non-existent, periodic watering ensures optimal growth and flowering.

GROUND PREPARATION

Start small when you begin a wildflower area. Working on a modest scale allows you to learn about native plants and how they will adapt to your site. Keep in mind that larger plantings are expensive and require a substantial amount of labor during site preparation, planting, and initial maintenance. If you do not have the time, money, or machinery to properly establish and maintain a large tract, it is best to try a smaller, more manageable plot. You need patience and flexibility, so that you can try new experiments when early ones fail. A certain amount of experimentation is usually necessary to identify the best plants for your site.

The steps you will need to take to prepare the ground prior to planting depend upon what is already growing at the site. Each person has a unique situation with his or her own expectations. A site should be assessed for its present value, and management plans should be tailored to the site.

First, identify the plants present and take time to determine their value to the site. You may need to merely enhance a grassland, for instance, or completely reestablish wildflowers and native grasses in an old pasture, vacant lot, or disturbed site. The seeds, roots, and rhizomes of weeds frequently lie dormant beneath the soil surface, and germinate quickly after they are exposed to moisture and light. If your site is full of weeds, it may require a year's lead time or more to kill them, and that may not even be feasible at an extremely disturbed site. It is easier, and often less expensive, to eliminate weeds as much as possible before planting, rather than trying to control them in a newly seeded meadow or other site.

Methods of ground preparation include:

• *interseeding into existing vegetation.* If your site is not weedy and you plan only to interseed wildflowers into existing vegetation, the efforts required to properly prepare your site will not be as great as for a highly disturbed, weedy site. An acre of grassland is an ideal site for many wildflower plantings if the grass is a warm-season species. Mow the vegetation as short as possible, and either roughen the soil surface or spread a thin layer of topsoil (one-half to one inch). A flail mower is often used to mow and lightly scalp or roughen the ground.

• *clearing the site before seeding.* An initial light tilling-watering cycle and/or herbicide treatment may be repeated as many times as needed in order to clear your site. The number of repetitions will depend on the size of the plot, existing weed competition problems, and the degree of weed control you desire.

If you prefer not to till or hand weed, two applications of Roundup may be sufficient to remove existing vegetation. Before you apply Roundup, water the site for a week or two to promote germination of weed seed. Allow the new seedlings to grow for one to two weeks, then apply Roundup. Repeat this process once more to ensure a fairly clean seed bed. Roundup is nonresidual; in other words, it does not continue its herbicidal activity in the soil and you can plant your wildflower and native grass seed as soon as you are sure competing vegetation is under control. Roundup will not affect seed germination, only the growing plants that you have treated.

SEEDING METHODS

One rule applies to all plantings: *good seed-soil contact is essential*. For starters, it provides protection from bird predation. In addition, soil helps retain moisture around the seed, which is necessary for germination, and provides a substrate for seedling growth. An *agricultural grain drill* or a *Cultipacker* planter can be used either to interseed wildflowers (one species at a time) into existing vegetation or plant seed into a clean bed. Both are effective in producing good seed-soil contact.

• *Grain drills,* used to plant grass seed, can also be used to plant wildflower seed. John Deere, Truax Co., and The Tye Co. are three well-known manufacturers of grain drills. These drills cut furrows into the ground, then drop seed into the furrows from seed boxes. Drills that accommodate more than one box allow you to plant different types of seed (e.g., fluffy, large or small seeds) at the recommended rates for each seed. A chain or rubber tire is attached behind the drill to work the seed into the soil by tamping it down. A grain drill is labor-efficient and provides an even seeding rate. A disadvantage of this method is that seed is distributed in rows.

• *Cultipackers* are used by ranchers to plant grasses and improve their pastures. The seed box can be set at a specified seeding rate to plant wildflowers and native grasses. An attached roller bar follows, packing the seed into the soil.

• *A mechanical seeder,* which is adjustable and hand-carried, is effective for many plant species. Some species produce small seed, which makes even distribution with a mechanical seeder difficult. Mixing small seed with fine, damp sand then distributing the seed-sand mixture should eliminate seed clumping.

• *Hand broadcasting* requires only a small investment and can be successful if you do it correctly. For better seed distribution, mix the seed with fine, damp sand in a proportion of four parts sand to one part seed. Seed into a prepared area, then rake or tamp seed into the soil to ensure good seed-soil contact. Other methods of working the seed into the soil include using a Cultipacker to roll the seed in, or dragging a section of chain link fence by tractor over the area.

Spreading a commercial wildflower mix evenly is difficult because of the different sizes and weights of seed. Purchasing the seed for each species separately and seeding one species at a time can eliminate this problem. *Do not attempt to plant a wildflower mix with a grain drill, Cultipacker, or mechanical seeder!*

The least effective method of wildflower seeding is the "feeding the chickens" technique, which is the random scattering of seed on unprepared ground. This process works in nature because it occurs repeatedly over a period of many years. The total amount of seed present in the soil each year is hundreds, sometimes thousands of times greater than there is time or money to duplicate.

The Texas Department of Highways and Public Transportation has utilized a version of the "feeding the chickens" technique for over 50 years with some success: roadsides lacking wildflowers have been covered with mown hay or mulch collected from areas with dense stands of wildflowers. This method, however, requires approximately five to ten years to produce populous stands of wildflowers.

HOW TO MANAGE YOUR SITE

Annuals germinate quickly and visually dominate the site during the first year. Although many perennials germinate in the first year, root growth will comprise two to three times the biomass of above-ground vegetation during that time. Perennials normally flower in the second or third year. Native grasses usually do not flower or set seed the first year, and can reach heights of only two or three inches by the end of the growing season, depending upon the species. *Schizachyrium scoparium* (little bluestem), for example, under favorable environmental conditions develops a two- to three-inch primary root system before an above-ground shoot appears.

If tall weeds are shading wildflower seedlings, mow above the seedlings several times the first year to help suppress annual weeds. A scythe or hand clipper will also do the job if a mower is unavailable, or mower blades cannot be set high enough. Most of the weeds will be annuals, and mowing before seed set destroys the seed crop. The exact time and height for mowing varies with each site, and mowing may also be necessary the second and third year. In many cases, hand weeding or spot application of an herbicide cannot be avoided, especially if aggressive species or perennial weeds are dominating the site.

You may choose to reseed or spot transplant to fill bare spots or increase the diversity of vegetation, especially in the second or third year after seeding. Transplant only when the plants are dormant, either late fall or early spring. Extricate as much of the root system as you can when digging up the plants. Shake soil clumps from the roots, and immediately place roots in a moist, protected environment. Some people fold transplants into dampened burlap; others place them in restaurant bussing pans with a low level of water. Sort the plants, divide, and root prune in a shady, protected place. All plants must be kept moist and protected from the sun. A cloudy, calm day is ideal for transplanting. Relocate transplants as soon after digging as possible.

Delay mowing your wildflower area until at least half of the latest blooming species have dropped seed. Annual and biennial wildflowers must be allowed to reseed in order to produce a strong stand the next year. Do not mow native grasses in late summer and early fall during their elongation, flowering and seed set periods. Never mow native grasses below six inches.

Coreopsis tinctoria

LOW-MAINTENANCE GARDENING AND LANDSCAPING

Native plants offer practical alternatives to home owners who seek a more naturalistic look for their landscapes. Once established, native plants can save time and money because they require less maintenance, water, fertilizer, and pesticide than traditional landscapes.

Yard work becomes a positive activity! Instead of eliminating plants to achieve a monoculture of turf grass, you add diversity, and anxiously await changes in your landscape. Your lawn care chores are redirected toward encouraging variety rather than discouraging it. *You work with nature rather than against it.*

Incorporating native plants into a landscape can be accomplished in a variety of ways, depending upon your preference and finances. At the lowest investment level, you can complement existing beds with native plants. Placement should be similar to that in a traditional design. Many native perennials make ideal border plants. These wildflowers can improve dramatically in appearance under cultivation, no longer having to compete for light, moisture and nutrients. Similarly, if you are looking for a shade tree, select a native over a nonnative species.

On a more ambitious scale, you might want to assess the environmental conditions (e.g., shady or sunny, adequate or inadequate drainage) on your property, and embellish those areas with groupings of native plants appropriate for the conditions. This is called *zoning*, and the results are well worth the time spent analyzing and matching species to site conditions.

On a higher level of complexity, you can let your imagination run wild and design a natural landscape by imitating associations found in specific plant communities in your region (e.g., a prairie area, wetland, or woodland edge). To varying degrees, all of these landscape options have the advantage of reflecting your region's natural landscape.

Whether old or new, any landscape can be made more water-efficient simply by utilizing the water-wise concepts of Xeriscape (zer-i-skape). "Xeriscaping" is a word coined originally by a special task force of the Denver Water Department, Associated Landscape Contractors of Colorado, and Colorado State University, to describe landscaping with conservation of water as a major objective. The word is derived from the Greek "xeros," which means "dry." Xeriscapes need not be cactus or rock gardens. They can be green, cool landscapes full of beautiful native plants. In fact, if a Xeriscape is well-planned, plants will flower successively throughout the growing season.

Xeriscape is now administered by the National Xeriscape Council, Inc. To learn about membership, publications, conferences, and various programs across the country, write to the Association and Society Management, Inc., 940 E. 51st St., Austin, Texas 78751.

Xeriscape follows seven steps to achieve a more water-efficient landscape. These steps also apply to landscaping with native plants and involve: *planning and design; limiting turf areas; irrigating efficiently; improving soil; mulching; selecting plants with low water demands* (native plants are recommended); and *maintaining the landscape.*

PLANNING AND DESIGN

The first step in landscaping with native plants is to analyze your site and determine your expectations and needs. Whether you are redesigning an old landscape or starting fresh with a new one, a plan is mandatory. It does not have to be elaborate, and can be installed in phases as money and time permit.

How do you use your yard? What kind of look do you hope to achieve? How can your yard become more water-efficient? These are questions to consider. Think in terms of zoning plants according to water usage and cultural requirements. For example, turf areas should be zoned and irrigated differently than areas with border shrubs or flower beds. Northern and eastern exposures need less water than southern and western exposures.

As a landscape designer, you need to observe native plants in their natural environment to learn about their cultural requirements and growth habits. A visit to local natural areas will help determine which species will grow well on your property. Even if it is unrealistic to expect to learn about all the plant species in your area, it is possible to learn about the dominant species. By duplicating at home what you see in nature, you will place native plants properly in your yard.

LIMITING TURF AREAS

Since turf is the highest water- and maintenance-demanding material in a landscape, it should be located only in areas where it provides functional benefits; in a play or recreational area, for example. If you need a turf area, you might choose *Buchloë dactyloides* (buffalo grass) or *Bouteloua gracilis* (blue grama), two native grasses that have low water needs and are appropriate for parts of the Southwest, High Plains and Midwest.

Turf can be converted to less water-demanding plant material such as ground cover or mulched beds or borders. Avoid designing narrow strips of turf, hard-to-maintain corners, and isolated islands of grass into your landscape plan. These areas are difficult to water and maintain efficiently.

IRRIGATING EFFICIENTLY

Plants should be grouped according to water needs. To conserve water, use sprinklers to irrigate turf areas, and water them separately from other plantings. The key to watering a lawn efficiently is to apply water infrequently, yet thoroughly. This creates a deep, well-rooted lawn that uses water stored in the soil.

Trees, shrubs, perennial wildflowers and ground covers are watered most efficiently with low-volume drip systems, in which water drips slowly from a tube placed near the root zone, or with spray or bubbler emitters. Water should be applied to slopes at a slower rate than to flat surfaces.

IMPROVING SOIL

Proper soil preparation is essential for water conservation and healthy plants. It provides better absorption of water, improved water-holding capacity, and adequate drainage. Soil texture should be crumbly to the touch; a loam soil is ideal. If the soil is clay or sand, you may need to improve its content by adding organic matter, such as compost. Prepare your beds two to three months before planting to allow the soil time to settle. To control weeds during the settling period, apply a four- to six-inch deep mulch.

Some plants will benefit from additional soil preparation. For example, many wildflowers require well-drained soil. You may need to supplement the prepared soil with sand, gravel, or other material that loosens it and permits good drainage. Some wild-flower species require moist soil, and adding large amounts of rotted leaves and peat moss accommodate those needs. Other wildflowers develop weak, rangy stems that cannot stay upright if planted in rich soil. These plants generally fare better in poor soil with a high mineral content.

MULCHING

Mulched plant beds and border areas are an ideal alternative to turf areas. Mulching island beds is a method of limiting turf areas and displaying perennials. Typically, island beds are oval or odd-shaped beds set in a lawn.

Mulching involves covering the soil with a coarse organic material, such as bark chips, compost, or pine leaves. Inorganic mulch is also available. Mulching these areas covers and cools the soil, minimizes evaporation, reduces weed growth, improves soil composition as the organic material decays, and slows erosion. Apply mulch three to four inches deep for the best results.

SELECTING PLANTS

Plant selection involves consideration of aesthetics, function, adaptability, and commercial availability. You may be attracted to the flower color or size; the leaf shape, texture, or color; or the overall shape of a plant. An individual specimen or a complementary grouping of plants can accent your yard.

Plants often perform special functions. If you live in a hot climate, for example, shade trees have a cooling effect. In colder climates, trees are planted to form windbreaks. If you live on a busy street, plants can screen out loud noise and provide privacy.

Environmental conditions, especially climatic ones, should influence your selection of plant material for an area. Both the intensity and duration of sunlight should be taken into account. The amount of annual rainfall is also a critical factor. If you live in an arid region, choose xerophytic species to conserve water. Bear in mind that although some native plants benefit from supplemental watering, many xerophytic plants decline when planted in heavily irrigated sites. This is one reason that zoning or grouping plants according to similar water needs is essential in landscape design.

The commercial availability of native plants will ultimately determine what plants you are able to incorporate into your landscape. A demand for native plants will prompt the nursery industry to respond, and thus supply native species in large quantities. Keep asking your local nurseries to stock native plants!

MAINTAINING THE LANDSCAPE

Like any planned landscape, a naturalistic landscape or Xeriscape requires several years to become well-established. Once it has, maintenance requirements will be minimal. In the meantime, many maintenance practices that are effective for traditional, cultivated plants also work for native plants, depending on the look you wish to achieve. You may need to prune fast-growing species, or weed out undesirable plants. Clipping seed-heads encourages fullness and longer bloom periods for many perennials. Some perennial wildflowers and native shrubs respond well to severe pruning in the fall. However, many wildflowers do not need fertilizer, and may actually be chemically burned by an application of fertilizer. Indeed, many native plants thrive in poor soils.

During the summer, residents of urban areas consume 40 to 60 percent of the water supply in maintaining water-demanding landscapes. A well-designed landscape can decrease water use and maintenance by as much as 50 percent through reducing the need for mowing and replanting.

It is time we rethink the way we plan our landscapes, and begin to design them with an awareness of ecological as well as aesthetic values. Over the long term, native plant gardens hold great potential for conserving water, maintaining the ecological balance, and restoring regional character to planned landscapes.

Sisyrinchium sagittiferum

HOW TO ESTABLISH A BUFFALO GRASS LAWN

Buffalo grass provides an alternative, low-maintenance lawn that will thrive in areas, throughout the Great Plains states. Known scientifically as *Buchloë dactyloides* (buck-LOW-ee dact-tuh-LOY-dees), this warm-season perennial grass establishes itself as a short bunchgrass, and spreads by means of above-ground runners (stolons). The runners form a turf that is solid, yet loose enough to accommodate wildflowers and other native grasses. Found in native habitats from Minnesota to Montana, and south into Mexico, buffalo grass is exceptionally cold- and drought-tolerant. No other grass surpasses buffalo grass in suitability for sunny, dry-land lawns in heavy soil. It is also ideal for large landscaped areas, such as corporate grounds, parks or country homes.

Buffalo grass appears as bluish-green turf during periods of adequate rainfall. During summer drought periods and when temperatures are high, buffalo grass turns brown. This is a survival adaptation to conserve moisture, and buffalo grass turns green once again when sufficient moisture is available. With periodic rainfall or light watering, buffalo grass remains green throughout the summer. In winter months, it becomes dormant and again turns brown.

Buffalo grass must have full sun. Its one limitation is its intolerance of shade. Although it is adapted to a variety of soils, buffalo grass prefers heavier soils. Buffalo grass does not thrive in sandy soil. It is most productive in rich, well-drained clay soil, but also grows well in rocky, calcareous soil intermixed with *Bouteloua gracilis* (blue grama), *Bouteloua curtipendula* (side oats grama), *Sporobolus cryptandrus* (sand dropseed), *Schizachyrium scoparium* (little bluestem) and *Bouteloua hirsuta* (hairy grama).

Buffalo grass is dioecious, which means that male and female reproductive parts are on separate plants. The female plant blooms low to the ground, probably as an adaptation to prevent seed from being grazed. Flowers on the male plant reach a height of five to six inches and are more conspicuous, protruding above the foliage. The male flowers, often called flags, add a speckled look to the lawn.

Buffalo grass seed is contained within a hard protective coat called a burr. You should buy double-treated seed for an increased germination rate during the first year. Double treatment involves soaking the seed for 24 hours in a 0.5 percent solution of potassium nitrate (saltpeter), then storing it in a moist environment at 41 degrees Fahrenheit for 4 to 6 weeks. The seed is then dried rapidly at temperatures not exceeding 110 degrees Fahrenheit. While the germination rate of nontreated seed can be as low as 10 percent, treated seed often has a germination rate above 70 percent.

Since buffalo grass is a warm-season grass, it will not germinate until warm spring days arrive. Sow the seeds after the danger of frost has passed, when soil temperatures are 70 to 80 degrees Fahrenheit. A seeding rate of 3 to 4 pounds per 1,000 square feet is recommended. Although this rate will not immediately produce a dense lawn, buffalo grass does produce aboveground runners about 4 weeks after germination; and the runners will eventually fill in sparse areas. If economics are no concern, try seeding at a higher rate to speed up the appearance of turf grass. For larger or disturbed sites, such as reclamation projects, the recommended rate is 32 pounds per acre.

The germination and establishment rate for buffalo grass can be characterized as good to fair. However, proper watering can maximize the performance of buffalo grass. Buffalo grass seed, like any other seed, needs water to germinate. Water new plantings regularly for 1 to 2 weeks to assure germination and root establishment. Optimum growing temperatures range from 80 to 95 degrees Fahrenheit during the day; 68 degrees Fahrenheit is the optimum nighttime temperature.

Seedbed preparation for buffalo grass differs little from preparation for other lawn grasses. Till the soil no deeper than 2 inches. Rake level, and roll the soil lightly to firm the seedbed. Remove all existing weeds. As tilling often stimulates weed seed to germinate, it is advisable to water the seedbed for 1 to 2 weeks before planting. This encourages the weed seed present to germinate. Weed seedlings can then be eliminated by hand weeding, or by using herbicides with no soil-residual activity, which would also affect the grass seed. This procedure may need to be repeated several times to ensure a clean seedbed. Since it is much easier to eliminate weeds before planting, start with a fairly clean seedbed.

Planting can be done by hand broadcasting or with a garden planter. In large areas, planting seed in rows 1 foot apart enables you to weed with a hoe or garden cultivator. If you hand broadcast the seed, be sure to distribute it evenly, covering the seed with 1/2 inch or less of soil. This can be accomplished by raking in two different directions in loose topsoil. Water the bed to keep the soil moist until germination occurs, 4 to 6 days later.

Compared to other turf grass seeds, buffalo grass seeds are large. A pound contains about 50,000 seeds, whereas a pound of common Bermuda grass seed contains about 1.5 million seeds. The large seed size makes even distribution of buffalo grass seed relatively easy. Double-treated seed is stained with a dye (commonly purple or blue) that makes it visible on top of the soil.

Weeds invariably appear after seeding, and controlling them is one of the most difficult problems in establishing buffalo grass. Seedbeds that accommodate grass also accommodate most weeds. Since weeds grow faster than grass seedlings, you must control them, or the competition they provide will reduce the stand of grass. Shading seedlings and competing with them for moisture are the most harmful growth activities of weeds.

Weed control involves proper watering and mowing. Watered lawns often require more frequent mowing to prevent undesirable weeds and grasses from becoming established. Watering too early or late in the season, and overwatering, are practices that encourage weeds to grow. Weeds will establish while the grass is dormant if too much water is applied.

Buffalo grass lawns should be mowed occasionally, but never shorter than 2 inches. Mowing at least once a year will ensure a healthier lawn. An established lawn, if not mowed periodically, will actually become choked and decline over several years. If you desire a clean, uniform appearance, you may want to mow more often. Otherwise, an annual mowing is sufficient since buffalo grass only reaches 6 to 8 inches in height.

Once established, buffalo grass is virtually indestructible. Neither fertilization nor irrigation is necessary, but a timely, minimal application of either should produce a dense stand of grass. To produce thicker turf, in the spring apply fertilizer with a nitrogen-phosphorus-potassium (NPK) ratio of 3-1-2. Use cautiously, since heavy fertilization encourages weeds and Bermuda grass to grow.

Verbena bipinnatifida

A GUIDE TO RECREATING A PRAIRIE

The tallgrass prairie once covered 250 million acres of land, from Texas to Canada and from Ohio to Kansas. It was the largest ecosystem or natural area in the country. Unfortunately, today only about 1 million acres remain, making the tallgrass prairie one of our most threatened natural areas. Only Oklahoma's Osage Hills and the rocky Flint Hills of Kansas still retain significant examples of the nation's original tallgrass prairie.

As increasing numbers of settlers moved west, they transformed the tallgrass prairie into what is known as "America's Breadbasket." The few remaining sites are a part of our heritage that is fast diminishing, making it paramount that we protect, manage and learn from the few prairie remnants left, and incorporate prairie plants in future restoration projects and landscape designs.

The prairie landscape is a unique complex of associations so subtle they are easily overlooked. To the untrained eye, a native prairie may look like just another domestic pasture from a distance, but in reality a prairie is an amazingly diverse garden that may contain 200 to 300 different species of grasses and forbs.

Beginning with prairie restoration efforts at the University of

Wisconsin Arboretum in the 1930s, and the reestablishment of native pastures following the Dust Bowl, the restoration movement has spread to commercial, government and private property throughout North America's prairie biome. The early efforts at Wisconsin and in the Great Plains proved it was possible to produce vegetation resembling the native prairies, although it may be impossible to create a prairie in a strict scientific sense. Most prairies were not studied until they had been greatly altered or eradicated, making it difficult to determine what they were, and therefore, how exactly to recreate them. In addition, prairie soil structure and composition may have been irreversibly changed, preventing total restoration of prairie communities.

Since it is unrealistic to expect that such a complex ecosystem can be totally reinstated, prairie restorations are simplifications in that there will almost always be fewer species present than in natural prairies. This exemplifies why restoration is never a substitute for conservation, but rather a process that complements it.

Reasons for starting a prairie restoration are varied. The benefits of landscaping with prairie plants include the natural beauty of grasses and forbs, the attraction of wildlife, the relatively low maintenance required after the plants are established, and the personal satisfaction of encouraging a landscape that is ecologically supportive.

Before trying a restoration project, look at relict prairie sites and read studies that have been done on such sites. Since there is not a single procedure to follow in establishing a prairie, it is extremely important to observe and read about natural prairie communities. A state listing of prairie preserves is at the end of this chapter and should lead you to one in your area. Only a few of the relict prairie areas that have been acquired for preservation are in a pristine or truly native condition. After 150 years of farming and westward expansion in North America, very little natural grassland prairie remains. Rocky soil, steep hillsides, pioneer cemeteries, wet meadows and railroad/roadside embankments comprise most of the areas that have not been plowed. Those remnant prairie sites that are the best examples of natural prairies have experienced a relatively small amount of mowing or domestic grazing and only periodic burns. The number of pristine sites for scientific study continues to decrease, however.

Plant diversity in a restoration project initially will not be as great as in a natural prairie, but should increase in the following five to ten years. Many plantings will give the outward appearance of a prairie, but may contain only ten or so prevalent species. Of course, the *more diversity the better the restoration project*, and if these sites can be supplemented with an additional ten to fifteen species, so much toward improvement.

Native grasses are the framework of the prairie. As much as 50 to 95 percent of the vegetation is grass, and it supplies a unifying element. Forbs, or broad-leaved flowers, are seasonally codominant features of the plant community, providing the majority of species diversity. There are more differences in types of forbs in different regions than in types of grasses.

The major tallgrass prairie species are:

1. *Andropogon gerardi* (big bluestem): Grows robustly, up to six feet tall where moisture is plentiful. Dense root system extends six to seven feet underground. Attractive turkey-foot shaped inflorescence makes the species easy to identify. Found in dry, mesic or wet prairies.

2. *Bouteloua curtipendula* (side oats grama): Attractive clump grass which grows three to four feet high. Inflorescence typically large with numerous spikelets. Spikelet color ranges from bronze to yellow and the anthers are usually orange. Found in dry prairies.

3. *Elymus canadensis* (Canada wild rye): A two- to four-foot tall bunchgrass with wide leaf blades and seedheads resembling wheat. Seedheads drop or nod when mature. Found in mesic prairies.

4. *Koeleria pyramidata* (Junegrass): A short attractive plant with a dense, fluffy seedhead. Immature seedhead is silvery green and turns fluffy at maturity. Found in dry prairies.

5. *Panicum virgatum* (switchgrass): A three- to six-foot tall clump grass. Large, robust plants with bluish leaf blades. Inflorescence is pyramid-shaped with purplish spikelets. Found in mesic prairies.

6. *Schizachyrium scoparium* (little bluestem): At one time, it was the most abundant grass in mid-America. Very attractive

clumps cast a reddish color in the fall, topped with fluffy seeds. Found in dry or mesic prairies.

7. *Sorghastrum nutans* (Indian grass): A three- to eight-foot tall clump grass with wide leaf blades and large inflorescence. Turns a handsome bronze to yellowish color in fall. Found in dry or mesic prairies.

8. *Sporobolus heterolepis* (prairie dropseed): A one- to two-foot tall graceful and fine-textured grass which grows into fountain-head clumps. Found in dry or mesic prairies.

Grasses perform many functions. Among them are:

- *providing support and protection for tall flowers*
- *forming a dense cover that resists penetration by intro-duced weeds*
- *lending color and texture to the landscape, especially in the fall when grasses turn golden*
- *preventing soil erosion*

SPECIES SELECTION AND DISTRIBUTION PATTERNS

The amount of moisture in the soil determines which grass-land species will grow best. Soil factors, such as pH and soil type, can determine what the dominant species are as well as their proportions and distribution patterns. Often, botanists classify prairies into the following five types: *dry* (xeric); *dry-mesic; mesic; wet-mesic;* and *wet* (hydric). Generally, dry prairies have shallow sandy, gravelly, or limestone soil and cover hilltops and slopes; dry-mesic prairies develop on moderate slopes with deep mineral soil; mesic prairies are found on flat, well-drained silt-loam with a deep organic layer; wet-mesic and wet prairies occur on low, flat land near rivers and marshes, and often flood in the spring.

Haphazard placement of prairie grasses and forbs into the landscape is ineffective. Plan carefully to match species to types of soil conditions — this is an important step. Think of the prairie as a highly complex plant community with unique distribution patterns. One approach to planting a prairie is to plant a homogeneous seed mix of appropriate native species on a site, since over a period of time a natural sorting out occurs. A more scientific approach is to analyze the site's soil and microhabitats to determine the natural distribution patterns, and match the site with specific groups of species for each microhabitat.

SOIL PREPARATION

It is advisable to start small when you begin a prairie restoration project. Working on a modest scale gives you an opportunity to learn about prairie plants and how they adapt to your site. Keep in mind that larger restorations will require a considerable amount of labor during site preparation, planting, and initial maintenance. If you do not have the time, money and machinery to establish and maintain a large tract, it is best to establish a smaller, more manageable plot.

Preparation of the seedbed is one of the most important steps in recreating a prairie. Proper preparation reduces weeds, facilitates planting, and provides a suitable seedbed.

A year's lead time is necessary to allow preparatory steps in weed control. The seeds, roots and rhizomes of weeds are frequently present in large numbers, and germinate quickly after plowing. Since prairie species grow slowly above ground the first year, usually starting growth in spring, cool-season grasses and weeds have a distinct advantage the first two years and will readily choke out young plants. After two to three years, prairie plants will be able to successfully compete with most invading weeds.

The following options can be used to prepare the ground:

• *Lightly disk the site throughout the growing season whenever a new crop of weed seeds germinates.* This may need to be repeated several times before planting. Weed rhizomes will die when exposed to sun and frost during this repetitive process. It is generally recommended not to disk too deeply because dormant weed seed will then be continually exposed, creating continuing weed problems.

• *Prior to planting, if cool-season species are present lightly disk again and seed immediately.*

- *If you do not have a year's notice of planting time, lightly disk your site in the spring* and follow up with one or two additional light diskings to remove weeds that have germinated. Disk immediately prior to planting.

- *Applications of Roundup may be incorporated* if you are working on a small scale. Water the site for a week or two to promote germination of weed seed. Allow the new seedlings to grow for one to two weeks, then apply Roundup. Repeat this process once more to ensure a fairly clean seed bed. Roundup is nonresidual; in other words, it does not continue its herbicidal activity in the soil and you can plant your wildflower and native grass seed as soon as you are sure competing vegetation is under control. Roundup will not affect seed germination, only the growing plants that you have treated.

PLANTING TIMES

Upper Midwest: Last half of May until June 15 (or about the same time corn is planted)

Midwest: May (or about the same time corn is planted)

Southern Plains: Late February and March

Planting at these designated times allows for removal of cool-season weeds. If weeds are not an extreme problem, an earlier spring or late fall planting (late enough so seed will remain dormant during winter) provides for more natural stratification of seed.

Seeding later than these optimal spring planting dates increases the chance of inadequate rainfall. Seeds for prairie species are like any others: *all seeds require adequate water to germinate.* It is also important that once the seeds begin to imbibe water, they are not allowed to dry out, or they will lose their viability.

Although it is more labor-intensive, transplanting can speed up the establishment process. Prairie transplants should be treated like any other transplants and watered regularly for several weeks or until they are well-established. Transplant only when the plants are dormant, either in late fall or early spring. Extricate as much of the root system as you can when digging the plants up. Shake soil clumps from the root system, and immediately place the roots in a moist, protected environment. Fold transplants into dampened burlap, or put them in restaurant bussing pans with a low level of water. Sort the plants, divide, and root prune in a shady, protected place. All plants must be kept moist and protected from the sun. A cloudy, calm day is ideal for transplanting. Relocate transplants as soon after digging as possible.

Transplants can be obtained from several sources. Keep an eye out for local prairie remnants threatened by highway or building construction, improper maintenance, or farming. Seedlings may also be raised in greenhouses and transplanted to the field. In this case, they can be introduced in the early spring before lush growth appears, or in the fall.

PLANTING TECHNIQUES

The basic seeding techniques are *hand broadcasting, seeding with a Cultipacker* and *drill seeding*. All have advantages and disadvantages.

• *hand broadcasting*. Hand broadcast seed into a prepared seedbed, and follow by raking the seed into the soil, and then compacting with a Cultipacker or other roller to ensure good seed-soil contact.
  Advantage: Small investment in equipment; seed not distributed in rows.
  Disadvantage: Difficult to achieve uniform distribution of seed.

• *seeding with a Cultipacker*. Cultipackers are used by ranchers to plant grasses and improve their pastures. They are designed with a seed box that can be set at a specified seeding rate to plant wildflowers and native grasses. A roller bar on the Cultipacker packs the seed into the soil, ensuring good seed-soil contact.
  Advantages: Labor efficient; provides even seeding rates and depths.
  Disadvantages: Limited availability of equipment; sizing to a tractor may be difficult.

• *drill seeding:* Drill seeders are available to plant grass seed. (John Deere, Truax Co. and The Tye Co. are three well-known manufacturers.) Drill seeders cut furrows in the ground into which seeds are dropped at the recommended rate. Often a chain drags behind or a rubber tire follows, to work the seed into the soil and tamp it down. Running the drill seeder in one direction and then making a second pass over the same area, perpendicular to the first pass, is effective.

Advantages: Labor-efficient; provides even seeding rates and depths.

Disadvantage: Seed planted in rows. (More even coverage can be achieved by removing the double-disk opening and disconnecting the tube. The tube can be left hanging or removed.)

Another planting method that utilizes equipment many farms already have is to use a spreader to plant seed, followed by a *spike-tooth harrow*. A spike-tooth harrow is an implement that can be dragged behind a tractor or attached to another piece of equipment such as a drill seeder. It is a light covering device that helps work seed into the soil.

The recommended seeding depth is one-fourth to one-half inch. A good rule of thumb is to cover seed with soil at a depth that is one to three times the diameter of one of the seeds. Small seeds should be pressed into the soil surface only.

SEEDING RATES

Seeding rates vary depending on the species and the viability of that year's seeds. Generally, planting 11 to 13 pure live seeds (PLS) per square foot is recommended. (The PLS percentage should be commercially available for most species.) In critical areas where erosion control is a concern, the standard seeding rate is generally doubled. The proportion of grass seed should be no less than 60 percent grass to 40 percent wildflowers.

THE FIRST YEAR

If you have included annuals in your mix, they will germinate the first year and visually dominate the site. Although many perennials also germinate the first year, their root growth comprises two to three times the biomass of above-ground vegetation during the first year. Usually, grasses will not flower or set seed the first year, and probably will grow only two to three inches tall by the end of the growing season. *Schizachyrium scoparium* (little bluestem), for example, under favorable environmental conditions, develops a two- to three-inch primary root system before an above-ground shoot appears.

If tall weeds are shading the prairie seedlings, mow above the seedlings several times the first year to help suppress annual weeds. A scythe or hand clipper will also do the job if a mower is not available or mower blades cannot be set high enough. Most of the weeds will be annuals, and mowing before seed set destroys the seed crop. Optimum mowing time and height varies with each site. Mowing may also be necessary the second and third years. In many cases, hand weeding or spot application of an herbicide cannot be avoided, especially if aggressive species or perennial weeds are dominating the site.

THE SECOND YEAR

Most grass species will flower and produce seed the second year with an average amount of moisture. Several biennial and perennial wildflower species will also bloom. If optimum conditions for germination did not exist the first year, seeds will continue to germinate in the second year.

THE THIRD YEAR

By the third or fourth year, your prairie will benefit from a spring burn. *Fire is a natural process within the prairie ecosystem* and is important in reducing woody plants and other invaders. Burning also stimulates prairie grasses to produce above-ground vegetation the next growing season, and induces some dormant seeds to germinate. It is a management tool that should be incorporated every three or four years.

You may choose to reseed, or spot transplant species to fill in bare spots or increase the diversity of vegetation in the prairie planting, especially in the second or third year after seeding.

Once established, a restored prairie is less expensively managed and requires fewer resources than maintaining a traditional landscape. Having survived thousands of years, prairie plants are proven performers.

BIBLIOGRAPHY

Ahrenhoerster, R. & T. Wilson. 1981. *Prairie Restoration for the Beginner*. Prairie Seed Source, P.O. Box 83, North Lake, Wisc. 53064.

Costello, David. 1969. *The Prairie World*. Minneapolis, Minn.: University of Minnesota Press.

Diekelmann, John & R. Schuster. 1982. *Natural Landscaping: Designing with Native Plant Communities*. New York: McGraw-Hill.

McClain, William. 1986. *Illinois Prairie: Past and Future. A Restoration Guide*. Springfield, Ill.: Illinois Department of Conservation, Division of Natural Heritage.

Rock, Harold. 1981. *Prairie Propagation Handbook*. Milwaukee, Wisc.: Wehr Nature Center, Whitnall Park.

Smith, J. & B. Smith. 1980. *The Prairie Garden: 70 Native Plants You Can Grow in Town or Country*. Madison, Wisc.: The University of Wisconsin Press.

PRAIRIE PRESERVES

ILLINOIS: Many representative prairie samples remain. For an extensive listing, write: Illinois Department of Conservation, 605 Wm. G. Stratton Building, 400 S. Spring Street, Springfield, Ill. 62706. *Goose Lake Prairie Nature Preserve*, located in Grundy County southeast of Morris on Jugtown Road, has 1,500 acres, and is the largest of Illinois remnants. *Illinois Beach State Park* at Zion protects 829 acres of prairie and has trails and an interpretative center. *James Woodworth Prairie* in surburban Glenview on the east side of Milwaukee Avenue, and one-half mile north of Golf Road, is a 5-acre virgin prairie with trails and guides.

INDIANA: The 300-acre *Hoosier Prairie* is a national landmark and is located west of Griffith in Lake County within an industrial area. This is the last example of the Indiana sand prairie that covered the northwestern part of the state.

IOWA: Iowa once had more tallgrass prairie than any other state. Currently, 17 prairie preserves exist, totalling only 1,400 acres. *Hayden Prairie* is the largest preserve, with 240 acres. It is located 4 miles west and 5 miles north of the junction of Hwy. 9 and Hwy. 63 near Cresco. *Cayler Prairie* is located in Dickinson County, southeast of Lake Park; *Kalsow Prairie* is in north central Iowa near Fort Dodge, and has 160 acres with 240 types of plants.

KANSAS: The rolling *Flint Hills* of eastern Kansas contain one of the last large expanses of unplowed prairie. The Grassland Heritage Foundation, 5450 Buena Vista, Shawnee Mission, Kans. 66205, publishes a Flint Hills Scenic Route booklet. *Konza Prairie* is owned by Kansas State University. This 8,600-acre area south of Manhattan is used for research purposes with access by permit only. *Tuttle Creek Reservoir* near Manhattan offers camping and prairie hikes.

MINNESOTA: Sherburne National Wildlife Refuge, northwest of Minneapolis, offers a diversity of prairie species, both plant and animal. *Pipestone National Monument,* near the South Dakota border, has 200 acres of restored prairie with trails. *Blue Mounds, Buffalo River* and *Glacial Lakes State Parks* all manage areas of tallgrass prairie.

MISSOURI: Taberville Prairie in St. Clair county, 2 1/2 miles north of Taberville, is the largest preserve in Missouri, with a total of 1,650 acres. *Golden Prairie* is 16 miles northeast of Carthage near Golden City. *Tucker Prairie* is in Callaway County, 7 miles northwest of Fulton.

NEBRASKA: Willa Cather Memorial Prairie is 5 miles south of Red Cloud. It is a 610-acre site including the historic home of the novelist. The *Nebraska National Forest* preserves the grass-covered Sand Hills. *Homestead National Monument,* on the west edge of Beatrice on Route 4, has a 90-acre tract of restored prairie with trails and a visitor center.

NORTH and SOUTH DAKOTA: Both states possess great expanses of grassland, although heavy grazing has reduced its quality. The Nature Conservancy manages the *Samuel H. Ordway, Jr. Memorial Prairie* in McPherson County near the North and South Dakota boundary, 9 miles west of Leola. It is the second largest prairie preserve in the country. Its primary purpose is research, and field trips are available only by advance arrangement. In *Wind Cave National Park* and the *Theodore Roosevelt National Memorial Park,* near the Montana-North Dakota border, bison and antelope still graze in the mixed-grass prairie.

WISCONSIN: One of the larger remnants, *Avoca Prairie* in Iowa County, can be reached off of Hwy. 133, 1.5 miles east of Avoca. Hiking one-fourth mile to reach this 900-acre national landmark is well worth the effort. *Dewey Heights Prairie* in Nelson Dewey State Park at Cassville is located along the banks of the Mississippi River. *Brady's Bluff Prairie* near La Crosse within Perrot State Park is a 10-acre prairie. Of course, the *University of Wisconsin Arboretum* in Madison has one of the finest examples of restored prairie in the country.

Eschscholzia californica

HOW TO ORGANIZE A ROADSIDE WILDFLOWER PROJECT

Roadside beautification projects offer communities an excellent opportunity to unite diverse groups of people and motivate them to work toward a common goal. When citizens work together for beautification of their highways and communities, there is no limit to what they can accomplish. Highways are a visitor's introduction to a community, and first impressions can be lasting.

Highway beautification extends beyond mowing and spraying with herbicides in order to achieve a clean, green appearance. It is no longer a matter of removing plants, but one of encouraging desired species to diversify and beautify roadsides.

In the early 1900s, roadsides were covered by predominantly native vegetation. Rights-of-way were filled with native flowers, grasses, shrubs, and trees. Conditions changed in the 1930s, as truck-drawn mowers replaced horses and the federal government hired the unemployed to remove woody vegetation. Highway departments became involved in maintaining the appearance of the roadsides. An additional concern was maintaining safety strips along roadsides. Intensive right-of-way management became an increasingly standard practice.

The advent of herbicides in the 1950s provided another management tool, and many states adopted a fairly aggressive spraying policy to eradicate broadleaf vegetation. During this time aesthetics emphasized neat, lawn-like roadsides, and roadsides lost a great deal of their natural vegetation.

Prior to 1970, highway departments in many states mowed five or six times a year, from fence row to fence row. In urban areas, roadsides were sometimes mown nine or ten times annually. The energy crisis during the 1970s gradually forced many highway departments to reduce the number of times they mowed per year. As a result, some rural areas were allowed to naturalize, and slowly returned to a semblance of their native vegetation. Many of the first wildflower planting projects were also undertaken at this time, with varying degrees of success.

After the Texas Department of Highways and Public Transportation was formed in 1917, observers noted that highways were never built on natural ground, but rather over areas that highway engineers characterize as "cut or fill." And in many cases, wildflowers were the first vegetation to reappear on the disturbed land. Letting the wildflowers grow was considered by the Highway Department to be an acceptable means of erosion control, and by 1929 the department had recognized that wildflowers also serve beautification purposes. It is generally agreed that Texas' highway department was the first to recognize wildflowers as a roadside asset.

THE PLANNING PROCESS

A wildflower planting project begins with a bit of research. The first step in the planning process is to find out more about the state highway department's policies and practices. Is the state divided by districts, vegetation, or other types of zones? What are the mowing standards? Are there any "no-mow" areas? In areas where full-width mowing will be necessary, can it be deferred until the wildflower seeds have matured? Does the highway department already encourage or plant wildflowers and native grasses along roadsides? What types of grass are commonly planted? What is the department's herbicide spraying cycle, and will this interfere with wildflower plantings?

Urban areas, rural areas, interstates, and highways all undergo different mowing and herbicide routines. Analyze the various management policies and determine if plantings at certain locations are feasible. Types of mowing routines include *shoulder strip, safety, full-width,* and *non-mow.* Types of herbicide application routines include *edge-of-pavement, guardrail, signpost,* and *overspray* of undesirable plants. Before planting, it is necessary to determine if the current vegetation management policies are compatible with your goals.

If you have selected a particular route, determine whether it is under city, county or state jurisdiction. Arrange a meeting with the governing entity to discuss the possibility of undertaking a roadside beautification project. If the roadside is managed by the state highway department, meet with a representative, such as the district manager, to receive permission for your planting. If you can provide seed, many states will assist in planting and manage the area as well. Sometimes cost-sharing is possible.

Try to determine if the highway department has done any research on wildflower plantings. Contact more than one person in the highway department. These departments are often very large governmental agencies, and employees may not be aware of projects that are in progress within the agency, but outside of their sections. In addition, check with university departments, extension agents, experimental stations or other groups to learn of research activities. Listen closely to accounts of both successful and unsuccessful trial plantings. It could save you time and money later on.

SETTING UP PLOTS

Do not expect to plant the entire state, or try to interfere with existing landscaped areas. Start small; you can expand plantings in time, using techniques and species that are successful in initial plantings. If there have been few wildflower plantings in your state, starting small permits you to experiment and determine what works best in your area. Keep in mind, plantings that cover one linear mile may be too ambitious! Following are some additional recommendations:

• *Mark out small areas and use signage.* This informs motorists that they are driving through a wildflower area.

• *Select eight to ten indigenous species.* Check on commercial availability of seed by referring to seed catalogs. This is also a good way to become familiar with the cost per pound. Observation of nearby natural areas with similar soil type, slope, drainage, and exposure will help you select the most appropriate species to plant. Native species are usually well-adapted for field plantings and often grow in the poor soil that occurs along roadsides. However, roadsides are altered habitats and can also be hostile to plant life. The soil often contains a mixture of rock and other debris, and can be highly compacted, poorly drained, and high in salt and oil content. Other problems include competing vegetation such as cool-season grasses, construction activity, and mowing and spraying routines. Select a site at which these conditions occur minimally.

• *Select species to provide a blooming period of at least two months, and include both annuals and perennials.* Generally, annuals germinate and flower the first year, while perennials often take two to three years to become established and begin to flower. The Nebraska Department of Roads developed the following criteria for evaluating the potential usefulness of a wildflower species:

- *it must not be a noxious weed*
- *it must not be poisonous*
- *it should be a perennial or it must self-seed and reestablish readily if it is an annual or biennial*
- *it must have showy foliage or flowers*
- *it must have a good root system to help stabilize the soil*
- *it must associate and compete well with other vegetation*

• *If you are unsure of which indigenous species to plant, contact a botanist* or someone from the highway department, a nearby botanic garden, a local chapter of a native plant society, or a university. Use your local resources!

• *In selecting a planting site, choose a highly visible area.* Rest areas, interchanges, park turnouts, or approaches to cities or towns are highly visible sites. Form a committee to plan the development and promotion of scenic resources of the city or county. Survey roadsides and scenic areas to formulate a master plan, which you can expand each year. Be sure to define the governing entity for the site(s) selected.

• *Existing vegetation at the site should not be tight turf.* Warm-season, clump- or bunch-forming grasses are highly desirable. Many states have planted cool-season grasses, such as fescue or ryegrass, on roadsides. These grasses pose competition problems for interseeded wildflowers. Areas where cool-season grasses occur may need to be periodically replanted with wildflower seed.

Areas along newly constructed highways are prime sites for wildflower planting projects, since seed germinates more readily in loose soil than in hard, compacted soil. A newly prepared seedbed makes it easier for a highway department to plant a grass seed mixture that is compatible with wildflowers.

• *Use effective weed control techniques.* Weed control techniques, such as mowing and spraying, affect grasses as well as weeds. Often these techniques are short-term solutions and actually contribute to the weed problem. A more permanent method of eradicating many annual weeds is to limit soil disturbance and promote a well-managed grass cover. Countless numbers of weed seed exist in the soil and lie dormant until a disturbance exposes seed to light and moisture. Soil disturbances also weaken or eliminate established grasses, creating an opportunity for weeds to establish, free from competition.

Perennial weeds have extensive root systems and any technique used against them must kill the roots. Mowing too low or spraying them indiscriminately weakens the grass cover, but perennial weeds quickly respond by sending up more shoots than before. Again, failing to kill the entire weed results in more weeds, due to a less competitive grass cover. A grass cover prevents weeds from germinating, and also chokes out perennial weeds. Keeping wildflowers and native grasses vigorous is the key to controlling weeds.

• *Prepare the ground properly.* This requires equipment, time, and labor. Highway departments usually own flail mowers or other equipment that lightly scalps the ground, scratching the topsoil loose. Properly preparing the ground permits good seed-soil contact.

• *To determine planting methods, consider the size of the planting site.* In small areas, hand broadcast the seed in the fall. In northern states, try both a spring and fall planting to compare results. Mix seed with sand to ensure even distribution. Work the seed into the soil with a hand rake, or drag a section of a chain link fence by tractor across the area. Scout groups or other service organizations can be organized to help. For large areas, consult the chapter on large-scale wildflower planting to determine what methods are best for you.

• *After the blooming season, wait four to six weeks for the seed to mature before mowing.* Ask a botanist to view the plots to determine if the majority of the seed is mature. Leave the plots staked so they can be monitored over a three-year period, which is sufficient time to determine what species will flower in subsequent years and to assess your planting's long-term success. In certain parts of the country, you may need to mow again to control woody shrubs.

AWARDS PROGRAMS

You may want to develop an awards program that recognizes outstanding contributions of highway department personnel. The Lady Bird Johnson Award for Highway Beautification program, which began in Texas in 1969, was the first of its kind. In recognition of contributions in two categories, this program:

• *salutes maintenance supervisors at the county level* for contributing significantly to the traveling public's aesthetic enjoyment and recreational opportunities;

• *commends those who contribute to the natural scenic beauty* of Texas highways through preservation of native plant species.

Georgia, Florida and Michigan have patterned awards programs after the Lady Bird Johnson Award program. The Garden Club of Georgia, Inc., sponsors a Highway Wildflower Awards Luncheon. The Florida Department of Transportation started the Paths of Sunshine Awards, and the Michigan Department of Transportation sponsors an awards program for district maintenance personnel.

The National Council of State Garden Clubs spearheads a program called "Operation Wildflower," which incorporates an awards program. Each year cash grants are awarded members to encourage preservation and propagation of wildflowers and native grasses. The types of projects the awards recognize include: rural highway, urban highway, safety rest area, and civic project. The awards program began in 1973, and is carried out in cooperation with state departments of transportation. To determine whether an active chapter exists in your area, contact "Operation Wildflower," 4401 Magnolia Ave., St. Louis, Mo. 63110. A bimonthly newsletter, *The Columbine*, is available to members, and provides valuable news about projects throughout the country.

FUND-RAISING IDEAS

Exemplary of imaginative fund-raising are the efforts of an Oklahoma group, Oklahoma City Beautiful, Inc. The group conducted a penny collection campaign to raise money for a wildflower program. Penny collection canisters were placed in shopping malls throughout the city. All the money raised was used to buy wildflower seed for community plantings. Oklahoma City Beautiful also held a contest to devise a unique design for the canister.

Other ways to raise funds include encouraging civic or fraternal organizations to donate money for seed, or to formally adopt a section of roadway for beautification plantings. Local businesses may want to "sponsor a species," and donate money to buy seed. School children or scout troops can be organized to help plant the seed. Foundations with charitable trusts are also potential sources of funds.

Echinocereus pectinatus

CREATING A WILDLIFE GARDEN In recent years there has been a trend in garden styles, away from highly formalized, labor-intensive landscapes of European plants toward lower-maintenance yards and gardens with native vegetation. This changing attitude is resulting in gardens that are more sympathetic to existing ecosystems. A beneficiary of this trend, whether by design or not, is wildlife. In a world rapidly becoming fragmented into cultivated landscapes to the detriment of natural habitats, patches of wildflowers and native plants provide wildlife corridors for birds, insects, and small mammals.

You can make a garden more attractive to wildlife in a variety of ways. Keep in mind that even minor changes, such as mowing less frequently, can increase the number of nonhuman visitors. The size of your garden does not matter; even tiny yards or porches can become mini-zoos. Wildlife should enhance your garden, however, rather than become its focus. Design your garden to please yourself first, then garnish it for "critters."

The basic needs of wildlife include food, shelter, and water. A wildlife garden should provide all three. The key to creating an optimum habitat is diversity. A diverse habitat attracts a wider variety of species, offers more choices for forage and shelter, and ensures a constant food supply. Ideally, a garden should offer a mixture of meadow, woods and wet areas.

FOOD SOURCES

When deciding what to plant, include food sources for developmental needs of wildlife. Larval stages of insects, for instance, may feed on completely different plants from what the adults prefer. Some butterflies have highly species-specific needs; they may only feed on one or two types of plants. Select plants to maximize flowering and fruiting. Nectar-rich wildflowers often provide more nutritious meals for wildlife than do showy but often sterile cultivars.

Observe birds and butterflies in the wild or on untended land to discover their food preferences. Color attracts both hummingbirds and butterflies. Hummingbirds prefer bright red and orange, while butterflies seem to select primarily yellow, purple or pink over other colors. They often favor flowers that match their own coloration. To encourage butterflies, plant flowers in masses rather than singly, and separate flowers by color. Butterflies tend to frequent single flowers as opposed to double, and medium to pale colors rather than dark. The adults rarely feed on flowers in shady areas. Coarse plants like thistles and docks are good nectar sources for butterflies, and later form seedheads that attract finches and other birds.

Be sure to include trees and shrubs with berries, to provide winter forage for birds and small mammals. Vines and grasses also provide seed and nesting materials. Other provisions you can offer wildlife include pollen and sap from native plants, or fungi or compost.

SHELTER SOURCES

In planning shelter for wildlife, think layering. Wooded areas usually include overlapping canopies of trees, shrubs and forbs. The edges of woods are usually rich with wildlife. Cover provides them with protection from the elements and from predators. Different forms of wildlife can occupy specific niches within a habitat. For example, warblers, according to what species they are, may inhabit the top, middle, or lower branches of spruce trees.

In designing shelter areas, including shrubs may be more important than adding trees, since shrubs grow faster. Shrubs provide nesting sites for many different species. To provide maximum cover, curb your pruning impulse! Though dense shrubbery, tangled vines, and dead-standing trees may be incongruous with your vision of an orderly yard, they do create ideal sites for nesting and forage.

In a small yard, a single tree or a few vines can provide shelter for nesting wrens or blackbirds, as well as cover for snails and butterflies. And don't overlook what's underfoot. Brush piles, hollow logs, and compost heaps offer a range of habitats to suit many organisms.

WATER SOURCES

The third component for a wildlife garden is water. A significant portion of wildlife activity centers around water. A water source, such as a small pond, provides a home for amphibians and aquatic insects, a bathing facility for birds, and refreshing drinks for them all! Many insects have aquatic larval stages of growth, during which they require a water source. Migrant wildlife especially will find an aquatic service station quite convenient. On the smallest scale, even a birdbath can be a valuable addition to your garden or yard.

Once you allow wildlife into your garden, you must allow nature a bit of freedom in ruling it. In the words of Chris Baines, an innovative British landscaper, "The secret of a successful wildlife garden depends on understanding the way in which your various gardening activities will distort the balance." Try to minimize disturbance and refrain from using chemicals such as herbicides, pesticides, or fungicides, which adversely affect delicately balanced interactions between organisms and their environment. Allowing your garden more autonomy will leave you plenty of time to observe, enjoy and learn from your creation.

BIBLIOGRAPHY
FOR WILDLIFE GARDENING

Baines, C. 1985. *How to Make a Wildlife Garden*. London: Elm Tree Books.

Barrington, R. 1972. *A Garden for Your Birds*. New York: Grosset & Dunlap.

Burke, K. & J. Wood (eds.) 1983. *How to Attract Birds*. San Francisco: Ortho Books.

Carr, A. 1983. *Rodale's Color Handbook of Garden Insects*. Emmaus, Pa.: Rodale Press.

Damrosh, B. 1982. *Theme Gardens*. New York: Workman Publishing Co.

DeGraff, R.M. & G.M. Whitman. 1979. *Trees, Shrubs, and Vines for Attracting Birds*. Amherst, Mass.: University of Massachusetts Press.

Dennis, J.W. 1985. *The Wildlife Gardener*. New York: Alfred A. Knopf.

Gellner, S., ed. 1974. *Attracting Birds to the Garden*. Stanford, Calif.: Lane Books.

Gutierrez, R.J., D.J. Decker, R.A. Howard, Jr., & J.P. Lassoie. 1976. *Managing Small Woodlands for Wildlife*. Ithaca, N.Y.: Cornell University Extension Service, Information Bulletin 157: 1-32.

Halls, L.K. 1977. *Southern Fruit-Producing Woody Plants Used by Wildlife*. USDA Forest Service General Technical Report SO-16: 1-235.

Herzog, D.A. 1977. *How to Invite Wildlife into Your Backyard*. Brighton, Mich.: Great Lakes Living Press.

Kindilien, C.T. 1979. *Natural Birdscaping*. New York: Dell Publishing Co.

Logsdon, Gene. 1983. *Getting Food from Water: A Guide to Backyard Aquaculture*. Emmaus, Pa.: Rodale Press.

—— 1983. *Wildlife in Your Garden*. Emmaus, Pa.: Rodale Press.

Martin, A.C., H.S. Zim, A.L. Nelson. 1951. *American Wildlife and Plants: A Guide to Wildlife Food Habits*. New York: Dover.

Peterson, R.T. et al. 1974. *Gardening with Wildlife*. Washington D.C.: National Wildlife Federation.

Roth, C.E. 1982. *The Wildlife Observer's Guidebook*. Englewood Cliffs, N.J.: Prentice-Hall.

Rothschild, M., & C. Farrell. 1983. *The Butterfly Gardener*. London: Michael Joseph Ltd./Rainbow.

Schutz, W.E. 1974. *How to Attract, House, and Feed Birds*. New York: MacMillian Publishing Co.

Smyser, C.A. 1982. *Nature's Design*. Emmaus, Pa.: Rodale Press.

Tufts, Craig. 1988. *The Backyard Naturalist*. Washington D.C.: National Wildlife Federation.

Vanderpoel, R. "How We Created a Backyard Wilderness". National Wildlife 15(1):50-53. Dec.-Jan. 1977.

Warren. E.J.M. 1988. *The Country Diary Book of Creating A Butterfly Garden*. New York: Henry Holt & Co.

Wasowski, S. & J. Ryan. 1985. *Landscaping with Texas Native Plants*. Austin, Tex.: Texas Monthly Press.

Wilson, W.H.W. 1984. *Landscaping with Wildflowers and Native Plants*. San Francisco: Ortho Books.

Gaillardia pulchella

HOW TO BUY WILDFLOWER SEED IN BULK

While most seed companies can recommend an amount of seed for you to buy and plant in a given area, it is important to remember to ask about *seed quality*. Seed quality is a relevant factor for anyone producing, importing, selling or buying seed. What follows is a guide to understanding the two most important indicators of seed quality — *germination percentage* and *purity* — and a third indicator that combines these percentages, *pure live seed (PLS)*.

Wildflower seed varies considerably in both price and quality. It is important to begin shopping early and to shop carefully. Consult seed packets, obtain seed catalogs, or contact seed producers to determine the germination percentage, the date the germination test was conducted, and seed purity. You can then calculate the PLS to compare seed quality and price.

GERMINATION PERCENTAGE

Germination percentage refers to the proportion of seed that will germinate under optimum conditions in a seed-testing laboratory. To determine the germination percentage, tests are conducted on small samples of seed. The germination percentage may overestimate the actual success of germination in the field, but in all cases, the higher the percentage the better the quality of seed.

A substantial portion of wild seed is highly dormant. Dormancy is a characteristic that has been bred out of traditionally cultivated flower species. A seed may be dormant due to an impenetrable seed coat, chemical inhibitors, or other factors. Overcoming dormancy mechanisms can be a challenge in germination testing.

Seeds that do not germinate immediately may germinate in the future. It is not unusual for seeds to lie dormant in the soil for a year or more. *Lupinus texensis* (Texas bluebonnet) is an example of a species that produces hard seeds with a low first-year germination rate. Bluebonnet seeds have the appearance and feel of pea gravel. As the hard seed coats become more and more worn by the soil and are rinsed by successive rains, more seeds sprout. The dormancy mechanism helps ensure survival of the species through drought years.

Wildflower seeds do not always mature simultaneously. This is termed *indeterminate maturity*. A proportion of the seed may be immature when harvested, which can contribute to poor germination test results.

Unlike seed purity, germination percentage can change over time depending on how the seeds have been stored. High temperature and high humidity can have detrimental effects on seed germination. It is important to find out when seed was harvested, if it was harvested more than a year ago, and how has it been stored.

PURITY

Purity is a measure of the proportion of wildflower seed a given sample contains. Wildflower seed has many shapes and sizes, and this often makes the seeds difficult to clean. The portion of a sample that is not from the stated species may include seed for other crops, noxious weed seed, or inert matter such as chaff and broken seeds.

PLS OR PURE LIVE SEED

PLS combines germination percentage and purity. It is obtained by multiplying together the numerals for germination percentage and purity measure, and dividing by 100. As a general rule, the higher the PLS, the better the quality of seed, although it is important to check germination percentage and purity individually. For example:

Seed Lot A:

$$\frac{80(\%)\ \text{germination percentage} \times 90(\%)\ \text{purity measure}}{100} = 72\%\ \text{PLS}$$

Seed Lot B:

$$\frac{90(\%)\ \text{germination percentage} \times 80(\%)\ \text{purity measure}}{100} = 72\%\ \text{PLS}$$

Seed lots A and B have the same PLS, but if you desired a high germination rate, seed from lot B would be your best buy. To minimize contamination with weed seed, consumers should have samples checked for noxious weed seed content. If a sample from lot B were found to contain a high proportion of noxious weed seed, for example, then seed from lot A would be the better buy, for it would minimize weed eradication costs.

The PLS is an estimate of the amount of viable seed in a given lot. For example, in a seed lot with a 72% PLS, 72 pounds of a 100-pound sack of seed will germinate. The value of the PLS measure becomes clear when you are shopping for seed and comparing PLS with price-per-pound. Inexpensive seed with a low PLS may actually cost more per pound of viable seed than higher priced seed with a higher PLS. Compare the two batches of seed below:

Seed Lot C:

$$\frac{50(\%)\ \text{germination percentage} \times 70(\%)\ \text{purity measure}}{100} = \begin{array}{l} 35\%\ \text{PLS} \\ \text{at \$3 per lb.} \end{array}$$

Seed Lot D:

$$\frac{70(\%)\ \text{germination percentage} \times 80(\%)\ \text{purity measure}}{100} = \begin{array}{l} 56\%\ \text{PLS} \\ \text{at \$4 per lb.} \end{array}$$

Do the following calculations to determine how much seed you must buy from lot C to yield 100 pounds of pure live seed. Divide the PLS percentage (in this case 35% or .35) into 100 pounds. The resulting quotient is 286, so you would need to buy 286 pounds of seed from lot C to yield 100 pounds of pure live seed. Multiply 286 by $3 (the price per pound of seed from lot C), divide the product by 100, and you find that you would pay $8.58 for a pound of pure live seed.

For lot D, 178 pounds of seed are needed to yield 100 PLS pounds. Again this is calculated by dividing the PLS percentage (in this case 56% or .56) into 100. After multiplying 178 by $4, and dividing the product by 100, you find that the seed costs $7.12 per pound of pure live seed. The seed from lot D, though more expensive per pound ($4 per pound), by price per pure live seed ($7.12) is the better buy.

Although seed quality for vegetable and forage crops has been regulated for many years, wildflower seed quality has not. Seed testing standards developed by the Association of Official Seed Analysis (AOSA) exist for most agricultural crop species, but only a few standards exist for wildflower species. Seed testing laboratories recognize the need to develop tests, and are conducting the necessary research when time and staff are available.

Aster novae-angliae

HOW TO PROPAGATE WILDFLOWERS FROM SEED

Successful propagation of wildflowers from seed is a matter of understanding what a seed needs in order to germinate. Seed germination requirements are known for many wildflower species. However, if you collect seed from the wild for propagation, you may have to determine what some of these requirements are yourself.

Observing the natural growing conditions of the plant and physical characteristics of the seed will provide clues as to what is needed for seed germination. For example, a seed from a shade-loving plant will probably not germinate if exposed to light. Light will indicate to the seed that it is in the sun, where a mature plant cannot survive. Conversely, darkness will signal to seeds planted too deep in the soil that seedlings cannot survive.

Spring-germinating seeds often have a chilling requirement. This means that the seeds must be cold-stratified (exposed to a prescribed amount of cold) before they will germinate. This mechanism protects the seeds from being fooled into germination by an early, temporary warm spell. During a warm winter, seeds requiring cold-stratification may not germinate.

A hard seed may require scarification (nicking or breaking open of the seed coat). Scarification is achieved in nature through microbial decay, abrasion or freeze-thaw action, and may take years. Seeds with a hard coat will have a low germination rate the first year if they are not scarified.

The germination requirement common to all seeds is water. A seed must imbibe water before it can respond to other environmental conditions. Once a seed has been allowed to dry out, it loses its viability. Keep seeds moist from the beginning and throughout pretreatments. Sowing seeds in flats makes it easier to keep them moist.

Due to the variety of germination requirements, it is important to observe seeds carefully to make certain they have germinated. If they have not, pretreatment may be necessary. Sowing seeds in flats is a way of providing the proper environmental conditions needed for germination, and monitoring the germination rate. After seeds have been cleaned and dried, place them in a flat containing equal parts of peat, perlite, and vermiculite. Tiny seeds should be kept on the surface of the medium in order to be exposed to the light. Other seeds should be placed at varying depths; some on the surface, some deeper. This will ensure that at least some seeds are at the proper depth and receive the required amount of light. If no seeds germinate, try other treatments, such as placing seeds in a cooler for several weeks, or keeping them in a warm place.

Once germination has occurred, and seedlings have developed true leaves and are growing, it is time to transplant the seedlings. Seedlings may be transplanted directly into the landscape, or into a container such as a two- or four-inch pot. Temporarily planting seedlings in pots allows more observation of their growth habits and more environmental control. It also allows the seedlings to reach a size that may better survive fluctuations in environmental conditions once they are planted into the landscape. In addition, transplanting larger plants also allows more control of your planting design. You can set plants out while taking size, color, and spacing requirements into account.

Transplanting seedlings into a large-scale wildflower planting may not be economically feasible. Usually, direct seeding is most effective; plugs will help to fill in gaps. However, for smaller plantings such as gardens or for planting wild-collected seed, sowing seeds into flats and then planting seedlings into the landscape can provide more control and better results.

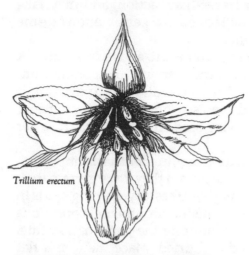

Trillium erectum

GUIDELINES FOR COLLECTING SEED

HOW AND WHERE TO COLLECT

• *Collecting wildflower seed is done largely by hand* because native species usually do not grow in pure stands. Also, topography often limits the use of mechanical equipment.

• *Tools and materials are determined by the size of the harvest.* Basic equipment includes gloves, boots, drop cloths, pruning shears, boxes, baskets, paper or canvas bags (no plastic bags). Many plants can be stripped by hand, or the seeds can be beaten onto drop cloths. Screens with large openings are often used to sort seed or fruit from other plant parts. This reduces the amount of plant material that must be dried before thrashing. Commercial operations use machines such as vacuum strippers, mechanical harvesters and tractor-drawn seed strippers to gather large quantities of seed.

• *Mark native plants during their flowering season*, when they are most noticeable. This is an important step. Seldom will plants growing in the wild catch your attention when they are in fruit, and dried seed stalks are difficult to find. Use surveyor's flagging to mark individual plants. Record landmarks (e.g., six miles from town on U.S. 12 by an "Adopt a Highway " sign on the south side of the road) so that you can find plant communities again when it is time to collect seed.

• *Always obtain permission from the landowner* when collecting seed on private land. Never collect on public land.

• *Areas scheduled to be developed or where native plants will be destroyed in the near future are excellent* sites for seed collection.

• *Avoid collecting seed from rare or endangered species.* Collect only from plants that you find growing abundantly in a given area so that you will not eradicate an isolated population. Never collect seed from plants that have not been identified.

• *At the most, take only one-third of the seed* to ensure that enough remains to reseed and increase the stand. Seeds traded commercially must number in the millions. Sellers grow seed for some species, and collect seed from native plant habitats for the rest. Ordinarily, seed collection is not likely to deplete a species, particularly if it is an annual. However, if a large proportion of the seed is collected from a site where there is a limited population of the species, or if the site is on the edge of its range and collection continues over a period of years, seed collection could deplete the population.

SEED MATURATION

• *Successful harvesting requires an understanding of seed ripening,* dispersal mechanisms, and the weather's influence on the timing of seed maturation. Collectors must be familiar with approximate flowering and fruiting dates and also should be able to recognize a mature fruit or seed. Experience is often the best teacher in learning to assess seed maturation. Since production of mature seed is weather-dependent, flowering and fruiting dates vary from year to year. For example, an early spring and dry summer may cause seed to set, or mature early. Seed quality also varies from year to year and from location to location.

• *After you have determined the approximate time period in which the fruit or seed will ripen, the next step is careful observation.* Collection should begin when fruit and seed are mature. A delay of only a few days can result in an unsuccessful harvest, especially of seeds that are dispersed quickly or are attractive to birds and other animals. Delayed harvesting, even of persistent pods, may also result in insect- or mold-infested pods and seed.

• *Many pods or capsules dehisce (break open and expel seed) when ripe and at staggered intervals,* making collection difficult. Once maturation begins, these plants may need to be checked every few days for newly matured seed. Or you may invert a paper sack over the blooms and tie the sack off with a twist-tie. Enough light and air will reach the plant to allow it to continue growing, but the sack will collect seeds as they mature and drop. This way, you will only need to collect seed once, at the end of seed set.

• *Collect seeds as soon as they are mature.* Mature seeds are usually dark in color, firm and dry. Seeds that are green and moist are immature and generally will not germinate, or will produce unhealthy seedlings. Legume pods should be collected just before or as the pod turns brown, and before it dehisces. The flesh of pulpy fruit often becomes soft and changes from green or yellow to red or blue-purple when ripe. Seeds are often mature a week or more before the fleshy fruit turns color and falls from the plant. Seed maturity can be determined by cutting open the fruit and examining the seed for firmness, fullness and dark color.

• *Gather fruit from the ground only if it has dropped recently.* Fruit or seed that has been on moist ground for some time should be rejected because they probably will have begun to decay or become infested with insects. They could ruin the rest of the harvest if combined with other seed during storage.

SEED CLEANING AND PREPARATION

• *Pods should be dried in single layers spread thinly* on a canvas cloth. Or dry them on screens or trays raised from the ground. Air-drying seed takes from one to three days, depending on humidity. Once pods are dry, seeds may be extracted by beating or threshing the pods. Often a mature pod will twist and split open to drop the seeds. Store seeds in a sealed container in a cool, dry place. Be sure that they are thoroughly dry.

• *It is not necessary to clean all seed before storage, but seed with pulpy fruit attached should be cleaned* to prevent molding. Remove pulp of large fruit by hand, by rubbing the fruit on a screen, or by mashing it with a wooden block, rolling pin or fruit press. Smaller fruit may be detached from seeds in a blender if care is taken not to damage the seeds. Blend a small portion of the seed with water in a two-to-one ratio. Brief, intermittent agitation at low speed and subsequent straining of the mixture to separate seed from pulp is effective.

• *Threshing seed (separating seeds from the rest of the collected plant material) is optional,* but has two advantages: the volume of seed to be stored is reduced, minimizing the space needed for storage; and mold spores, seed-predators such as insects, and other causes of seed deterioration may be removed when the chaff is discarded.

Threshing is most commonly accomplished by the simple method of rubbing the collected material against a coarse screen (wear a glove). Another procedure is to use one or more paddles covered with rubber matting to rub the plant material on the screen.

Commercial operations use mechanical threshers or hammermills. Hammermills are used on tough fruit where hand rubbing is impossible. Finger-like hammers rotate inside a section of a perforated metal cylinder. Seed processed in the mill is subjected to a vigorous beating or rolling action by the hammers and a perforated screen; this removes appendages and forces seed through the screen holes.

SEED STORAGE

• *The two most critical factors in seed storage are constant temperature and humidity.* Ideally, both should be low: 50 degrees Fahrenheit or less for temperature and 50 percent or less for humidity. In general, fluctuating temperature and humidity do more harm to seed than slightly higher, *constant* values of each. The key to storing seed is to find a cool, dry place that *remains* cool and dry throughout the storage period.

• *Dusting seed with a mild insecticide will help prevent insect infestation* and kill pests collected with the seed. Another tip:

insert a pest strip in each sackful of seed for several days while leaving the sacks open to allow insects to escape.

- **Store seed in paper sacks** for optimum air circulation and to prevent molding. Do not store in plastic bags or other nonporous containers *unless thoroughly air dried first*.

- **Store seed in your refrigerator,** not your freezer, until you are ready to plant. Low temperature, humidity and light levels promote seed longevity. If it is not practical to store seed in your refrigerator, store it in any place that is cool, dark and dry, protecting it from insects as much as possible.

- **Seed from fleshy fruit should be kept in a moist condition** to maintain viability. If allowed to dry out, the seeds will either germinate prematurely or not at all. This type of seed should be planted immediately or mixed in a one-to-one ratio with moist sand, sphagnum moss, or a peat-perlite medium, and stored in a cool place. If the radicle (root) emerges from the seed during storage, the seedling should be removed and planted immediately.

- **Longevity in storage varies from species to species.** Some seeds may be viable after being stored for ten years, and others may fail to germinate after a second year of storage. Ideally, seeds should be planted within one year of collection.

SEED COLLECTING BIBLIOGRAPHY

Embertson, Jane. 1979. *Pods: Wildflowers and Weeds in their Final Beauty*. New York: Charles Scribner's Sons.

Nokes, Jill. 1986. *How to Grow Native Plants of Texas and the Southwest*. Austin, Tex.: Texas Monthly Press.

Phillips, Harry. 1985. *Growing and Propagating Wild Flowers*. Chapel Hill, N.C.: The University of North Carolina Press.

Young, James & Cheryl. 1986. *Collecting, Processing and Germinating Seeds of Wildland Plants*. Portland, Oreg.: Timber Press.

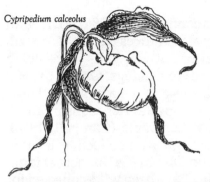

Cypripedium calceolus

WILDFLOWER CONSERVATION AND THE NURSERY TRADE

When the U.S. Congress passed the Endangered Species Act in 1973, the extent to which native plant species were in danger was not fully realized. Up until that time, the term *endangered species* was quickly associated with animals such as eagles or panda bears, rather than orchids or grasses. It was only after Congress directed the Smithsonian Institution to inventory and list endangered and threatened plants in the United States that the full extent of plant endangerment was exposed.

In 1978, the Smithsonian Plant Conservation Unit listed 3,187 plant species as extremely rare, threatened, endangered, or already extinct. This number represented approximately 15 percent of the total native flora in the United States, with the exception of Hawaii. Over 50 percent of Hawaii's native plant species were listed (Thibodeau & Falk, 1986).

Habitat loss as a result of human activity has occurred at an astonishing pace in recent decades, threatening many plants and animals. As sessile organisms (organisms that cannot move about), plants are extremely susceptible to physical disturbances such as grazing, off-road vehicles, cultivation, logging, or clearing of the land for construction. Collection of wild plants for commercial trade — for example, woodland species, cacti and other succulents, bulbs, and orchids — has placed additional pressure on many species.

A number of plants offered for sale at nurseries or through mail-order catalogs are not being distributed through propagation, the process of growing large quantities of plants from a small amount of plant material. Instead, they have been collected from the wild.

A survey of 46 catalogs that was conducted in 1986 by Dr. Faith Thompson Campbell, of the Natural Resources Defense Council, discovered that over 600 species of native plants were being offered for sale by various nurseries or catalogs. One of the 600 wildflower species sold through these 46 catalogs was listed under the United States Endangered Species Act. Conservationists consider several others to be vulnerable (Campell, 1988). Plants that have been retailed through wild-collection include species from the Lily (Liliaceae) and Orchid (Orchidaceae) families. In the Lily family, the following have been wild-collected for retail purposes: *Trillium* spp. (snow trillium and large-flowered trillium), *Erythronium* spp. (trout lily), *Polygonatum biflorum* (Solomon's seal), *Lilium* spp. (wild lily), and *Uvularia* spp. (bellwort). (Scott, 1986) and (Campbell, 1988).

Orchids that have been listed in catalogs and have been reported as being wild-collected include: *Cypripedium acaule* (pink ladyslipper orchid), *Orchis spectabilis* (showy orchid), and *Goodyera* spp. (rattlesnake plantain). In addition, *Iris* spp. (wild iris), *Arisaema triphyllum* (Jack-in-the-pulpit), and *Dodecatheon* spp. (shooting star) have been commercially available through wild-collection (Scott, 1986) and (Campbell, 1988).

Propagation of ferns can be a slow process, as spores must develop into a tiny plant called a prothallus before fertilization can occur. Some fern species are more threatened than others. Consumers should determine whether the fern they wish to buy grows in a widespread range and can be easily propagated by division. If not, the species could be vulnerable.

Conservation should be a major consideration for consumers in purchasing native plants. Even the most conservation-minded gardeners can unknowingly contribute to the wild-collection trade. It has been estimated that over 100,000 herbaceous plants are removed annually from the woodlands of North Carolina and Tennessee (Scott, 1986) and (Campbell, 1988). Equally dis-turbing is the fact that many wild-dug species do not survive transplanting. Some wildflowers are difficult to establish for even the most educated gardeners. Many species are habitat-specific, and often require mycorrhizal associations (an associa-tion between a fungus and the root system of a plant) or difficult-to-create soil conditions. The following plants are among those that usually do not survive transplanting: gentians, lilies, or-chids, parasitic Indian paintbrushes, trilliums, hepaticas, blood-root, Dutchman's breeches, and squirrel corn. These species should be enjoyed only where they occur naturally — in their native habitats!

What can *you* do to prevent buying wild-collected plants? Use the price charged as an indication of whether plants are nursery-propagated or wild-collected. Trilliums, for example, may take up to ten years to bloom. If trilliums are offered at a low price, they may have been wild-collected (Scott, 1986) and (Brumback, 1988).

Ask if the plant has been nursery-propagated or wild-col-lected. Nurseries that propagate their own plants are usually very knowledgeable about plant species and can offer good advice on how to successfully reestablish them. Nursery-pro-pagated plants have the advantage of a fully developed and compact root system. They have already been transplanted at least once, so they are able to withstand the transfer to a garden without shock to the plant, and are ready to grow immedi-ately.

Some nurseries collect plants in areas that are destined to be destroyed. Plants that are rescued from these sites can often be used for breeding stock, and the more common species can be immediately sold for use in a landscape.

LITERATURE CITED

Brumback, William. Spring 1988. "Collection of Plants From the Wild: One Propagator's View." *Wildflower*.

Campbell, Faith T. Jan./Feb. 1988. "Boycotting the Wild-Plant Trade." *Garden*.

Jones-Roe, Charlotte A. Jan. 1986. "A Commitment to Conservation at the North Carolina Botanical Garden." *The Public Garden*.

Scott, Jane. June 1986. "Native Plants and the Nursery Trade." *American Horticulturist*.

Thibodeau, Frank & Don Falk. Jan. 1986. "A New Response to Endangerment." *The Public Garden*.

Erythronium americanum

BIBLIOGRAPHIES

GENERAL BIBLIOGRAPHY

Aiken, George. 1968. *Pioneering with Wildflowers*. Englewood Cliffs, N.J.: Prentice-Hall.

Art, Henry. 1986. *A Garden of Wildflowers: 101 Native Species & How To Grow Them*. Pownal, Vt.: Storey Communications, Inc.

Berger, John. 1987. *Restoring the Earth. How Americans Are Working to Renew Our Damaged Environment*. New York: Doubleday.

Birdseye, Clarence & G. Eleanor. 1951. *Growing Woodland Plants*. New York: Oxford University Press.

Brooklyn Botanic Garden. 1962. *Handbook on Gardening with Wildflowers*. Vol. 18(1). Brooklyn, N.Y.

Brown, Lauren. 1976. *Weeds in Winter*. New York: Norton.

Bruce, Hal. 1976. *How to Grow Wildflowers and Wild Shrubs and Trees in your Own Garden*. New York: Alfred Knopf.

Crockett, James U., E. Oliver & the editors of Time-Life Books. 1977. *Wildflower Gardening*. Time-Life Encyclopedia of Gardening, Vol. 14. Alexandria, Va.: Time-Life Books.

Damrosch, Barbara. 1982. *Theme Gardens*. New York: Workman.

Diekelmann, John & R. Schuster. 1982. *Natural Landscaping: Designing with Native Plant Communities*. New York: McGraw-Hill.

Ecological Studies, Vol. 58. 1986. *Ecology of Biological Invasions of North America and Hawaii*. Edited by H.A. Mooney and J.A. Drake. New York: Springer-Verlag.

Gottehrer, Dean. 1982. *Natural Landscaping*. New York: McGraw-Hill.

Harrington, H. D. & L. W. Durrell. 1979. *How to Identify Plants*. Athens, Ohio: Swallow Press.

Hersey, Jean. 1964. *Wild Flowers to Know and Grow*. Princeton, N. J.: Van Nostrand.

Johnson, Lady Bird & Carlton Lees. 1988. *Wildflowers Across America*. New York: Abbeville Press.

Kramer, Jack. 1973. *Natural Gardens: Gardening with Native Plants*. New York: Charles Scribner & Sons.

McHarg, Ian. 1971. *Design With Nature*. Garden City, N.Y.: Natural History Press.

Martin, Laura. 1986. *The Wildflower Meadow Book*. Charlotte, N.C.: East Woods Press.

Naveh, Zev & Arthur Lieberman. 1984. *Landscape Ecology, Theory and Application*. New York: Springer-Verlag.

Penn, Cordelia. 1982. *Landscaping with Native Plants*. Winston-Salem, N.C.: John Blair.

Phillips, Harry. 1985. *Growing and Propagating Wild Flowers*. Chapel Hill, N.C.: North Carolina University Press.

Smith, James. 1977. *Vascular Plant Families*. Eureka, Calif.: Mad River Press.

Smith, Robert & Beatrice Smith. 1980. *The Prairie Garden: 70 Native Plants You Can Grow in Town or Country*. Madison, Wisc.: University of Wisconsin Press.

Smyser, Carol. 1981. *Nature's Design*. Emmaus, Pa.: Rodale Press.

Stokes, Donald. 1981. *The Natural History of Wild Shrubs & Vines*. New York: Harper & Row Publishers.

Sperka, Marie. 1973. *Growing Wildflowers: A Gardener's Guide*. New York: Harper & Row.

Steffek, Edwin. 1983. *The New Wild Flowers and How to Grow Them*. Portland, Oreg.: Timber Press.

Stevenson, Violet. 1985. *The Wild Garden: Making Natural Gardens Using Wild & Native Plants*. New York: Penguin Books.

Tatum, Billy Joe. 1976. *Wild Foods Field Guide and Cookbook*. New York: Workman Publishing Co.

Twenty-fourth Symposium of the British Ecological Society. 1986. *Ecology and Design in Landscape*. Edited by A.D. Bradshaw, D.A. Goode and E. Thorp. Palo Alto, Calif.: Blackwell Scientific Publications.

Wilson, William. 1984. *Landscaping with Wildflowers and Native Plants*. San Francisco, Calif.: Ortho Books.

Young, James and Cheryl Young. 1986. *Collecting, Processing and Germinating Seeds of Wildland Plants*. Portland, Oreg.: Timber Press.

CALIFORNIA BIBLIOGRAPHY

Abrams, Leroy. 1940. *Illustrated Flora of the Pacific States*. Vol. 1 - 4. Stanford, Calif.: Stanford University Press.

Barbour, Michael & Jack Major, eds. 1988. *Terrestrial Vegetation of California*. Davis, Calif.: California Native Plant Society.

Beauchamp, Mitchel R. 1986. *A Flora of San Diego County, California*. National City, Calif.: Sweetwater River Press.

Becking, Rudolf. 1982. *Pocket Flora of the Redwood Forest*. Covelo, Calif.: Island Press.

Benson, Lyman. 1969. *The Native Cacti of California*. Stanford, Calif.: Stanford University Press.

Benson, Lyman and Robert Darrow. 1981. *Trees and Shrubs of the Southwestern Desert*. Tucson, Ariz.: University of Arizona Press.

Clark, Lewis J. 1976. *Wild Flowers of the Pacific Northwest from Alaska to Northern California*. Sidney, British Columbia: Gray's Publishing Ltd.

Department of Water Resources. 1981. *Plants for California Landscapes: A Catalog of Drought-Tolerant Plants*. Revised. Bulletin 209; California Resources Agency, Department of Natural Resources, P.O. Box 388, Sacramento, Calif. 95802.

Duffield, Mary Rose and Warren Jones, 1981. *Plants for Dry Climates, How to Select, Grow and Enjoy*. Tucson, Ariz.: H. P. Books.

Editors of Sunset Books. 1979. *Sunset New Western Garden Book*. Menlo Park, Calif.: Lane Publishing Co.

Haskin, Leslie. 1977. *Wild Flowers of the Pacific Coast*. New York: Dover Publications.

Hood, Mary and Bill. 1969. *Yosemite Wildflowers and Their Stories*. Yosemite, Calif.: Flying Spur Press.

Johnson, Eric & David Harbison. 1985. *Landscaping to Save Water in the Desert*. Rancho Mirage, Calif.: E & H Products.

Kruckeberg, Arthur R. 1982. *Gardening with Native Plants of the Pacific Northwest*. Seattle, Wash.: University of Washington Press.

Labadie, Emile. 1978. *Native Plants for Use in the California Land-scape*. Sierra City, Calif.: Sierra City Press.

Lenz, Lee and John Dourley. 1981. *California Native Trees and Shrubs for Garden and Environmental Use in Southern California*. Claremont, Calif.: Rancho Santa Ana Botanic Garden.

Lloyd, Robert and Richard Mitchell. 1973. *A Flora of the White Mountains, California and Nevada*. Berkeley, Calif.: University of California Press.

McMinn, Howard and Evelyn Maino. 1963. *An Illustrated Manual of Pacific Coast Trees*. Berkeley, Calif.: University of California Press.

Martino, Steve & Vernon Swaback. 1986. *Desert Excellence: A Guide to Natural Landscaping*. Bellamah Community Development, 426 No. 44th St., Suite 350, Phoenix, Ariz. 85008.

Munz, Philip. 1961. *California Spring Wildflowers from the Base of the Sierra Nevada and Southern Mountains to the Sea*. Berkeley, Calif.: University of California Press.

Munz, Philip. 1962. *California Desert Wildflowers*. Berkeley, Calif.: University of California Press.

Munz, Philip. 1963. *California Mountain Wildflowers*. Berkeley, Calif.: University of California Press.

Munz, Philip A. 1973. *A California Flora*. Berkeley, Calif.: University of California Press.

Niehaus, Theodore and Charles Ripper. 1976. *A Field Guide to Pacific States Wildflowers*. Boston, Mass.: Houghton Mifflin Company.

Parsons, Mary Elizabeth. 1966. *The Wild Flowers of California*. New York: Dover.

Raven, Peter. 1966. *Native Shrubs of Southern California*. Berkeley, Calif.: University of California Press.

Schmidt, Marjorie. 1980. *Growing California Native Plants*. Berkeley, Calif.: University of California Press.

Thomas, John Hunter. 1961. *Flora of the Santa Cruz Mountains of California*. Stanford, Calif.: Stanford University Press.

BIBLIOGRAPHY
FOR THE MIDWESTERN
AND HIGH PLAINS STATES

Barr, Claude. 1983. *Jewels of the Plains: Wildflowers of the Great Plains, Grasslands & Hills*. Minneapolis, Minn.: University of Minnesota Press.

Costello, David. 1981. *The Prairie World*. Minneapolis, Minn.: University of Minnesota Press.

Currah, R., A. Smreciu & M. Van Dyk. 1983. *Prairie Wildflowers*. Edmonton, Alberta: Friends of the Devonian Botanic Garden.

Denison, Edgar. 1978. *Missouri Wildflowers*. Jefferson City, Mo.: Missouri Department of Conservation.

Edsall, Marian. 1985. *Roadside Plants and Flowers: A Traveler's Guide to the Midwest and Great Lakes Area*. Madison, Wisc.: The University of Wisconsin Press.

Great Plains Flora Association. 1986. *Flora of the Great Plains*. Lawrence, Kans.: University Press of Kansas.

Hitchcock, A. S. 1971. *Manual of Grasses of the United States*. New York: Dover.

Hunter, Carl G. 1984. *Wildflowers of Arkansas*. Little Rock, Ark.: The Ozark Society Foundation.

Kindscher, Kelly. 1987. *An Ethnobotanical Guide: Edible Wild Plants of the Prairie*. Lawrence, Kans.: University Press of Kansas.

Lommasson, Robert. 1973. *Nebraska Wild Flowers*. Lincoln, Nebr.: University of Nebraska Press.

Mohlenbrock, Robert. 1970. *The Illustrated Flora of Illinois*. Carbondale, Ill.: Southern Illinois University Press.

Moyle, John & Evelyn Moyle. 1977. *Northland Wild Flowers: A Guide for the Minnesota Region*. Minneapolis, Minn.: University of Minnesota Press.

Owensby, Clinton. 1980. *Kansas Prairie Wildflowers*. Ames, Iowa: Iowa State University Press.

Plants of South Dakota Grasslands: A Photographic Study. 1982. Bulletin 566; Agricultural Experiment Station: South Dakota State University, Brookings, S. Dak.

Preston, Richard, Jr. 1980. *North American Trees.* Ames, Iowa: Iowa State University Press.

Reichman, O.J. 1988. *Konza Prairie. A Tallgrass Natural History.* Lawrence, Kans.: University Press of Kansas.

Rock, Harold. *Prairie Propagation Handbook.* Milwaukee, Wisc.: Boerner Botanical Garden.

Smith, Helen. 1980. *Michigan Wildflowers.* Bloomfield, Mich.: Cranbrook Institute of Science.

Smith, J. Robert & Beatrice Smith. 1980. *The Prairie Garden: 70 Native Plants You Can Grow in Town or Country.* Madison, Wisc.: The University of Wisconsin Press.

Sperka, Marie. 1973. *Growing Wildflowers: A Gardener's Guide.* New York: Harper & Row.

Stephens, H.A. 1980. *Poisonous Plants of the Central United States.* Lawrence, Kans.: University Press of Kansas.

Stephens, H.A. 1973. *Woody Plants of the North Central Plains.* Lawrence, Kans.: The University Press of Kansas.

Stevens, O. A. 1963. *Handbook of North Dakota Plants.* Fargo, N. Dak.: Institute of Regional Studies.

Stubbendieck, J., Stephan Hatch & Kathie Hirsch. 1986. *North American Range Plants.* 3rd Edition. Lincoln, Nebr.: University of Nebraska Press.

Sweet, Muriel. 1975. *Common Edible and Useful Plants of the East & Midwest.* Happy Camp, Calif.: Naturegraph Publishers.

Swink, Floyd & Gerould Wilhelm. 1979. *Plants of the Chicago Region.* Lisle, Ill.: The Morton Arboretum.

Van Bruggen, Theodore. 1985. *The Vascular Plants of South Dakota.* 2nd Edition. Ames, Iowa: The Iowa State University Press.

Vance, F. R., J. R. Jowsey & J. S. McLean. 1984. *Wildflowers of the Northern Great Plains.* Minneapolis, Minn.: Minnesota University Press.

Voight, John & R. H. Mohlenbrock. 1964. *Plant Communities of Southern Illinois*. Carbondale, Ill.: Southern Illinois University Press.

Voss, Edward. 1972. *Michigan Flora*. Bloomfield, Mich.: Cranbrook Institute of Science.

Weaver, J.E. 1954. *North American Prairie*. Lincoln, Nebr.: Johnsen Publishing Co.

BIBLIOGRAPHY
FOR THE MID-ATLANTIC
& NORTHEASTERN STATES

Ahmadjian, Vernon. 1979. *Flowering Plants of Massachusetts.* Amherst, Mass.: University of Massachusetts Press.

Bruce, Hal. 1976. *How to Grow Wildflowers and Wild Shrubs and Trees in your Own Garden.* New York: Alfred Knopf.

Cox, Donald. 1985. *Common Flowering Plants of the Northeast: Their Natural History and Uses.* Albany, N.Y.: State University of New York.

Crow, Garrett. 1982. *New England's Rare, Threatened & Endangered Plants.* Washington D.C.: U.S. Government Printing Office.

DuPont, Elizabeth. 1978. *Landscaping with Native Plants in the Middle Atlantic Region.* Chadds Ford, Pa.: Brandywine Conservancy.

Gleason, Henry. 1952. *The New Britton & Brown Illustrated Flora of the Northeastern U.S. & Adjacent Canada.* Vol. 1-3. New York: Hafner Press.

Gupton, Oscar & Fred Swope. 1981. *Trees & Shrubs of Virginia.* Charlottesville, Va.: University Press of Virginia.

Gupton, Oscar & Fred Swope. 1982. *Wildflowers of the Shenandoah Valley & Blue Ridge Mountains.* Charlottesville, Va.: University Press of Virginia.

Gupton, Oscar & Fred Swope. 1982. *Wildflowers of Tidewater Virginia.* Charlottesville, Va.: University Press of Virginia.

Gupton, Oscar & Fred Swope. 1986. *Wild Orchids of the Middle Atlantic States.* Knoxville, Tenn.: The University of Tennessee Press.

Newcomb, Lawrence. 1977. *Newcomb's Wildflower Guide.* Boston: Little, Brown & Co.

Penn, Cordelia. 1982. *Landscaping with Native Plants.* Winston-Salem, N.C.: John Blair.

Peterson, Roger T. 1968. *Field Guide to Wildflowers of Northeastern & North Central North America*. Boston: Houghton-Mifflin.

Steffek, Edwin. 1983. *The New Wild Flowers and How to Grow Them*. Portland, Oreg.: Timber Press.

Stevenson, Violet. 1985. *The Wild Garden: Making Natural Gardens Using Wild & Native Plants*. New York: Penguin.

Stokes, Donald. 1985. *A Guide to Enjoying Wildflowers*. Boston: Little, Brown & Co.

Stokes, Donald. 1981. *The Natural History of Wild Shrubs & Vines*. New York: Harper & Row Publishers.

Strausbaugh, P.D. & Earl Core. 1977. *Flora of West Virginia*. Grantsville, W.Va.: Seneca Books, Inc.

Tenenbaum, Frances. 1973. *Gardening with Wild Flowers*. New York: Charles Scribner & Sons.

BIBLIOGRAPHY
FOR THE NORTHWESTERN STATES

Abrams, Leroy. 1940. *Illustrated Flora of the Pacific States*. Vols. 1-4. Stanford, Calif.: Stanford University Press.

Clark, Lewis. 1974. *Lewis Clark's Field Guide to Wild Flowers of Field and Slope in the Pacific Northwest*. Seattle, Wash.: University of Washington Press.

———. 1974. *Lewis Clark's Field Guide to Wild Flowers of Forest and Woodland in the Pacific Northwest*. Seattle, Wash.: University of Washington Press.

———. 1975. *Lewis Clark's Field Guide to Wild Flowers of the Arid Flatlands in the Pacific Northwest*. Sidney, British Columbia: Gray's Publishing Limited.

———. 1975 *Lewis Clark's Field Guide to Wild Flowers of the Mountains in the Pacific Northwest*. Seattle, Wash.: University of Washington Press.

———. 1974. *Lewis Clark's Field Guide to Wild Flowers of the Sea Coast in the Pacific Northwest*. Sidney, British Columbia: Gray's Publishing Limited.

———. 1976. *Wild Flower of the Pacific Northwest from Alaska to Northern Claifornia*. Sidney, British Columbia: Gray's Publishing Limited.

Haskin, Leslie. 1977. *Wild Flowers of the Pacific Coast*. Toronto, Ontario: General Publishing Co.

Hitchcock, A.S. 1971. *Manual of Grasses of the United States*. New York: Dover.

Jolley, Russ. 1988. *Wildflowers of the Columbia Gorge*. Portland, Oreg.: Oregon Historical Society Press.

Kruckeberg, Arthur R. 1982. *Gardening with Native Plants of the Pacific Northwest*. Seattle, Wash.: University of Washington Press.

McMinn, Howard and Evelyn Maino. 1963. *An Illustrated Manual of Pacific Coast Trees*. Berkeley, Calif.: University of California Press.

Niehaus, Theodore and Charles Ripper. 1976. *A Field Guide to Pacific States Wildflowers*. Boston: Houghton-Mifflin Co.

Rickett, Harold Williams. 1971. *Wild Flowers of the United States and the Northwestern States*. Vol. 5. New York: McGraw-Hill Book Co. for the New York Botanical Garden.

Sargent, Charles Sprague. 1965. *Manual of the Trees of North America*. Vols. 1 and 2. New York: Dover.

Spellenberg, Richard. 1985. *The Audubon Society Field Guide to North American Wildflowers: Western Region*. New York: Alfred A. Knopf.

Whitney, Steven. 1986. *The Audubon Society Nature Guides. Western Forests*. New York: Alfred A. Knopf.

BIBLIOGRAPHY
FOR THE ROCKY MOUNTAIN STATES

Costello, David. 1981. *The Prairie World*. Minneapolis, Minn.: University of Minnesota Press.

Craighead, John, Frank Craighead and Ray Davis. 1963. *A Field Guide to Rocky Mountain Wildflowers*. Boston: Houghton Mifflin Co.

Great Plains Flora Association. 1986. *Flora of the Great Plains*. Lawrence, Kans.: University Press of Kansas.

Harrington, H.D. 1979. *Manual of the Plants of Colorado*. Ann Arbor, Mich.: Grove Press.

Hitchcock, A.S. 1971. *Manual of Grasses of the United States*. New York: Dover.

Ingwersen, Will. 1986. *Manual of Alpine Plants*. Portland, Oreg.: Timber Press.

Kindscher, Kelly. 1987. *An Ethnobotanical Guide: Edible Wild Plants of the Prairie*. Lawrence, Kans.: University Press of Kansas.

Lamb, Samuel. 1977. *Woody Plants of the Southwest*. Santa Fe, N. Mex.: The Sunstone Press.

Moore, Michael. 1979. *Medicinal Plants of the Mountain West*. Santa Fe, N. Mex.: The Museum of New Mexico Press.

Phillips, Judith. 1987. *Southwestern Landscaping with Native Plants*. Santa Fe, N. Mex.: Museum of New Mexico Press.

Porslid, A.E. 1979. *Rocky Mountain Wild Flowers*. Ottawa: National Museums of Canada.

Preston, Richard, Jr. 1980. *North American Trees*. Ames, Iowa: Iowa State University Press.

Rickett, Harold Williams. 1973. *Wild Flowers of the United States: The Central Mountains and Plains*. Vol. 6. New York: McGraw-Hill Book Co. for the New York Botanical Garden.

Sargent, Charles Sprague. 1965. *Manual of the Trees of North America*. Vols. 1 and 2. New York: Dover.

Second Interim International Rock Garden Plant Conference. 1986. *Rocky Mountain Alpines*. Portland, Oreg.: Timber Press.

Spellenberg, Richard. 1985. *The Audubon Society Field Guide to North American Wildflowers: Western Region*. New York: Alfred A. Knopf.

Stubbendieck, J., Stephan Hatch and Kathie Hirsch. 1986. *North American Range Plants*. 3rd Edition. Lincoln, Nebr.: University of Nebraska Press.

Taylor, Ronald. 1982. *Rocky Mountain Wildflowers*. Seattle, Wash.: The Mountaineers.

Tierney, Gail and Phyllis Hughes. 1983. *Roadside Plants of Northern New Mexico*. Santa Fe, N. Mex.: The Lightning Tree.

Weaver, J.E. 1954. *North American Prairie*. Lincoln, Nebr.: Johnsen Publishing Co.

Weber, William. 1976. *Rocky Mountain Flora*. Boulder, Colo.: Colorado Associated University Press.

Whitney, Steven. 1986. *The Audubon Society Nature Guides. Western Forests*. New York: Alfred A. Knopf.

Zindahl, Robert. 1983. *Weeds of Colorado*. Cooperative Extension Service. Colorado State University. Fort Collins, Colo.: 80523 Bulletin 521A (revised).

BIBLIOGRAPHY
FOR THE SOUTHEASTERN STATES

Bell, C. Ritchie. 1982. *Florida Wild Flowers*. Chapel Hill, N.C.: Laurel Hill Press.

Brown, Clair. 1980. *Wildflowers of Louisiana & Adjoining States*. Baton Rouge, La.: Louisiana State University Press.

Bruce, Hal. 1976. *How to Grow Wildflowers & Wild Shrubs & Trees in Your Own Garden*. New York: Alfred Knopf.

Cronquist, Arthur. 1980. *Vascular Flora of the Southeastern United States*. Chapel Hill, N.C.: The University of North Carolina Press.

Dean, Blanche, Amy Mason & Joab Thomas. 1973. *Wildflowers of Alabama & Adjoining States*. University, Ala.: The University of Alabama Press.

Duncan, Wilbur & Leonard Foote. 1975. *Wildflowers of the Southeastern United States*. Athens, Ga.: The University of Georgia Press.

Gupton, Oscar & Fred Swope. 1981. *Trees & Shrubs of Virginia*. Charlottesville, Va.: University Press of Virginia.

Gupton, Oscar & Fred Swope. 1982. *Wildflowers of the Shenandoah Valley & Blue Ridge Mountains*. Charlottesville, Va.: University Press of Virginia.

Gupton, Oscar & Fred Swope. 1982. *Wildflowers of Tidewater Virginia*. Charlottesville, Va.: University Press of Virginia.

Gupton, Oscar & Fred Swope. 1986. *Wild Orchids of the Middle Atlantic States*. Knoxville, Tenn.: The University of Tennessee Press.

Justice, William & C. Ritchie Bell. 1983. *Wild Flowers of North Carolina*. Chapel Hill, N.C.: The University of North Carolina Press.

Odenwald, N. & J. Turner. 1987. *Identification Selection & Use of Southern Plants for Landscape Design*. Baton Rouge, La.: Claitors Publishing Division.

Parker, Lucile. 1981. *Mississippi Wildflowers*. Gretna, La.: Pelican Publishing Co.

Radford, Albert, Harry Ahles & C. Ritchie Bell. 1983. *Manual of the Vascular Flora of the Carolinas*. Chapel Hill, N.C.: The University of North Carolina Press.

Smith, Arlo. 1979. *A Guide to Wildflowers of the Mid-South*. Memphis, Tenn.: Memphis State University Press.

Steffek, Edwin. 1983. *The New Wild Flowers & How to Grow Them*. Portland, Oreg.: Timber Press.

Strausbaugh, P.D. & Earl Core. 1977. *Flora of West Virginia*. Grantsville, W.Va.: Seneca Books, Inc.

Stupka, Arthur. 1964. *Trees, Shrubs & Woody Vines of Great Smoky Mountains National Park*. Knoxville, Tenn.: The University of Tennessee Press.

Tondera, Bonnie, Laura French & Michael Gibson. 1987. *Wildflowers of North Alabama*. Huntsville, Ala.: DeskTop Publishing.

Workman, Richard. 1980. *Growing Native: Native Plants for Landscape Use in Coastal South Florida*. Sanibel, Fla.: The Sanibel-Captiva Conservation Foundation.

Zomlefer, Wendy. 1986. *Common Florida Angiosperm Families. Part I and II*. Gainesville, Fla.: Storter Printing Co.

BIBLIOGRAPHY
FOR THE SOUTHWESTERN STATES

Benson, Lyman & Robert Darrow. 1981. *Trees and Shrubs of the Southwestern Desert.* Tucson, Ariz.: University of Arizona Press.

Duffield, Mary Rose & Warren Jones. 1981. *Plants for Dry Climates, How to Select, Grow and Enjoy.* Tucson, Ariz.: H.P. Books.

Editors of Sunset Books. 1979. *Sunset New Western Garden Book.* Menlo Park, Calif.: Lane Publishing Company.

Johnson, Eric & David Harbison. 1985. *Landscaping to Save Water in the Desert.* Rancho Mirage, Calif.: E & H Products.

Kearney, Thomas, R. Peebles & collaborators. 1960. *Arizona Flora.* Berkeley, Calif.: University of California Press.

Lamb, Samuel. 1975. *Woody Plants of the Southwest.* Santa Fe, N.Mex.: The Sunstone Press.

Martino, Steve & Vernon Swaback. 1986. *Desert Excellence: A Guide to Natural Landscaping.* Bellamah Community Development, 426 No. 44th St., Suite 350, Phoenix, Ariz. 85008.

Nabhan, Gary Paul. 1985. *Gathering the Desert.* Tucson, Ariz.: The University of Arizona Press.

Natural Vegetation Committee. 1973. *Landscaping with Native Arizona Plants.* Tucson, Ariz.: Arizona Chapter of the Soil Conservation Society.

Niehaus, Thomas. 1984. *A Field Guide to Southwestern and Texas Wildflowers.* Boston: Houghton Mifflin Co.

Nokes, Jill. 1986. *How to Grow Native Plants of Texas and the Southwest.* Austin, Tex.: Texas Monthly Press.

Phillips, Judith. 1987. *Southwestern Landscaping with Native Plants.* Santa Fe, N.Mex.: Museum of New Mexico Press.

TEXAS WILDFLOWER BIBLIOGRAPHY

Abbott, Carroll. 1979. *How to Know and Grow Texas Wildflowers, Second Edition*. Kerrville, Tex.: Green Horizons Press.

Ajilvsgi, Geyata. 1984. *Wildflowers of Texas*. Bryan, Tex.: Shearer Publishing.

Ajilvsgi, Geyata. 1979. *Wildflowers of the Big Thicket, East Texas, and Western Louisiana*. College Station, Tex.: Texas A&M Press.

Cannatella, Mary. 1985. *Plants of the Texas Shore: A Beachcomber's Guide*. College Station, Tex.: Texas A&M Press.

Correll, Donovan & Marshall Johnston. 1979. *Manual of the Vascular Plants of Texas*. Richardson, Tex.: University of Texas.

Enquist, Marshall. 1987. *Wildflowers of the Texas Hill Country*. Austin, Tex.: Lone Star Botanicals.

Gould, Frank. 1975. *The Grasses of Texas*. College Station, Tex.: Texas A&M Press.

Graves, J. 1973. *Hard Scrabble: Observations on a Patch of Land*. Austin, Tex.: Texas Monthly Press.

Ham, Hal. 1984. *South Texas Wildflowers*. Kingsville, Tex.: The Conner Museum, Texas A&I University.

Irwin, Howard S. 1961. *Roadside Flowers of Texas*. Austin, Tex.: University of Texas Press.

Jones, Fred. 1975. *Flora of the Texas Coastal Bend*. Corpus Christi, Tex.: Mission Press.

Kutac, Edward A. and S. Christopher Caran. 1976. *A Bird Finding and Naturalist's Guide for the Austin, Texas, Area*. Austin, Tex.: The Oasis Press.

Loughmiller, Campbell and Lynn. 1984. *Texas Wildflowers: A Field Guide*. Austin, Tex.: The University of Texas Press.

Lynch, Brother Daniel, C.S.C. 1981. *Native & Naturalized Woody Plants of Austin & the Hill County*. Austin, Tex.: Saint Edward's University.

Niehaus, Theodore. 1984. *Field Guide to Southwestern & Texas Wildflowers*. Boston: Houghton-Mifflin Co.

Nixon, Elray. 1985. *Trees, Shrubs & Woody Vines of East Texas.* Nacogdoches, Tex.: Bruce Lyndon Cunningham Productions.

Nokes, Jill. 1986. *How to Grow Native Plants of Texas & the Southwest.* Austin, Tex.: Texas Monthly Press.

Odenwald, N. & J. Turner. 1987. *Identification Selection and Use of Southern Plants for Landscape Design.* Baton Rouge, La.: Claitors Publishing Division.

Phillips, Judith. 1987. *Southwestern Landscaping with Native Plants.* Santa Fe, N. Mex.: Museum of New Mexico Press.

Powell, Michael A. 1988. *Trees and Shrubs of Trans-Pecos Texas Including Big Bend and Guadalupe Mountains National Park.* Big Bend National Park, Tex.: Big Bend Natural History Association, Inc.

Vines, Robert. 1960. *Trees, Shrubs, and Woody Vines of the Southwest.* Austin, Tex.: University of Texas Press.

Warnock, Barton H. 1970. *Wildflowers of the Big Bend Country, Texas.* Alpine, Tex.: Sul Ross University Press.

Warnock, Barton H. 1977. *Wildflowers of the Davis Mountains and the Marathon Basin, Texas.* Alpine, Tex.: Sul Ross University Press.

Warnock, Barton H. 1974. *Wildflowers of the Guadalupe Mountains and the Sand Dune Country, Texas.* Alpine, Tex.: Sul Ross University Press.

Wasowski, Sally and Julie Ryan. 1985. *Landscaping with Texas Native Plants.* Austin, Tex.: Texas Monthly Press.

Wasowski, Sally. 1989. *Native Texas Plants: Landscaping Region by Region.* Austin, Tex.: Texas Monthly Press.

Weniger, Del. 1984. *Cacti of Texas & Neighboring States.* Austin, Tex.: University of Texas Press.

Rudbeckia laciniata

INFORMATION SOURCES

PLEASE NOTE: This list is computer sorted by two-letter
state postal abbreviation; e.g., PA for Pennsylvania.

ALASKA

Alaska Native Plant Society
P. O. Box 141613
Anchorage, AK 99514   (907)333-8212

Brief description: A nonprofit organization which promotes interest in native plants through newsletters, seed sales and field trips.

Publications: Newsletter (October - May)

Regional	Purpose:	Research Programs	Public Programs
City	Water conservation	Support research	✓ Educational programs
✓ State	Soil conservation	✓ Conduct research	✓ Field trips, seminars
National	✓ General conservation	Publish research	✓ Open to the public
	Prairie conservation		✓ Membership
	Restoration		
	Landscape design		

Wildflower Garden
c/o Verna Pratt, 7446 East 20th
Anchorage, AK 99504   (907)333-8212

Brief description: A small group of gardeners (25 members) who maintain a wildflower garden at a municipal park.

Publications:

Regional	Purpose:	Research Programs	Public Programs
✓ City	Water conservation	Support research	✓ Educational programs
State	Soil conservation	Conduct research	✓ Field trips, seminars
National	✓ General conservation	Publish research	✓ Open to the public
	Prairie conservation		✓ Membership
	Restoration		
	Landscape design		

ALABAMA

Alabama Wildflower Society, The
Rt. 2, Box 115
Northport, AL 35476   (205)339-2511

Brief description: A nonprofit organization which promotes the native plants of Alabama through field trips, special events and newsletters.

Publications: Newsletter

Regional	Purpose:	Research Programs	Public Programs
City	Water conservation	Support research	✓ Educational programs
✓ State	Soil conservation	Conduct research	✓ Field trips, seminars
National	✓ General conservation	Publish research	✓ Open to the public
	Prairie conservation		Membership
	Restoration		
	Landscape design		

Birmingham Botanical Garden
2612 Lane Park Rd.
Birmingham, AL 35223 (205)879-1227

Brief description: A municipally-owned plant collection used for research and public education; also a meeting place for several conservation groups.

Publications: Newsletter (6/yr.)

Regional	Purpose:	Research Programs	Public Programs
✓ City	Water conservation	Support research	✓ Educational programs
✓ State	Soil conservation	✓ Conduct research	✓ Field trips, seminars
National	✓ General conservation	Publish research	✓ Open to the public
	Prairie conservation		✓ Membership
	Restoration		
	Landscape design		

Huntsville/Madison County Botanical Garden Society
P. O. Box 281
Huntsville, AL 35804 (205)534-3270

Brief description: A nonprofit membership organization developing the first phase (35 acres) of a 110-acre botanical garden.

Publications:

Regional	Purpose:	Research Programs	Public Programs
✓ City	Water conservation	Support research	Educational programs
State	Soil conservation	Conduct research	✓ Field trips, seminars
National	✓ General conservation	Publish research	✓ Open to the public
	Prairie conservation		✓ Membership
	Restoration		
	Landscape design		

Troy State University Arboretum
212 Cowart Hall
Troy State University, AL 36082 (205)566-3000

Brief description: A 75-acre arboretum maintaining collections of native plants as well as representative habitats.

Publications:

Regional	Purpose:	Research Programs	Public Programs
City	Water conservation	Support research	✓ Educational programs
✓ State	Soil conservation	✓ Conduct research	✓ Field trips, seminars
National	✓ General conservation	Publish research	✓ Open to the public
	Prairie conservation		Membership
	Restoration		
	Landscape design		

University of Alabama Arboretum

P. O. Box 1927
University, AL 35486   (205)348-1803

Brief description: An arboretum which maintains four plant collections (ornamental, native woodland, wildflower, and herb/vegetable gardens).

Publications:

Regional	Purpose:	Research Programs	Public Programs
✓ City	Water conservation	Support research	✓ Educational programs
State	Soil conservation	Conduct research	✓ Field trips, seminars
National	✓ General conservation	Publish research	✓ Open to the public
	Prairie conservation		✓ Membership
	Restoration		
	Landscape design		

ARKANSAS

Arkansas Native Plant Society

c/o Dr. James Guldin, Dept. of Forest Resources, UAM
Monticello, AR 71655   (501)367-2835

Brief description: A nonprofit conservation group dedicated to the study, education, and promotion of wildflowers in Arkansas.

Publications:

Regional	Purpose:	Research Programs	Public Programs
City	Water conservation	✓ Support research	Educational programs
✓ State	Soil conservation	Conduct research	✓ Field trips, seminars
National	✓ General conservation	Publish research	✓ Open to the public
	Prairie conservation		✓ Membership
	Restoration		
	Landscape design		

Arkansas Natural Heritage Commission

The Heritage Center, Suite 200, 225 East Markham
Little Rock, AR 72201   (501)371-1706

Brief description: An agency which acquires and protects land with scenic value and natural resources, and maintains a registry of similar private land.

Publications: Arkansas's Natural Heritage; Annual Report

Regional	Purpose:	Research Programs	Public Programs
City	Water conservation	Support research	Educational programs
✓ State	Soil conservation	✓ Conduct research	✓ Field trips, seminars
National	✓ General conservation	✓ Publish research	✓ Open to the public
	Prairie conservation		Membership
	Restoration		
	Landscape design		

Nature Conservancy, The
Arkansas Office, 300 Spring Bldg. , #717
Little Rock, AR 72201   (501)372-2750

Brief description: A nonprofit conservation organization which works to protect biological diversity through preserving habitat.

Publications: The Nature Conservancy News (monthly), Chapter Newsletter

Regional	Purpose:	Research Programs	Public Programs
City	Water conservation	✓ Support research	Educational programs
✓ State	Soil conservation	✓ Conduct research	✓ Field trips, seminars
National	✓ General conservation	✓ Publish research	✓ Open to the public
	✓ Prairie conservation		✓ Membership
	Restoration		
	Landscape design		

ARIZONA

Arizona Native Plant Society
P. O. Box 41206, Sun Station
Tucson, AZ 85717

Brief description: A nonprofit organization which promotes a greater appreciation of native plants and the preservation of endangered species.

Publications: Plant Press (quarterly)

Regional	Purpose:	Research Programs	Public Programs
City	Water conservation	Support research	Educational programs
✓ State	Soil conservation	Conduct research	Field trips, seminars
National	✓ General conservation	Publish research	✓ Open to the public
	Prairie conservation		✓ Membership
	Restoration		
	Landscape design		

Arizona Nature Conservancy, The
300 E. University Blvd.
Tucson, AZ 85705   (602)622-3861

Brief description: A nonprofit conservation organization dedicated to protecting the natural diversity of the environment through land acquisition.

Publications: The Nature Conservancy News (monthly); Chapter Newsletter

Regional	Purpose:	Research Programs	Public Programs
City	Water conservation	Support research	Educational programs
✓ State	Soil conservation	Conduct research	✓ Field trips, seminars
✓ National	✓ General conservation	Publish research	✓ Open to the public
	Prairie conservation		✓ Membership
	Restoration		
	Landscape design		

Arizona-Sonora Desert Museum
Rt. 9, Box 900
Tucson, AZ 85704   (602)883-1380

Brief description: A nonprofit natural history institution which develops educational programs and conducts research on an international scale.

Publications: Sonorensis (3 times yearly)

Regional	Purpose:	Research Programs	Public Programs
✓ City	Water conservation	Support research	Educational programs
✓ State	Soil conservation	✓ Conduct research	✓ Field trips, seminars
✓ National	✓ General conservation	✓ Publish research	✓ Open to the public
	Prairie conservation		✓ Membership
	Restoration		
	Landscape design		

Boyce Thompson Southwestern Arboretum
P. O. Box AB
Superior, AZ 85273   (602)689-2811

Brief description: An aboretum affiliated with the University of Arizona and Arizona State Parks Board. Maintains a collection of plants adapted to the arid and semi-arid regions.

Publications: Desert Plants (quarterly journal)

Regional	Purpose:	Research Programs	Public Programs
City	✓ Water conservation	✓ Support research	✓ Educational programs
✓ State	Soil conservation	✓ Conduct research	✓ Field trips, seminars
✓ National	✓ General conservation	✓ Publish research	✓ Open to the public
	Prairie conservation		✓ Membership
	Restoration		
	✓ Landscape design		

C. F. Shuler, Inc.
15150 North Hayden Road
Scottsdale, AZ 85260   (602)483-0535

Brief description: A full-service landscape architectural firm which has extensive experience in using native plants.

Publications:

Regional	Purpose:	Research Programs	Public Programs
City	✓ Water conservation	Support research	Educational programs
✓ State	Soil conservation	✓ Conduct research	Field trips, seminars
National	✓ General conservation	✓ Publish research	Open to the public
	Prairie conservation		Membership
	Restoration		
	✓ Landscape design		

Desert Botanical Garden
1201 N. Galvin Parkway
Phoenix, AZ 85008   (602)941-1225

Brief description: A nonprofit organization devoted to the exhibition and conservation of arid-land plants, especially of the Southwest.

Publications: Agave (quarterly)

Regional	Purpose:	Research Programs	Public Programs
City	✓ Water conservation	✓ Support research	✓ Educational programs
✓ State	Soil conservation	✓ Conduct research	✓ Field trips, seminars
National	✓ General conservation	✓ Publish research	✓ Open to the public
	Prairie conservation		✓ Membership
	Restoration		
	Landscape design		

Nongame Wildlife Branch, Arizona Game and Fish Department
2222 West Greenway Road
Phoenix, AZ 85029-4399   (602)942-3000

Brief description: A state agency which oversees nongame wildlife and monitors endangered species.

Publications:

Regional	Purpose:	Research Programs	Public Programs
City	Water conservation	✓ Support research	Educational programs
✓ State	Soil conservation	✓ Conduct research	Field trips, seminars
National	✓ General conservation	Publish research	Open to the public
	Prairie conservation		Membership
	Restoration		
	Landscape design		

Tohono Chul Park
7366 North Paseo Del Norte
Tucson, AZ 85704   (602)742-6455

Brief description: A 35-acre preserve with nature trails, a demonstration garden and an exhibit hall housing a gallery, library and gift shop.

Publications:

Regional	Purpose:	Research Programs	Public Programs
City	Water conservation	Support research	Educational programs
✓ State	Soil conservation	Conduct research	✓ Field trips, seminars
National	✓ General conservation	Publish research	✓ Open to the public
	Prairie conservation		✓ Membership
	Restoration		
	Landscape design		

Transition Zone Horticulture Institute
P. O. Box 670
Flagstaff, AZ 86002   (602)774-1441

Brief description: A nonprofit organization which researches drought-tolerant plants of the Colorado plateau.

Publications:

Regional	Purpose:	Research Programs	Public Programs
City	Water conservation	Support research	✓ Educational programs
✓ State	Soil conservation	✓ Conduct research	✓ Field trips, seminars
National	✓ General conservation	✓ Publish research	✓ Open to the public
	Prairie conservation		✓ Membership
	Restoration		
	✓ Landscape design		

Tucson Botanical Gardens
2150 North Alverson Way
Tucson, AZ 85712   (602)326-9255

Brief description: A nonprofit institution with an active wildflower propagation and display program.

Publications: TGB Newsletter

Regional	Purpose:	Research Programs	Public Programs
✓ City	Water conservation	Support research	✓ Educational programs
State	Soil conservation	Conduct research	✓ Field trips, seminars
National	✓ General conservation	Publish research	✓ Open to the public
	Prairie conservation		✓ Membership
	Restoration		
	✓ Landscape design		

CALIFORNIA

California Department of Fish and Game, Endangered Plant Program
1416 9th Street
Sacramento, CA 95814   (916)324-3814

Brief description: An agency which identifies and works to conserve endangered plant species in California.

Publications:

Regional	Purpose:	Research Programs	Public Programs
City	Water conservation	✓ Support research	Educational programs
✓ State	Soil conservation	✓ Conduct research	Field trips, seminars
National	✓ General conservation	Publish research	Open to the public
	Prairie conservation		Membership
	Restoration		
	Landscape design		

California Native Plant Society
909 12th Street, #116
Sacramento, CA 95814   *(916)447-2677*

Brief description: A nonprofit organization which monitors and protects rare and endangered plants native to California.

Publications: Fremontia (monthly); The Bulletin (quarterly)

Regional	Purpose:	Research Programs	Public Programs
✓ City	✓ Water conservation	✓ Support research	✓ Educational programs
✓ State	✓ Soil conservation	✓ Conduct research	✓ Field trips, seminars
National	✓ General conservation	✓ Publish research	✓ Open to the public
	✓ Prairie conservation		✓ Membership
	Restoration		
	✓ Landscape design		

De Anza College Environmental Study Area
21250 Stevens Creek Blvd.
Cupertino, CA 95014   *(408)996-4525*

Brief description: A community college that maintains a small study area divided into twelve native California plant communities.

Publications: Plant list

Regional	Purpose:	Research Programs	Public Programs
City	Water conservation	Support research	✓ Educational programs
✓ State	Soil conservation	Conduct research	Field trips, seminars
National	✓ General conservation	Publish research	✓ Open to the public
	Prairie conservation		Membership
	Restoration		
	Landscape design		

Descanso Gardens Guild, Inc.
P. O. Box 778, 1418 Descanso Drive
La Canada, CA 91011   *(818)790-5414*

Brief description: A nonprofit organization which supports the Descano Gardens. The west section is a California native plant garden.

Publications:

Regional	Purpose:	Research Programs	Public Programs
City	Water conservation	Support research	✓ Educational programs
✓ State	Soil conservation	Conduct research	✓ Field trips, seminars
National	✓ General conservation	Publish research	✓ Open to the public
	Prairie conservation		✓ Membership
	Restoration		
	Landscape design		

East Bay Regional Parks Botanic Garden
Tilden Regional Park
Berkeley, CA 94708   (415)841-8732

Brief description: A botanic garden specializing in California native plants.

Publications: Four Seasons (quarterly)

Regional	Purpose:	Research Programs	Public Programs
City	Water conservation	Support research	✓ Educational programs
✓ State	Soil conservation	Conduct research	✓ Field trips, seminars
National	✓ General conservation	✓ Publish research	✓ Open to the public
	Prairie conservation		Membership
	Restoration		
	Landscape design		

Hortense Miller Garden
22511 Allview Terrace
Laguna Beach, CA 92657   (714)494-6740

Brief description: A 2 1/2 acre garden of native chaparral on steep land overlooking the Pacific Ocean.

Publications: Newsletter (quarterly)

Regional	Purpose:	Research Programs	Public Programs
✓ City	✓ Water conservation	Support research	✓ Educational programs
State	✓ Soil conservation	Conduct research	✓ Field trips, seminars
National	✓ General conservation	Publish research	✓ Open to the public
	Prairie conservation		✓ Membership
	Restoration		
	Landscape design		

Julian Woman's Club
P. O. Box 393
Julian, CA 92036   (619)765-1876

Brief description: A club which raises money for local educational projects and scholarships and also sponsors an annual wildflower show.

Publications:

Regional	Purpose:	Research Programs	Public Programs
✓ City	Water conservation	✓ Support research	Educational programs
State	Soil conservation	Conduct research	✓ Field trips, seminars
National	General conservation	Publish research	✓ Open to the public
	Prairie conservation		✓ Membership
	Restoration		
	Landscape design		

Lands and Natural Areas Project, California Department of Fish and Game
1416 Ninth Street, Room 1225
Sacramento, CA 95616   (916)322-2446

Brief description: An agency which identifies natural areas and encourages their long-term protection.

Publications:

Regional	Purpose:	Research Programs	Public Programs
City	Water conservation	Support research	Educational programs
✓ State	Soil conservation	Conduct research	Field trips, seminars
National	✓ General conservation	Publish research	Open to the public
	Prairie conservation		Membership
	Restoration		
	Landscape design		

Living Desert, The
P. O. Box 1775, 47900 South Portola Avenue
Palm Desert, CA 92661   (619)346-5694

Brief description: A nonprofit wild animal park and botanical garden with a collection of Sonoran Desert species.

Publications: Foxpaws (monthly)

Regional	Purpose:	Research Programs	Public Programs
✓ City	Water conservation	Support research	✓ Educational programs
State	Soil conservation	✓ Conduct research	✓ Field trips, seminars
National	✓ General conservation	Publish research	✓ Open to the public
	Prairie conservation		✓ Membership
	Restoration		
	Landscape design		

Lummis Garden Project, Historical Society of Southern California
200 East Avenue 43
Los Angeles, CA 90031   (213)222-0546

Brief description: A water-conserving garden, planted with California native plants or other water-conserving, drought-tolerant plants.

Publications: Southern California Quarterly Newsletter

Regional	Purpose:	Research Programs	Public Programs
✓ City	✓ Water conservation	Support research	✓ Educational programs
State	Soil conservation	Conduct research	✓ Field trips, seminars
National	General conservation	Publish research	✓ Open to the public
	Prairie conservation		✓ Membership
	Restoration		
	Landscape design		

Mendocino Coast Botanic Garden
18220 North Hwy. 1
Fort Bragg, CA 95437   (707)964-4352

Brief description: A botanic garden which collects and displays plants native to the Northern California coast.

Publications:

Regional	**Purpose:**	**Research Programs**	**Public Programs**
✓ City	Water conservation	Support research	✓ Educational programs
State	Soil conservation	Conduct research	Field trips, seminars
National	✓ General conservation	Publish research	✓ Open to the public
	Prairie conservation		✓ Membership
	Restoration		
	Landscape design		

Natural Reserve System, University of California
2120 University Avenue, 4th Floor
Berkeley, CA 94720   (415)644-4211

Brief description: Natural areas and field stations acquired for college-level teaching and research in field-oriented natural sciences.

Publications: Directory; The NRS Transect; Reserve descriptions

Regional	**Purpose:**	**Research Programs**	**Public Programs**
City	Water conservation	✓ Support research	Educational programs
✓ State	Soil conservation	✓ Conduct research	✓ Field trips, seminars
National	✓ General conservation	Publish research	✓ Open to the public
	Prairie conservation		✓ Membership
	✓ Restoration		
	Landscape design		

Nature Conservancy, The
California Field Office, 785 Market Street
San Francisco, CA 94103   (415)777-0487

Brief description: A nonprofit conservation organization dedicated to protecting the natural diversity of the environment through land acquistion and monitoring endangered species.

Publications: The Nature Conservancy News (quarterly); Chapter Newsletter

Regional	**Purpose:**	**Research Programs**	**Public Programs**
City	Water conservation	✓ Support research	Educational programs
✓ State	Soil conservation	✓ Conduct research	✓ Field trips, seminars
National	✓ General conservation	Publish research	✓ Open to the public
	Prairie conservation		✓ Membership
	✓ Restoration		
	Landscape design		

Rancho Santa Ana Botanic Garden
1500 North College Avenue
Claremont, CA 91711   (714)625-8767

Brief description: A botanic garden which emphasizes the vegetation of California, Mexico and countries with Mediterranean climates.

Publications: Newsletter (monthly)

Regional	Purpose:	Research Programs	Public Programs
City	Water conservation	Support research	✓ Educational programs
✓ State	Soil conservation	✓ Conduct research	✓ Field trips, seminars
National	✓ General conservation	✓ Publish research	✓ Open to the public
	Prairie conservation		✓ Membership
	Restoration		
	Landscape design		

San Joaquin Delta Community College, Natural Science Department
5151 Pacific Avenue
Stockton, CA 95207

Brief description: A community college which maintains a native plant demonstration garden.

Publications: Pamphlet

Regional	Purpose:	Research Programs	Public Programs
✓ City	Water conservation	Support research	Educational programs
State	Soil conservation	Conduct research	Field trips, seminars
National	✓ General conservation	Publish research	Open to the public
	Prairie conservation		Membership
	Restoration		
	Landscape design		

Santa Barbara Botanic Garden
1212 Mission Canyon Road
Santa Barbara, CA 93105   (805)682-4726

Brief description: A botanic garden which displays and studies native plants and fosters the protection of native plants of California.

Publications:

Regional	Purpose:	Research Programs	Public Programs
City	Water conservation	Support research	✓ Educational programs
✓ State	Soil conservation	✓ Conduct research	✓ Field trips, seminars
National	✓ General conservation	✓ Publish research	✓ Open to the public
	Prairie conservation		✓ Membership
	Restoration		
	Landscape design		

Southern California Botanists
California State University, Department of Biology
Fullerton, CA 92634   (714)773-3614

Brief description: A professional organization which sponsors activities such as field trips, plant sales and symposia.

Publications: Crossosoma (bimonthly)

Regional	Purpose:	Research Programs	Public Programs
City	Water conservation	✓ Support research	✓ Educational programs
✓ State	Soil conservation	Conduct research	✓ Field trips, seminars
National	✓ General conservation	Publish research	✓ Open to the public
	Prairie conservation		✓ Membership
	Restoration		
	Landscape design		

Strybing Arboretum and Botanic Garden
Golden Gate Park, 9th Avenue and Lincoln Way
San Francisco, CA 94122   (415)558-3622

Brief description: A botanic garden with collections from around the world, including a California rare and endangered plant walk.

Publications:

Regional	Purpose:	Research Programs	Public Programs
✓ City	Water conservation	Support research	✓ Educational programs
State	Soil conservation	Conduct research	✓ Field trips, seminars
National	✓ General conservation	Publish research	✓ Open to the public
	Prairie conservation		✓ Membership
	Restoration		
	✓ Landscape design		

Theodore Payne Foundation
10459 Tuxford Street
Sun Valley, CA 91352   (818)768-1802

Brief description: A nonprofit foundation devoted to preserving and propagating native plants. Also, publishes educational information and operates a native plant nursery.

Publications: Poppy Print (quarterly); Colorful California Natives

Regional	Purpose:	Research Programs	Public Programs
✓ City	✓ Water conservation	Support research	✓ Educational programs
✓ State	✓ Soil conservation	✓ Conduct research	✓ Field trips, seminars
National	✓ General conservation	Publish research	✓ Open to the public
	Prairie conservation		✓ Membership
	Restoration		
	✓ Landscape design		

University Arboretum
Department of Environmental Design, University of California
Davis, CA 95616   (916)752-2498

Brief description: A 100-acre arboretum with 2,000 species, most of which are
drought-tolerant plants, including many California natives.

Publications: Native California Plants; Indian Uses of Native Plants

Regional	Purpose:	Research Programs	Public Programs
City	✓ Water conservation	Support research	✓ Educational programs
✓ State	Soil conservation	Conduct research	✓ Field trips, seminars
National	General conservation	Publish research	✓ Open to the public
	Prairie conservation		✓ Membership
	Restoration		
	Landscape design		

University of California Botanic Gardens
Riverside, CA 92521   (714)787-4650

Brief description: A botanic garden specializing in plants that are adapted to
Mediterranean-like climates.

Publications: Newsletter (quarterly)

Regional	Purpose:	Research Programs	Public Programs
City	✓ Water conservation	Support research	✓ Educational programs
✓ State	Soil conservation	✓ Conduct research	✓ Field trips, seminars
National	✓ General conservation	Publish research	✓ Open to the public
	Prairie conservation		Membership
	Restoration		
	Landscape design		

University of California Botanical Garden
Centennial Drive
Berkeley, CA 94720   (415)642-3343

Brief description: A university botanic garden with over 8,000 species including a
Californian native plant collection.

Publications: Seed list; Newsletters; Brochures

Regional	Purpose:	Research Programs	Public Programs
City	Water conservation	Support research	✓ Educational programs
✓ State	Soil conservation	✓ Conduct research	✓ Field trips, seminars
✓ National	✓ General conservation	Publish research	✓ Open to the public
	Prairie conservation		✓ Membership
	Restoration		
	Landscape design		

COLORADO

Colorado Native Plant Society
P. O. Box 200
Fort Collins, CO 80522

Brief description: A nonprofit organization dedicated to the appreciation and conservation of Colorado's native plants.

Publications: Newsletter

Regional	Purpose:	Research Programs	Public Programs
City	Water conservation	✓ Support research	✓ Educational programs
✓ State	Soil conservation	Conduct research	✓ Field trips, seminars
National	✓ General conservation	Publish research	Open to the public
	Prairie conservation		✓ Membership
	Restoration		
	Landscape design		

Colorado Natural Areas Inventory, Department of Natural Resources
1313 Sherman Street, Room 718
Denver, CO 80203   (303)866-3311

Brief description: A state agency which identifies, monitors, and protects rare and endangered species.

Publications:

Regional	Purpose:	Research Programs	Public Programs
City	Water conservation	Support research	Educational programs
✓ State	Soil conservation	Conduct research	Field trips, seminars
National	✓ General conservation	Publish research	Open to the public
	Prairie conservation		Membership
	Restoration		
	Landscape design		

Denver Botanic Gardens
909 York
Denver, CO 80206   (303)575-3751

Brief description: A botanic garden with collections that include an alpine garden and landscape demonstration areas of low-maintenance plants.

Publications: Green Thumb (quarterly)

Regional	Purpose:	Research Programs	Public Programs
City	✓ Water conservation	Support research	✓ Educational programs
✓ State	Soil conservation	✓ Conduct research	✓ Field trips, seminars
National	✓ General conservation	✓ Publish research	✓ Open to the public
	Prairie conservation		✓ Membership
	Restoration		
	Landscape design		

Navajo Natural Heritage Program, The Nature Conservancy
1370 Pennsylvania, Suite 190
Denver, CO 80203   (303)860-9142

Brief description: A biological inventory of the Navajo Reservation, jointly performed by the Navajo Nation and The Nature Conservancy.

Publications:

Regional	Purpose:	Research Programs	Public Programs
City	Water conservation	Support research	Educational programs
State	Soil conservation	✓ Conduct research	Field trips, seminars
✓ National	✓ General conservation	Publish research	Open to the public
	Prairie conservation		✓ Membership
	Restoration		
	Landscape design		

Neils Lunceford, Inc.
Box 102
Dillon, CO 80435   (303)468-0340

Brief description: A landscape architectural firm specializing in high altitude plants.

Publications:

Regional	Purpose:	Research Programs	Public Programs
✓ City	Water conservation	✓ Support research	Educational programs
✓ State	Soil conservation	✓ Conduct research	Field trips, seminars
National	✓ General conservation	✓ Publish research	✓ Open to the public
	Prairie conservation		Membership
	Restoration		
	✓ Landscape design		

Upper Colorado Environmental Plant Center
Box 448
Meeker, CO 81641   (303)878-5003

Brief description: A soil conservation service plant material center that tests plant collections for potential use in conservation and release foundation seed to growers.

Publications:

Regional	Purpose:	Research Programs	Public Programs
City	✓ Water conservation	Support research	Educational programs
✓ State	✓ Soil conservation	✓ Conduct research	✓ Field trips, seminars
National	✓ General conservation	✓ Publish research	✓ Open to the public
	✓ Prairie conservation		Membership
	Restoration		
	Landscape design		

CONNECTICUT

Connecticut Arboretum
Connecticut College
New London, CT 06320   (201)447-1911

Brief description: An arboretum that emphasizes native woody plants and focuses research on ecology and vegetation management.

Publications: Connecticut Arboretum Bulletins No. 1-29

Regional	Purpose:	Research Programs	Public Programs
City	Water conservation	✓ Support research	✓ Educational programs
✓ State	Soil conservation	✓ Conduct research	✓ Field trips, seminars
✓ National	✓ General conservation	✓ Publish research	✓ Open to the public
	Prairie conservation		✓ Membership
	Restoration		
	Landscape design		

Connecticut Botanical Society
24 Cedarwood Lane
Old Saybrook, CT 06475   (203)388-6148

Brief description: A society which maintains an active herbarium of 30,000 specimens. Also documents flora and monitors critical natural areas.

Publications: Newsletter (quarterly)

Regional	Purpose:	Research Programs	Public Programs
City	Water conservation	Support research	✓ Educational programs
✓ State	Soil conservation	Conduct research	✓ Field trips, seminars
National	✓ General conservation	Publish research	✓ Open to the public
	Prairie conservation		✓ Membership
	Restoration		
	Landscape design		

Connecticut Natural Diversity Data Base
165 Capitol Avenue, Room 553
Hartford, CT 06106   (203)566-3540

Brief description: A cooperative governmental program which incorporates biological inventories of endangered species into a database.

Publications: Plant and Animal List

Regional	Purpose:	Research Programs	Public Programs
City	Water conservation	Support research	Educational programs
✓ State	Soil conservation	✓ Conduct research	Field trips, seminars
National	✓ General conservation	✓ Publish research	Open to the public
	Prairie conservation		Membership
	Restoration		
	Landscape design		

Fairfield Historical Society
636 Old Post Road
Fairfield, CT 06430   *(203)259-1598*

Brief description: A historical society of Fairfield which also operates a woodland wildflower garden at Ogden House.

Publications: Ogden Farm Book

Regional	Purpose:	Research Programs	Public Programs
✓ City	Water conservation	Support research	✓ Educational programs
State	Soil conservation	Conduct research	✓ Field trips, seminars
National	✓ General conservation	Publish research	✓ Open to the public
	Prairie conservation		✓ Membership
	Restoration		
	Landscape design		

Flanders Nature Center, Inc.
P. O. Box 702
Woodbury, CT 06798   *(203)263-3711*

Brief description: A nature center featuring guided nature walks, classes and programs for adults and children.

Publications: Ferns and Fern Allies of the Botany Trail

Regional	Purpose:	Research Programs	Public Programs
City	Water conservation	✓ Support research	✓ Educational programs
State	Soil conservation	✓ Conduct research	✓ Field trips, seminars
National	✓ General conservation	Publish research	✓ Open to the public
	Prairie conservation		✓ Membership
	Restoration		
	Landscape design		

Nature Conservancy, The
Connecticut Field Office. 55 High Street
Middletown, CT 06457   *(203)344-0716*

Brief description: A nonprofit conservation organization dedicated to the preservation of natural diversity through land acquisition.

Publications: The Nature Conservancy News (monthly); Chapter Newsletter

Regional	Purpose:	Research Programs	Public Programs
City	Water conservation	Support research	Educational programs
✓ State	Soil conservation	Conduct research	Field trips, seminars
National	✓ General conservation	Publish research	Open to the public
	Prairie conservation		✓ Membership
	Restoration		
	Landscape design		

New Canaan Nature Center
144 Oenoke Ridge
New Canaan, CT 06840   *(203)966-9577*

Brief description: A 40-acre sanctuary including an arboretum and native plant garden; also provides horticultural and natural history programs

Publications: Newsletter; Brochure

Regional	Purpose:	Research Programs	Public Programs
✓ City	Water conservation	Support research	✓ Educational programs
State	Soil conservation	Conduct research	✓ Field trips, seminars
National	✓ General conservation	Publish research	✓ Open to the public
	Prairie conservation		✓ Membership
	Restoration		
	Landscape design		

DISTRICT OF COLUMBIA

Environmental Defense Fund
1616 P Street, NW, Suite 150
Washington, DC 20009   *(202)387-3500*

Brief description: A nonprofit organization working for environmental issues such as state and federal plant conservation policies.

Publications: EDF Letter (quarterly)

Regional	Purpose:	Research Programs	Public Programs
City	Water conservation	Support research	Educational programs
✓ State	Soil conservation	✓ Conduct research	Field trips, seminars
✓ National	✓ General conservation	✓ Publish research	✓ Open to the public
	Prairie conservation		✓ Membership
	Restoration		
	Landscape design		

Fern Valley Native Plant Garden, U. S. National Arboretum
3501 New York Avenue, NE
Washington, DC 20002   *(202)475-4815*

Brief description: A 6.6 acre garden planted with native wildflowers, ferns, shrubs and trees.

Publications:

Regional	Purpose:	Research Programs	Public Programs
City	Water conservation	Support research	✓ Educational programs
State	Soil conservation	✓ Conduct research	✓ Field trips, seminars
✓ National	✓ General conservation	Publish research	✓ Open to the public
	Prairie conservation		✓ Membership
	Restoration		
	Landscape design		

Natural Resources Defense Council
1350 New York Avenue, NW
Washington, DC 20005   (202)783-7800

Brief description: A nonprofit organization which influences public policy on environmental issues through advocacy and lobbying.

Publications: Brochures; Bulletins; Newsline (bimonthly newsletter)

Regional	Purpose:	Research Programs	Public Programs
City	Water conservation	Support research	Educational programs
State	Soil conservation	Conduct research	Field trips, seminars
✓ National	✓ General conservation	Publish research	✓ Open to the public
	Prairie conservation		✓ Membership
	Restoration		
	Landscape design		

U. S. National Arboretum
3501 New York Avenue, NE
Washington, DC 20003   (202)475-4815

Brief description: A public garden with displays of woody and herbaceous species, including a native plant collection from the eastern forests.

Publications:

Regional	Purpose:	Research Programs	Public Programs
City	Water conservation	Support research	Educational programs
State	Soil conservation	✓ Conduct research	✓ Field trips, seminars
✓ National	✓ General conservation	Publish research	✓ Open to the public
	Prairie conservation		✓ Membership
	Restoration		
	Landscape design		

DELAWARE

Central Atlantic Region, Operation Wildflower
2513 Raven Road
Wilmington, DE 19810   (302)478-4185

Brief description: A nonprofit organization promoting wildflowers through public education and roadside planting projects.

Publications:

Regional	Purpose:	Research Programs	Public Programs
City	Water conservation	Support research	✓ Educational programs
✓ State	Soil conservation	Conduct research	Field trips, seminars
National	✓ General conservation	Publish research	Open to the public
	Prairie conservation		✓ Membership
	Restoration		
	Landscape design		

Delaware Federation of Garden Clubs
2016 Naamans Road / F10
Wilmington, DE 19810   *(302)475-7626*

Brief description: A total of 34 garden clubs working together to preserve wildflowers, beautify Delaware and preserve natural areas.

Publications:

Regional	Purpose:	Research Programs	Public Programs
City	✓ Water conservation	✓ Support research	Educational programs
✓ State	✓ Soil conservation	Conduct research	Field trips, seminars
National	✓ General conservation	Publish research	Open to the public
	✓ Prairie conservation		✓ Membership
	Restoration		
	Landscape design		

Delaware Natural Heritage Inventory, Division of Parks and Recreation
89 Kings Highway
Dover, DE 19903   *(302)736-5285*

Brief description: An agency that promotes preservation of natural areas and rare plant conservation, and computerizes heritage data.

Publications:

Regional	Purpose:	Research Programs	Public Programs
City	Water conservation	✓ Support research	Educational programs
✓ State	Soil conservation	Conduct research	✓ Field trips, seminars
National	✓ General conservation	Publish research	✓ Open to the public
	Prairie conservation		Membership
	Restoration		
	Landscape design		

Mt. Cuba Center
Box 3570
Greenville, DE 19807-0570   *(302)239-4244*

Brief description: A 230-acre private estate with 10 acres of wildflower gardens, soon to become a public garden with a native plant focus.

Publications:

Regional	Purpose:	Research Programs	Public Programs
City	Water conservation	Support research	✓ Educational programs
✓ State	Soil conservation	Conduct research	✓ Field trips, seminars
National	✓ General conservation	Publish research	Open to the public
	Prairie conservation		Membership
	Restoration		
	Landscape design		

FLORIDA

Flamingo Gardens
3750 Flamingo Road
Ft. Lauderdale, FL 33330   (305)473-2955

Brief description: A nonprofit display garden in the hammocks and everglades of
Florida.

Publications: Flamingo Garden Bulletin

Regional	Purpose:	Research Programs	Public Programs
City	Water conservation	Support research	Educational programs
✓ State	Soil conservation	Conduct research	✓ Field trips, seminars
National	✓ General conservation	Publish research	✓ Open to the public
	Prairie conservation		✓ Membership
	Restoration		
	Landscape design		

Florida Federation of Garden Clubs, Inc.
P. O. Drawer 1604
Winter Park, FL 32790   (305)647-7016

Brief description: A state-wide organization of 1,000 clubs working for the
beautification of Florida. Some clubs have a native plant focus.

Publications: The Florida Gardener

Regional	Purpose:	Research Programs	Public Programs
✓ City	Water conservation	Support research	✓ Educational programs
State	Soil conservation	Conduct research	✓ Field trips, seminars
National	✓ General conservation	Publish research	✓ Open to the public
	Prairie conservation		✓ Membership
	Restoration		
	✓ Landscape design		

Florida Native Plant Society
Suncoast Chapter
Seffner, FL 33584   (813)621-5605

Brief description: A nonprofit conservation organization offering programs and
field trips.

Publications:

Regional	Purpose:	Research Programs	Public Programs
✓ City	Water conservation	Support research	✓ Educational programs
State	Soil conservation	Conduct research	✓ Field trips, seminars
National	✓ General conservation	Publish research	✓ Open to the public
	Prairie conservation		✓ Membership
	Restoration		
	✓ Landscape design		

Florida Native Plant Society
1133 West Morse Blvd., Suite 201
Winter Park, FL 32789   (305)647-8839

Brief description: A nonprofit organization supporting preservation, conservation and restoration of native plants and communities.

Publications: The Palmetto (quarterly)

Regional	Purpose:	Research Programs	Public Programs
City	Water conservation	✓ Support research	✓ Educational programs
✓ State	Soil conservation	Conduct research	✓ Field trips, seminars
National	✓ General conservation	Publish research	✓ Open to the public
	Prairie conservation		✓ Membership
	✓ Restoration		
	Landscape design		

Florida Natural Areas Inventory, The Nature Conservancy
254 East Sixth Avenue
Tallahassee, FL 32303   (904)224-8207

Brief description: A program with an information management system which monitors rare species and communities for biological diversity.

Publications:

Regional	Purpose:	Research Programs	Public Programs
City	Water conservation	✓ Support research	Educational programs
✓ State	Soil conservation	✓ Conduct research	✓ Field trips, seminars
National	✓ General conservation	✓ Publish research	✓ Open to the public
	Prairie conservation		Membership
	Restoration		
	Landscape design		

Marie Selby Botanical Gardens
811 Palm Avenue
Sarasota, FL 33577   (813)366-5730

Brief description: A tropical botanical garden devoted to research and education, especially of epiphytes and endangered tropical plants.

Publications: Selbyana; Selby Bulletin

Regional	Purpose:	Research Programs	Public Programs
✓ City	Water conservation	Support research	Educational programs
State	Soil conservation	✓ Conduct research	✓ Field trips, seminars
National	✓ General conservation	✓ Publish research	✓ Open to the public
	Prairie conservation		✓ Membership
	Restoration		
	Landscape design		

Nature Conservancy, The
Florida State Office, 1353 Palmetto Avenue, Suite 205
Winter Park, FL 32789   (305)628-5887

Brief description: A nonprofit conservation organization dedicated to the
preservation of natural diversity through land acquistion and
monitoring rare species.

Publications: The Nature Conservancy News (monthly); Chapter Newsletter

Regional	**Purpose:**	**Research Programs**	**Public Programs**
City	Water conservation	✓ Support research	Educational programs
✓ State	Soil conservation	✓ Conduct research	✓ Field trips, seminars
National	✓ General conservation	Publish research	✓ Open to the public
	Prairie conservation		✓ Membership
	Restoration		
	Landscape design		

Sanibel Captive Conservation Foundation, Native Plant Nursery
3333 Sanibel-Captive Road
Sanibel, FL 33957   (813)472-1932

Brief description: A nature center with trails, a gift shop and a native plant nursery.

Publications: Growing Native

Regional	**Purpose:**	**Research Programs**	**Public Programs**
City	✓ Water conservation	✓ Support research	Educational programs
✓ State	✓ Soil conservation	✓ Conduct research	✓ Field trips, seminars
National	✓ General conservation	✓ Publish research	✓ Open to the public
	Prairie conservation		✓ Membership
	Restoration		
	✓ Landscape design		

GEORGIA

Atlanta Botanical Garden
Box 77246, 1345 Piedmont Road
Atlanta, GA 30357   (404)876-5858

Brief description: A 60-acre urban botanical garden with experimental wildflower
research plots.

Publications:

Regional	**Purpose:**	**Research Programs**	**Public Programs**
✓ City	Water conservation	Support research	✓ Educational programs
State	Soil conservation	Conduct research	✓ Field trips, seminars
National	✓ General conservation	Publish research	✓ Open to the public
	Prairie conservation		✓ Membership
	Restoration		
	Landscape design		

Atlanta Historical Society
3101 Andrews Drive, NW
Atlanta, GA 30305   (404)261-1837

Brief description: A historical society which owns and operates: Swan House, Tullie Smith Farm, McElreath Hall and 26 acres of gardens and woods.

Publications: Newsletter (bimonthly); Journal (quarterly)

Regional	Purpose:	Research Programs	Public Programs
✔ City	Water conservation	Support research	✔ Educational programs
State	Soil conservation	Conduct research	✔ Field trips, seminars
National	✔ General conservation	Publish research	✔ Open to the public
	Prairie conservation		✔ Membership
	Restoration		
	Landscape design		

Callaway Gardens
U. S. Highway 27
Pine Mountain, GA 31822   (404)663-2281

Brief description: A naturalistic garden with a greenhouse floral display, four landscaped walking trails and wildflower research plots.

Publications: Newsletter (quarterly)

Regional	Purpose:	Research Programs	Public Programs
City	Water conservation	Support research	✔ Educational programs
✔ State	Soil conservation	Conduct research	✔ Field trips, seminars
National	✔ General conservation	Publish research	✔ Open to the public
	Prairie conservation		Membership
	Restoration		
	Landscape design		

Fernbank Science Center
156 Heaton Park Drive NE
Atlanta, GA 30307-1398   (404)378-4311

Brief description: A museum, classroom and 65 acres of native forest supported by the DeKalb County School System and Fernbank, Inc.

Publications: Fernbank Quarterly

Regional	Purpose:	Research Programs	Public Programs
✔ City	Water conservation	Support research	✔ Educational programs
State	Soil conservation	Conduct research	✔ Field trips, seminars
National	✔ General conservation	Publish research	✔ Open to the public
	Prairie conservation		Membership
	Restoration		
	Landscape design		

Garden Club of Georgia, Inc.
325 South Lumpkin Street
Athens, GA 30602

Brief description: The state headquarters for the Garden Club of Georgia.

Publications:

Regional	**Purpose:**	**Research Programs**	**Public Programs**
City	Water conservation	Support research	✓ Educational programs
✓ State	Soil conservation	Conduct research	✓ Field trips, seminars
National	✓ General conservation	Publish research	✓ Open to the public
	Prairie conservation		✓ Membership
	Restoration		
	Landscape design		

Georgia Department of Natural Resources, Protected Plant Program
205 Butler, East Tower #1362
Atlanta, GA 30334   (404)656-3523

Brief description: A state agency that identifies, monitors and protects rare and endangered species.

Publications:

Regional	**Purpose:**	**Research Programs**	**Public Programs**
City	Water conservation	✓ Support research	Educational programs
✓ State	Soil conservation	✓ Conduct research	✓ Field trips, seminars
National	✓ General conservation	Publish research	Open to the public
	Prairie conservation		Membership
	Restoration		
	Landscape design		

Georgia Experiment Station
Department of Horticulture
Experiment, GA 30212   (404)228-7243

Brief description: An agricultural experiment station with an evaluation program to access plants for low maintenance areas.

Publications:

Regional	**Purpose:**	**Research Programs**	**Public Programs**
City	Water conservation	✓ Support research	Educational programs
✓ State	Soil conservation	✓ Conduct research	Field trips, seminars
National	✓ General conservation	✓ Publish research	✓ Open to the public
	Prairie conservation		Membership
	Restoration		
	Landscape design		

Georgia Natural Heritage Program, Department of Natural Resources
Rt. 2, Box 119-D
Social Circle, GA 30279   (404)557-2514

Brief description: A joint program of The Nature Conservancy and a state agency that monitors and protects rare and endangered species.

Publications:

Regional	Purpose:	Research Programs	Public Programs
City	Water conservation	Support research	Educational programs
✓ State	Soil conservation	✓ Conduct research	✓ Field trips, seminars
National	✓ General conservation	✓ Publish research	Open to the public
	Prairie conservation		Membership
	Restoration		
	Landscape design		

Nature Conservancy, The
Georgia Chapter, 3179 Maple Drive, NE, Suite 8
Atlanta, GA 30305   (404)266-8525

Brief description: A nonprofit organization working to preserve biological diversity through habitat protection.

Publications: The Nature Conservancy News (monthly); Chapter Newsletter

Regional	Purpose:	Research Programs	Public Programs
City	Water conservation	Support research	Educational programs
✓ State	Soil conservation	✓ Conduct research	✓ Field trips, seminars
National	✓ General conservation	Publish research	Open to the public
	Prairie conservation		✓ Membership
	Restoration		
	Landscape design		

Outdoor Activity Center
1442 Richland Road SW
Atlanta, GA 30310   (404)752-5385

Brief description: A nonprofit environmental education learning center with 26 acres of forest located in the inner city of Atlanta.

Publications: Leaves Newsletter (quarterly)

Regional	Purpose:	Research Programs	Public Programs
✓ City	Water conservation	Support research	✓ Educational programs
State	Soil conservation	Conduct research	✓ Field trips, seminars
National	✓ General conservation	Publish research	✓ Open to the public
	Prairie conservation		✓ Membership
	Restoration		
	✓ Landscape design		

State Botanical Garden of Georgia, The
The University of Georgia, 2450 South Milledge Avenue
Athens, GA 30605   (404)542-1244

Brief description: A 293-acre university affiliated botanical garden with five miles of trails, a conservatory and visitor center.

Publications: The Garden Leaflet

Regional	Purpose:	Research Programs	Public Programs
City	Water conservation	✓ Support research	✓ Educational programs
✓ State	Soil conservation	✓ Conduct research	✓ Field trips, seminars
National	✓ General conservation	✓ Publish research	✓ Open to the public
	Prairie conservation		Membership
	Restoration		
	Landscape design		

HAWAII

H. L. Lyon Arboretum
3860 Manoa Road
Honolulu, HI 96822   (808)988-3177

Brief description: A university-affiliated botanical garden and arboretum.

Publications:

Regional	Purpose:	Research Programs	Public Programs
City	Water conservation	Support research	✓ Educational programs
✓ State	Soil conservation	✓ Conduct research	✓ Field trips, seminars
National	✓ General conservation	✓ Publish research	✓ Open to the public
	Prairie conservation		Membership
	Restoration		
	Landscape design		

Hawaii Heritage
1116 Smith Street, #201
Honolulu, HI 96817   (808)537-4508

Brief description: A state agency which identifies, monitors, and protects rare and endangered species.

Publications:

Regional	Purpose:	Research Programs	Public Programs
City	Water conservation	Support research	Educational programs
✓ State	Soil conservation	Conduct research	Field trips, seminars
National	✓ General conservation	Publish research	Open to the public
	Prairie conservation		Membership
	Restoration		
	Landscape design		

Honolulu Botanic Gardens
50 North Vineyard Blvd.
Honolulu, HI 96839   (808)533-3406

Brief description: A collection of four sites comprising 650 acres with 9,000 species planted and maintained by city and county park departments.

Publications: Friends of Foster Garden newsletter

Regional	Purpose:	Research Programs	Public Programs
✓ City	Water conservation	Support research	✓ Educational programs
State	Soil conservation	Conduct research	✓ Field trips, seminars
National	✓ General conservation	Publish research	✓ Open to the public
	Prairie conservation		✓ Membership
	Restoration		
	Landscape design		

Kula Botanical Gardens
RR 2, Box 288
Kula, HI 96790   (808)878-1715

Brief description: A botanical garden with collections of proteas, orchids and other native plants.

Publications:

Regional	Purpose:	Research Programs	Public Programs
✓ City	Water conservation	Support research	Educational programs
State	Soil conservation	Conduct research	✓ Field trips, seminars
National	✓ General conservation	Publish research	✓ Open to the public
	Prairie conservation		Membership
	Restoration		
	Landscape design		

Nature Conservancy, The
Hawaii Field Office, 1116 Smith Street, Suite 201
Honolulu, HI 96817   (808)537-4508

Brief description: A nonprofit conservation organization devoted to the protection of Hawaii's native lands and wildlife.

Publications: The Nature Conservancy News (monthly); Chapter Newsletter

Regional	Purpose:	Research Programs	Public Programs
City	Water conservation	Support research	Educational programs
✓ State	Soil conservation	✓ Conduct research	✓ Field trips, seminars
National	✓ General conservation	✓ Publish research	✓ Open to the public
	Prairie conservation		✓ Membership
	Restoration		
	Landscape design		

Pacific Tropical Botanic Garden
P. O. Box 340
Lanai, HI 96765   *(808)332-7324*

Brief description: A botanical garden which focuses on research, education and preservation of tropical plant species.

Publications: The Bulletin; Allertonia; occasional papers

Regional	Purpose:	Research Programs	Public Programs
City	Water conservation	✓ Support research	✓ Educational programs
State	Soil conservation	✓ Conduct research	✓ Field trips, seminars
✓ National	✓ General conservation	✓ Publish research	✓ Open to the public
	Prairie conservation		✓ Membership
	Restoration		
	Landscape design		

USDA Soil Conservation Service
Plant Material Center, P. O. Box 236
Hoolehua, HI 96729   *(808)567-6378*

Brief description: A plant materials center that tests plant collections for potential use in conservation and produces foundation seed for growers.

Publications: Numerous

Regional	Purpose:	Research Programs	Public Programs
City	✓ Water conservation	Support research	✓ Educational programs
✓ State	✓ Soil conservation	✓ Conduct research	Field trips, seminars
National	General conservation	✓ Publish research	✓ Open to the public
	Prairie conservation		Membership
	Restoration		
	Landscape design		

Waimea Arboretum and Botanical Garden
59-864 Kamehameha Highway
Haleiwa, HI 96712   *(808)638-8655*

Brief description: A garden with over thirty botanical collections within a 1,800-acre nature park with emphasis on threatened tropical plants.

Publications: Notes from Waimea Arboretum (periodically updated)

Regional	Purpose:	Research Programs	Public Programs
City	Water conservation	Support research	Educational programs
✓ State	Soil conservation	✓ Conduct research	✓ Field trips, seminars
National	✓ General conservation	✓ Publish research	✓ Open to the public
	Prairie conservation		✓ Membership
	Restoration		
	Landscape design		

IOWA

Bickelhaupt Arboretum
340 South 14th Street
Clinton, IA 52732   (319)242-4771

Brief description: An arboretum which includes a Midwest prairie as one of its collections.

Publications:

Regional	**Purpose:**	**Research Programs**	**Public Programs**
City	Water conservation	Support research	✓ Educational programs
✓ State	Soil conservation	✓ Conduct research	Field trips, seminars
National	✓ General conservation	✓ Publish research	✓ Open to the public
	✓ Prairie conservation		Membership
	Restoration		
	Landscape design		

Nature Conservancy, The
424 10th Street, Suite 311
Des Moines, IA 50309   (515)244-5044

Brief description: A private nonprofit land preservation organization.

Publications: The Nature Conservancy News (monthly); Chapter Newsletter

Regional	**Purpose:**	**Research Programs**	**Public Programs**
City	Water conservation	Support research	Educational programs
✓ State	Soil conservation	✓ Conduct research	✓ Field trips, seminars
National	✓ General conservation	Publish research	✓ Open to the public
	Prairie conservation		✓ Membership
	Restoration		
	Landscape design		

Project Green
Civic Center
Iowa City, IA 52240   (319)351-5625

Brief description: A citizens' group dedicated to effective improvement of community landscape, especially roadside beautification.

Publications: Newsletter (quarterly)

Regional	**Purpose:**	**Research Programs**	**Public Programs**
✓ City	Water conservation	Support research	✓ Educational programs
State	Soil conservation	Conduct research	✓ Field trips, seminars
National	General conservation	Publish research	✓ Open to the public
	✓ Prairie conservation		Membership
	Restoration		
	✓ Landscape design		

State Preserves Advisory Board
Wallace State Office Building
Des Moines, IA 50319-0034   *(515)281-7614*

Brief description: A state agency that confers state preserve designation on natural, geological, historical or archaeological sites.

Publications:

Regional	Purpose:	Research Programs	Public Programs
City	Water conservation	✓ Support research	Educational programs
✓ State	Soil conservation	✓ Conduct research	✓ Field trips, seminars
National	✓ General conservation	Publish research	Open to the public
	Prairie conservation		Membership
	Restoration		
	Landscape design		

University of Northern Iowa Biological Preserves
Cedar Falls, IA 50614-0421   *(319)273-2456*

Brief description: A nature preserve with diverse natural lands and reconstructed prairies and forests.

Publications:

Regional	Purpose:	Research Programs	Public Programs
City	Water conservation	✓ Support research	✓ Educational programs
✓ State	Soil conservation	✓ Conduct research	✓ Field trips, seminars
National	✓ General conservation	Publish research	✓ Open to the public
	✓ Prairie conservation		Membership
	Restoration		
	Landscape design		

IDAHO

Don Brigham Plus Associates
Suite 412, Weisgerber Bldg.
Lewiston, ID 83501   *(208)743-7553*

Brief description: A private consulting firm which specializes in all phases of landscape architectural design and land use planning.

Publications:

Regional	Purpose:	Research Programs	Public Programs
✓ City	Water conservation	Support research	Educational programs
State	Soil conservation	✓ Conduct research	Field trips, seminars
National	✓ General conservation	Publish research	Open to the public
	Prairie conservation		Membership
	Restoration		
	✓ Landscape design		

Idaho Native Plant Society, Pahove Chapter
Box 9451
Boise, ID 83707   (208)375-8740

Brief description: A nonprofit organization concerned with conservation and promotion of native plants. Also sponsors programs and field trips.

Publications: Sage Notes

Regional	Purpose:	Research Programs	Public Programs
City	Water conservation	Support research	Educational programs
✔ State	Soil conservation	✔ Conduct research	✔ Field trips, seminars
National	✔ General conservation	Publish research	✔ Open to the public
	Prairie conservation		✔ Membership
	Restoration		
	Landscape design		

Idaho Natural Heritage Program
4696 Overland Road, Room 576
Boise, ID 83705   (208)334-3402

Brief description: A state agency which identifies, monitors, and protects rare and endangered species.

Publications:

Regional	Purpose:	Research Programs	Public Programs
City	Water conservation	Support research	Educational programs
✔ State	Soil conservation	Conduct research	Field trips, seminars
National	✔ General conservation	Publish research	Open to the public
	Prairie conservation		Membership
	Restoration		
	Landscape design		

Intermountain Resources
P. O. Box 1724
Sandpoint, ID 83864   (208)263-9391

Brief description: A consulting firm which specializes in reclamation, revegetation and erosion control.

Publications:

Regional	Purpose:	Research Programs	Public Programs
✔ City	✔ Water conservation	Support research	Educational programs
✔ State	✔ Soil conservation	✔ Conduct research	Field trips, seminars
National	✔ General conservation	Publish research	Open to the public
	Prairie conservation		Membership
	Restoration		
	✔ Landscape design		

National Council of State Federated Garden Clubs, Pacific Region
Rt. 2, Box 10
Kamiah, ID 83536   (208)935-2313

Brief description: Regional garden clubs working with the Idaho Department of
Transportation to develop wildflower plots along the highway.

Publications:

Regional	Purpose:	Research Programs	Public Programs
City	Water conservation	✓ Support research	✓ Educational programs
✓ State	Soil conservation	Conduct research	✓ Field trips, seminars
National	✓ General conservation	Publish research	✓ Open to the public
	Prairie conservation		✓ Membership
	Restoration		
	✓ Landscape design		

Nature Conservancy, The
Idaho Field Office, P.O. Box 64
Sun Valley, ID 83353   (208)726-3007

Brief description: A nonprofit conservation organization dedicated to the
preservation of natural diversity through land acquisition.

Publications: The Nature Conservancy News (monthly); Chapter Newsletter

Regional	Purpose:	Research Programs	Public Programs
City	Water conservation	Support research	Educational programs
✓ State	Soil conservation	Conduct research	Field trips, seminars
National	✓ General conservation	Publish research	Open to the public
	Prairie conservation		✓ Membership
	Restoration		
	Landscape design		

USDA Soil Conservation Service, Plant Materials Center
P. O. Box AA
Aberdeen, ID 83210   (208)397-4181

Brief description: A plant materials center that tests plant collections for potential
use in conservation, and produces foundation seed for growers.

Publications: Numerous

Regional	Purpose:	Research Programs	Public Programs
City	Water conservation	✓ Support research	✓ Educational programs
✓ State	✓ Soil conservation	Conduct research	✓ Field trips, seminars
National	General conservation	Publish research	✓ Open to the public
	Prairie conservation		✓ Membership
	Restoration		
	✓ Landscape design		

ILLINOIS

Chicago Botanic Gardens
P. O. Box 400
Glencoe, IL 60022   (312)835-5440

Brief description: A botanic garden with 300 acres of gardens, islands, and lakes managed by the Chicago Horticultural Society.

Publications: Garden Talk (monthly)

Regional	**Purpose:**	**Research Programs**	**Public Programs**
City	Water conservation	Support research	✓ Educational programs
✓ State	Soil conservation	Conduct research	✓ Field trips, seminars
National	✓ General conservation	Publish research	✓ Open to the public
	✓ Prairie conservation		✓ Membership
	Restoration		
	Landscape design		

Citizens for Conservation
Box 435, 132 West Station
Barrington, IL 60010   (312)382-SAVE

Brief description: A nonprofit group with principal interests in natural areas, open space, conservation, education and recycling.

Publications: CFC News (quarterly)

Regional	**Purpose:**	**Research Programs**	**Public Programs**
✓ City	Water conservation	Support research	✓ Educational programs
State	Soil conservation	Conduct research	✓ Field trips, seminars
National	✓ General conservation	Publish research	✓ Open to the public
	✓ Prairie conservation		✓ Membership
	Restoration		
	Landscape design		

Edward Ryerson Conservation Area, Lake County Forest Preserve
21950 North Riverwoods Road
Deerfield, IL 60015   (312)948-7750

Brief description: A 550-acre preserve of deciduous forest including a large variety of native trees and wildflowers.

Publications: The Ryerson Almanac (quarterly)

Regional	**Purpose:**	**Research Programs**	**Public Programs**
✓ City	Water conservation	✓ Support research	✓ Educational programs
State	Soil conservation	✓ Conduct research	✓ Field trips, seminars
National	✓ General conservation	Publish research	✓ Open to the public
	Prairie conservation		✓ Membership
	Restoration		
	Landscape design		

Evanston Environmental Association
2024 McCormick
Evanston, IL 60201   (312)864-5181

Brief description: A nonprofit association which sponsors environmental education programs for all ages.

Publications:

Regional	Purpose:	Research Programs	Public Programs
✓ City	Water conservation	Support research	✓ Educational programs
State	Soil conservation	Conduct research	✓ Field trips, seminars
National	✓ General conservation	Publish research	✓ Open to the public
	Prairie conservation		✓ Membership
	Restoration		
	✓ Landscape design		

Forest Park Nature Center
5809 Forest Park Drive
Peoria, IL 61614   (309)688-6413

Brief description: An interpretive nature center with 800 acres of forests and prairies, including seven miles of trails.

Publications: Tracks and Trails (bimonthly)

Regional	Purpose:	Research Programs	Public Programs
✓ City	Water conservation	Support research	✓ Educational programs
State	Soil conservation	Conduct research	✓ Field trips, seminars
National	✓ General conservation	Publish research	✓ Open to the public
	✓ Prairie conservation		✓ Membership
	Restoration		
	Landscape design		

Friends of Ryder's Woods
P. O. Box 81
Woodstock, IL 60098

Brief description: A support group for Ryder's Woods, a city-owned nature preserve within the city limits.

Publications:

Regional	Purpose:	Research Programs	Public Programs
✓ City	Water conservation	Support research	Educational programs
State	Soil conservation	Conduct research	✓ Field trips, seminars
National	✓ General conservation	Publish research	✓ Open to the public
	✓ Prairie conservation		✓ Membership
	Restoration		
	Landscape design		

Friends of the Fen
c/o Steve Byers, McGraw Wildlife, Box 194
Dundee, IL 60118   (312)741-8000

Brief description: A nonprofit organization dedicated to preservation and wise stewardship of Bluff Spring Fen.

Publications: Fenship Newsletter (annually)

Regional	Purpose:	Research Programs	Public Programs
✓ City	Water conservation	Support research	✓ Educational programs
State	Soil conservation	✓ Conduct research	✓ Field trips, seminars
National	General conservation	Publish research	Open to the public
	✓ Prairie conservation		Membership
	Restoration		
	Landscape design		

Grand Prairie Friends of Illinois
P. O. Box 36
Urbana, IL 61801   (217)896-2698

Brief description: A nonprofit group working to preserve and educate the public about prairies with a focus on southern Illinois.

Publications: Proceedings of 1st Central Illinois Prairie Conference

Regional	Purpose:	Research Programs	Public Programs
City	Water conservation	Support research	✓ Educational programs
✓ State	Soil conservation	✓ Conduct research	✓ Field trips, seminars
National	General conservation	✓ Publish research	✓ Open to the public
	✓ Prairie conservation		✓ Membership
	Restoration		
	Landscape design		

Green Earth, Inc.
P. O. Box 441
Carbondale, IL 62901   (618)549-4310

Brief description: A nonprofit group dedicated to the preservation of local natural areas.

Publications: Green Earth (quarterly)

Regional	Purpose:	Research Programs	Public Programs
✓ City	Water conservation	Support research	✓ Educational programs
State	Soil conservation	Conduct research	✓ Field trips, seminars
National	✓ General conservation	Publish research	✓ Open to the public
	Prairie conservation		✓ Membership
	Restoration		
	Landscape design		

Illinois Department of Conservation, Botany Program
524 South 2nd Street
Springfield, IL 62701-1787   (217)785-8774

Brief description: A state agency for natural resource conservation and a division of the Natural Heritage Program.

Publications:

Regional	Purpose:	Research Programs	Public Programs
City	Water conservation	Support research	Educational programs
✓ State	Soil conservation	✓ Conduct research	✓ Field trips, seminars
National	✓ General conservation	✓ Publish research	✓ Open to the public
	Prairie conservation		Membership
	Restoration		
	Landscape design		

Illinois Dunesland Preservation Society
2098 North Avenue
Waukegan, IL 60087   (312)336-9053

Brief description: A nonprofit society which supports the Illinois Beach State Park's nature center, prairie preserve, and trails.

Publications: Plants of the Illinois Duneslands

Regional	Purpose:	Research Programs	Public Programs
City	Water conservation	Support research	✓ Educational programs
✓ State	Soil conservation	Conduct research	✓ Field trips, seminars
National	General conservation	Publish research	✓ Open to the public
	✓ Prairie conservation		✓ Membership
	Restoration		
	Landscape design		

Illinois Native Plant Society
Southern Illinois University. Botany Department
Carbondale, IL 62901   (618)536-2331

Brief description: A nonprofit organization which promotes the preservation, conservation and study of native plants and communities.

Publications: Journal; newsletter (quarterly)

Regional	Purpose:	Research Programs	Public Programs
City	Water conservation	Support research	Educational programs
✓ State	Soil conservation	Conduct research	✓ Field trips, seminars
National	✓ General conservation	Publish research	Open to the public
	Prairie conservation		✓ Membership
	Restoration		
	Landscape design		

Illinois Nature Preserves Commission
Lincoln Tower Plaza, 524 South 2nd Street
Springfield IL 62701-1787   (217)785-8686

Brief description: A state agency which designates and manages the State Nature Preserves System.

Publications: Minutes of Commission Meetings

Regional	Purpose:	Research Programs	Public Programs
City	Water conservation	✓ Support research	Educational programs
✓ State	Soil conservation	Conduct research	Field trips, seminars
National	✓ General conservation	Publish research	✓ Open to the public
	Prairie conservation		Membership
	Restoration		
	Landscape design		

Illinois Prairie Path
P. O. Box 1086
Wheaton, IL 60189

Brief description: A nonprofit organization which maintains a 36-mile recreational trail owned by Dupage County Highway Department.

Publications: Illinois Prairie Path Newsletter

Regional	Purpose:	Research Programs	Public Programs
✓ City	Water conservation	Support research	✓ Educational programs
State	Soil conservation	Conduct research	✓ Field trips, seminars
National	✓ General conservation	Publish research	✓ Open to the public
	✓ Prairie conservation		✓ Membership
	Restoration		
	Landscape design		

Land Preservation, Inc., Nelson Lake Advocates
1141 Woodland Avenue
Batavia, IL 60510   (312)879-2991

Brief description: A nonprofit organization formed for the purpose of preserving the Nelson Lake Marsh as a natural area.

Publications:

Regional	Purpose:	Research Programs	Public Programs
City	Water conservation	Support research	Educational programs
✓ State	Soil conservation	✓ Conduct research	Field trips, seminars
National	✓ General conservation	Publish research	✓ Open to the public
	Prairie conservation		Membership
	Restoration		
	Landscape design		

Lee County SWCD, Lee County Natural Area Guardians
319 South Mason
Amboy, IL 61310   (815)857-3623

Brief description: A subcommittee of the Lee County SWCD whose primary goal is to locate and preserve natural areas and educate the public.

Publications:

Regional	Purpose:	Research Programs	Public Programs
✓ City	Water conservation	Support research	Educational programs
State	Soil conservation	✓ Conduct research	✓ Field trips, seminars
National	✓ General conservation	✓ Publish research	✓ Open to the public
	Prairie conservation		Membership
	Restoration		
	Landscape design		

Lincoln Memorial Garden and Nature Center
2301 East Lake Drive
Springfield, IL 62707   (217)529-1111

Brief description: A garden that recreates the Illinois landscape which existed during Lincoln's time. All plants are native to Illinois.

Publications: Nature Center News (bimonthly)

Regional	Purpose:	Research Programs	Public Programs
City	Water conservation	Support research	✓ Educational programs
✓ State	Soil conservation	Conduct research	✓ Field trips, seminars
National	✓ General conservation	Publish research	✓ Open to the public
	✓ Prairie conservation		✓ Membership
	Restoration		
	✓ Landscape design		

McHenry County Defenders
Box 603
Crystal Lake, IL 60050

Brief description: An environmental organization which trys to influence governmental actions that affect the environment, mostly through education.

Publications: McHenry County Defenders Newsletter

Regional	Purpose:	Research Programs	Public Programs
✓ City	✓ Water conservation	Support research	✓ Educational programs
State	✓ Soil conservation	Conduct research	✓ Field trips, seminars
National	General conservation	Publish research	✓ Open to the public
	✓ Prairie conservation		✓ Membership
	Restoration		
	Landscape design		

Morton Arboretum, The
Route 53
Lisle, IL 60532   *(312)968-0074*

Brief description: A nonprofit arboretum devoted to the growth and display of woody plants from around the world, also manages a restored prairie.

Publications: The Morton Arboretum Quarterly

Regional	Purpose:	Research Programs	Public Programs
City	Water conservation	✓ Support research	✓ Educational programs
✓ State	Soil conservation	✓ Conduct research	✓ Field trips, seminars
National	✓ General conservation	Publish research	✓ Open to the public
	Prairie conservation		✓ Membership
	Restoration		
	✓ Landscape design		

Native Landscapes
124 Dawson Avenue
Rockford, IL 61107   *(815)399-5475*

Brief description: A consultant involved in natural area assessment, management and restoration, also designs and installs landscapes.

Publications:

Regional	Purpose:	Research Programs	Public Programs
City	Water conservation	Support research	Educational programs
✓ State	Soil conservation	✓ Conduct research	Field trips, seminars
National	✓ General conservation	✓ Publish research	Open to the public
	✓ Prairie conservation		Membership
	Restoration		
	✓ Landscape design		

Natural Areas Association
320 South Third Street
Rockford, IL 61108   *(815)964-6666*

Brief description: An association working for the preservation of natural areas through the exchange of technical information, publications, and an annual conference.

Publications: Natural Areas Journal (quarterly)

Regional	Purpose:	Research Programs	Public Programs
City	Water conservation	Support research	✓ Educational programs
State	Soil conservation	Conduct research	Field trips, seminars
✓ National	✓ General conservation	✓ Publish research	✓ Open to the public
	Prairie conservation		✓ Membership
	Restoration		
	Landscape design		

Natural Areas Guardians, Mercer County Committee
30B SE 8th Avenue
Aledo, IL 61231   (309)852-5154

Brief description: A subcommittee of Mercer County Soil and Water Conservation District which manages natural areas for conservation and educational purposes.

Publications:

Regional	Purpose:	Research Programs	Public Programs
✓ City	Water conservation	Support research	✓ Educational programs
State	Soil conservation	Conduct research	✓ Field trips, seminars
National	✓ General conservation	Publish research	✓ Open to the public
	✓ Prairie conservation		Membership
	Restoration		
	Landscape design		

Natural Land Institute
320 South Third Street
Rockford, IL 61108   (815)964-6666

Brief description: A nonprofit institution which promotes natural areas through land acquisition, management, inventory and long-term planning.

Publications:

Regional	Purpose:	Research Programs	Public Programs
City	Water conservation	Support research	Educational programs
✓ State	Soil conservation	Conduct research	Field trips, seminars
National	✓ General conservation	Publish research	✓ Open to the public
	Prairie conservation		Membership
	Restoration		
	Landscape design		

Nature Conservancy, The
Illinois Field Office, 79 West Monroe Street, Suite 708
Chicago, IL 60603   (312)346-8166

Brief description: A nonprofit conservation organization working to preserve natural areas through land acquisition.

Publications: The Nature Conservancy News (monthly); The Conservator

Regional	Purpose:	Research Programs	Public Programs
City	Water conservation	Support research	Educational programs
✓ State	Soil conservation	Conduct research	✓ Field trips, seminars
National	✓ General conservation	Publish research	✓ Open to the public
	✓ Prairie conservation		✓ Membership
	Restoration		
	Landscape design		

Nature Foundation, The
79 West Monroe Street, Suite 710
Chicago, IL 60603   (312)236-7523

Brief description: A nonprofit organization working to acquire or help others acquire land worthy of protection for ecological reasons.

Publications:

Regional	Purpose:	Research Programs	Public Programs
City	Water conservation	Support research	Educational programs
✓ State	Soil conservation	Conduct research	Field trips, seminars
National	✓ General conservation	Publish research	Open to the public
	Prairie conservation		Membership
	Restoration		
	Landscape design		

Pecatonica Prairie Path
c/o David Derwent, 1213 South Oak Avenue
Freeport, IL 61032   (815)235-2103

Brief description: A nonprofit group developing a nature trail for public use along an old railroad right-of-way.

Publications:

Regional	Purpose:	Research Programs	Public Programs
✓ City	Water conservation	Support research	✓ Educational programs
State	Soil conservation	Conduct research	Field trips, seminars
National	✓ General conservation	Publish research	✓ Open to the public
	✓ Prairie conservation		✓ Membership
	Restoration		
	Landscape design		

Prairie Sun Consultants
612 Staunton Road
Naperville, IL 60565   (312)983-8404

Brief description: A consultant involved in land evaluation and management, restoration of natural areas, and education through nature studies.

Publications:

Regional	Purpose:	Research Programs	Public Programs
✓ City	Water conservation	Support research	✓ Educational programs
✓ State	Soil conservation	✓ Conduct research	✓ Field trips, seminars
National	✓ General conservation	Publish research	Open to the public
	✓ Prairie conservation		Membership
	Restoration		
	✓ Landscape design		

Save the Prairie Society
10327 Elizabeth
Westchester, IL 60153   *(312)865-8736*

Brief description: A nonprofit organization which manages the 80-acre Wolf Road Prairie.

Publications: Wolf Road Prairie (booklet); Prairie Pointer (quarterly)

Regional	Purpose:	Research Programs	Public Programs
✓ City	Water conservation	Support research	Educational programs
State	Soil conservation	✓ Conduct research	✓ Field trips, seminars
National	General conservation	Publish research	✓ Open to the public
	✓ Prairie conservation		✓ Membership
	Restoration		
	Landscape design		

Starhill Forest
Rt. 1, Box 272
Petersburg, IL 62675

Brief description: A private arboretum with a collection that stresses native plants.

Publications:

Regional	Purpose:	Research Programs	Public Programs
City	Water conservation	Support research	Educational programs
✓ State	Soil conservation	✓ Conduct research	✓ Field trips, seminars
National	✓ General conservation	Publish research	✓ Open to the public
	Prairie conservation		Membership
	Restoration		
	Landscape design		

INDIANA

Division of Nature Preserves, Department of Natural Resources
605B State Office Building
Indianapolis, IN 46204   *(317)232-4052*

Brief description: A state agency which identifies and protects natural areas and rare and endangered species.

Publications: Outdoor Indiana (monthly)

Regional	Purpose:	Research Programs	Public Programs
City	Water conservation	Support research	Educational programs
✓ State	Soil conservation	✓ Conduct research	✓ Field trips, seminars
National	✓ General conservation	✓ Publish research	✓ Open to the public
	✓ Prairie conservation		Membership
	Restoration		
	Landscape design		

Hayes Regional Arboretum, The
801 Elks Road
Richmond, IN 47374   (317)962-3745

Brief description: A 355-acre arboretum with primary emphasis on education and secondary focus on management and preservation.

Publications:

Regional	Purpose:	Research Programs	Public Programs
City	Water conservation	Support research	✓ Educational programs
✓ State	Soil conservation	Conduct research	✓ Field trips, seminars
National	✓ General conservation	Publish research	✓ Open to the public
	Prairie conservation		Membership
	Restoration		
	Landscape design		

Huntington College Arboretum and Botanical Garden
2303 College Avenue
Huntington, IN 46750   (219)356-6000

Brief description: A composite facility of Thornhill Nature Preserve, Pinkerton Natural Area and the Upper Wabash Basin Resource Center.

Publications:

Regional	Purpose:	Research Programs	Public Programs
City	Water conservation	Support research	✓ Educational programs
✓ State	Soil conservation	✓ Conduct research	✓ Field trips, seminars
National	✓ General conservation	✓ Publish research	✓ Open to the public
	Prairie conservation		Membership
	Restoration		
	✓ Landscape design		

Nature Conservancy, The
Indiana Field Office, 4200 North Michigan Road
Indianapolis, IN 46208   (317)923-7547

Brief description: A nonprofit organization which identifies and protects natural areas and rare species; also manages a stewardship program.

Publications: The Nature Conservancy News (monthly); Chapter Newsletter

Regional	Purpose:	Research Programs	Public Programs
City	Water conservation	Support research	Educational programs
✓ State	Soil conservation	✓ Conduct research	✓ Field trips, seminars
National	✓ General conservation	Publish research	✓ Open to the public
	Prairie conservation		✓ Membership
	Restoration		
	Landscape design		

KANSAS

Dyck Arboretum of the Plains, Hesston College
P. O. Box 3000
Hesston, KS 67062   (316)327-8127

Brief description: An arboretum which depicts the native Kansas prairie, but also
includes an area for adapted plants.

Publications:

Regional	Purpose:	Research Programs	Public Programs
City	Water conservation	Support research	✔ Educational programs
✔ State	Soil conservation	Conduct research	Field trips, seminars
National	General conservation	Publish research	✔ Open to the public
	✔ Prairie conservation		Membership
	Restoration		
	✔ Landscape design		

Kansas Natural Heritage Program, Biological Survey, University of Kansas
2291 Irving Hill Drive/ Campus West
Lawrence, KS 66045-2969   (913)864-3453

Brief description: A cooperative program between The Nature Conservancy and
the State Biological Survey to inventory the biodiversity in
Kansas.

Publications:

Regional	Purpose:	Research Programs	Public Programs
City	Water conservation	Support research	Educational programs
✔ State	Soil conservation	✔ Conduct research	Field trips, seminars
National	✔ General conservation	✔ Publish research	✔ Open to the public
	Prairie conservation		Membership
	Restoration		
	Landscape design		

Kansas Wildflower Society
Mulvane Art Center, Washburn University
Topeka, KS 66621

Brief description: A nonprofit society which sponsors lectures, field trips and
workshops on identification and conservation of native species.

Publications: Kansas Wildflowers (book); Newsletter (quarterly); brochures

Regional	Purpose:	Research Programs	Public Programs
City	Water conservation	Support research	✔ Educational programs
✔ State	Soil conservation	Conduct research	✔ Field trips, seminars
National	✔ General conservation	Publish research	✔ Open to the public
	✔ Prairie conservation		✔ Membership
	Restoration		
	Landscape design		

Kauffman Museum
Bethel College
North Newton, KS 67117   *(316)283-1612*

Brief description: A cultural and natural history museum with a prairie reconstruction project.

Publications:

Regional	Purpose:	Research Programs	Public Programs
City	Water conservation	Support research	✔ Educational programs
✔ State	Soil conservation	✔ Conduct research	✔ Field trips, seminars
National	General conservation	Publish research	✔ Open to the public
	✔ Prairie conservation		✔ Membership
	Restoration		
	✔ Landscape design		

KENTUCKY

Bernheim Forest Arboretum and Nature Center
Clermont, KY 40110   *(502)543-2451*

Brief description: A nonprofit 10,000-acre forest and nature preserve with a visitor's center and 250-acre arboretum. Open March 15 - September 15.

Publications:

Regional	Purpose:	Research Programs	Public Programs
City	Water conservation	Support research	✔ Educational programs
✔ State	Soil conservation	Conduct research	Field trips, seminars
National	✔ General conservation	Publish research	✔ Open to the public
	Prairie conservation		✔ Membership
	Restoration		
	Landscape design		

Eastern Kentucky University
Division of Natural Areas
Richmond, KY 40475   *(606)622-1476*

Brief description: A university system of protected natural areas/preserves cooperating with other agencies' protection efforts.

Publications: Papers in scientific journals

Regional	Purpose:	Research Programs	Public Programs
City	Water conservation	✔ Support research	✔ Educational programs
✔ State	Soil conservation	✔ Conduct research	Field trips, seminars
National	✔ General conservation	✔ Publish research	Open to the public
	Prairie conservation		Membership
	Restoration		
	Landscape design		

Kentucky Heritage Program, Kentucky Nature Preserves Commission
407 Broadway
Frankfort, KY 40601   (502)564-2886

Brief description: A state agency mandated to identify and protect natural areas in Kentucky.

Publications:

Regional	Purpose:	Research Programs	Public Programs
City	Water conservation	Support research	Educational programs
✓ State	Soil conservation	✓ Conduct research	✓ Field trips, seminars
National	✓ General conservation	✓ Publish research	Open to the public
	Prairie conservation		Membership
	Restoration		
	Landscape design		

Kentucky Native Plant Society, c/o Dr. Ronald Jones,
Dept. of Biological Sciences, Eastern Kentucky University
Richmond, KY 40475   (606)622-1476

Brief description: A nonprofit organization dedicated to conservation of native plants and habitats through educational programs and trips.

Publications:

Regional	Purpose:	Research Programs	Public Programs
City	Water conservation	Support research	✓ Educational programs
✓ State	Soil conservation	Conduct research	Field trips, seminars
National	✓ General conservation	Publish research	✓ Open to the public
	Prairie conservation		✓ Membership
	Restoration		
	Landscape design		

Kentucky Native Plant Society
Department of Biological Sciences, Eastern Kentucky University
Richmond, KY 40475   (606)622-6257

Brief description: A botanical organization interested in conservation of native plants and natural plant communities.

Publications: Newsletter

Regional	Purpose:	Research Programs	Public Programs
City	Water conservation	Support research	✓ Educational programs
✓ State	Soil conservation	Conduct research	✓ Field trips, seminars
National	✓ General conservation	✓ Publish research	✓ Open to the public
	Prairie conservation		✓ Membership
	Restoration		
	Landscape design		

Nature Conservancy, The
Kentucky Chapter, P.O. Box 1605
Frankfort, KY 40602   (502)564-2886

Brief description: A nonprofit conservation organization dedicated to the preservation of natural diversity through land acquisition.

Publications: The Nature Conservancy News (monthly); Chapter Newsletter

Regional	Purpose:	Research Programs	Public Programs
City	Water conservation	Support research	Educational programs
✓ State	Soil conservation	Conduct research	Field trips, seminars
National	✓ General conservation	Publish research	Open to the public
	Prairie conservation		✓ Membership
	Restoration		
	Landscape design		

LOUISIANA

Acadiana Native Plant Society
637 Girard Park Drive
Lafayette, LA 70503   (318)261-8348

Brief description: An affiliate chapter of the Louisiana Native Plant Society with a primary focus on conservation of native plants.

Publications:

Regional	Purpose:	Research Programs	Public Programs
City	Water conservation	Support research	✓ Educational programs
✓ State	Soil conservation	Conduct research	✓ Field trips, seminars
National	✓ General conservation	Publish research	✓ Open to the public
	Prairie conservation		✓ Membership
	Restoration		
	✓ Landscape design		

Lafayette Natural History Museum
637 Girard Park Drive
Lafayette, LA 70503   (318)261-8350

Brief description: A natural history museum with exhibits and programs, also maintains a nature station and trail.

Publications: Plants and Planets Newsletter (bimonthly); checklists; books

Regional	Purpose:	Research Programs	Public Programs
City	Water conservation	Support research	✓ Educational programs
✓ State	Soil conservation	✓ Conduct research	✓ Field trips, seminars
National	✓ General conservation	Publish research	✓ Open to the public
	Prairie conservation		✓ Membership
	Restoration		
	Landscape design		

Louisiana Natural Heritage Program, Department of Natural Resources
P.O. Box 44124
Baton Rouge, LA 70804-4124   (504)342-4602

Brief description: A state agency which identifies, monitors, and protects rare and endangered species.

Publications:

Regional	**Purpose:**	**Research Programs**	**Public Programs**
City	Water conservation	Support research	Educational programs
✓ State	Soil conservation	Conduct research	Field trips, seminars
National	✓ General conservation	Publish research	Open to the public
	Prairie conservation		Membership
	Restoration		
	Landscape design		

Louisiana Nature and Science Center
11000 Lake Forest Blvd.
New Orleans, LA 70127   (504)241-9606

Brief description: A nature center with programs on landscaping with native plants, wildflower identification, and field trips.

Publications: Floral and Faunal Notes (quarterly); Brochures

Regional	**Purpose:**	**Research Programs**	**Public Programs**
City	Water conservation	Support research	✓ Educational programs
✓ State	Soil conservation	✓ Conduct research	✓ Field trips, seminars
National	✓ General conservation	✓ Publish research	✓ Open to the public
	Prairie conservation		✓ Membership
	Restoration		
	Landscape design		

Louisiana Project Wildflower, Lafayette Natural History Museum
637 Girard Park Drive
Lafayette, LA 70503   (318)261-8350

Brief description: A private, statewide network for preserving, collecting data on and encouraging use of native trees, shrubs and wildflowers, especially along roadsides.

Publications: Newsletter (quarterly)

Regional	**Purpose:**	**Research Programs**	**Public Programs**
City	Water conservation	Support research	✓ Educational programs
✓ State	Soil conservation	✓ Conduct research	✓ Field trips, seminars
National	✓ General conservation	✓ Publish research	✓ Open to the public
	Prairie conservation		✓ Membership
	Restoration		
	Landscape design		

Natives Landscape Corporation
P. O. Box 2355, 303 North Columbia Street
Covington, LA 70434   (504)892-5424

Brief description: A landscape architectural firm which designs and installs
landscapes using native species.

Publications:

Regional	Purpose:	Research Programs	Public Programs
✓ City	Water conservation	Support research	Educational programs
State	Soil conservation	Conduct research	✓ Field trips, seminars
National	✓ General conservation	Publish research	Open to the public
	Prairie conservation		Membership
	Restoration		
	✓ Landscape design		

MASSACHUSETTS _____

Center for Plant Conservation
125 The Arborway
Jamaica Plains, MA 02130   (617)524-6988

Brief description: A nonprofit organization created to develop and maintain a
national network of programs at botanical gardens to study
endangered species.

Publications: Newsletter

Regional	Purpose:	Research Programs	Public Programs
City	Water conservation	✓ Support research	Educational programs
State	Soil conservation	✓ Conduct research	Field trips, seminars
✓ National	✓ General conservation	Publish research	Open to the public
	Prairie conservation		Membership
	Restoration		
	Landscape design		

_____

Chesapeake Audubon Society, Inc.
P. O. Box 3173
Baltimore, MA 21228   (301)766-4616

Brief description: A nonprofit organization working towards conservation in all
aspects of the environment.

Publications: Newsletter

Regional	Purpose:	Research Programs	Public Programs
✓ City	Water conservation	Support research	✓ Educational programs
✓ State	Soil conservation	Conduct research	✓ Field trips, seminars
National	✓ General conservation	Publish research	✓ Open to the public
	Prairie conservation		✓ Membership
	Restoration		
	Landscape design		

Massachusetts Horticultural Society
300 Massachusetts Avenue
Boston, MA 02115   (617)536-9280

Brief description: A nonprofit educational service organization dedicated to encouraging the science and practice of horticulture.

Publications: Bimonthly newsletter

Regional	Purpose:	Research Programs	Public Programs
City	Water conservation	Support research	✓ Educational programs
✓ State	Soil conservation	Conduct research	✓ Field trips, seminars
National	✓ General conservation	Publish research	✓ Open to the public
	Prairie conservation		✓ Membership
	Restoration		
	✓ Landscape design		

Massachusetts Natural Heritage Program
100 Cambridge Street
Boston, MA 02202   (617)727-9194

Brief description: A state agency which inventories, monitors and protects rare and endangered species.

Publications:

Regional	Purpose:	Research Programs	Public Programs
City	Water conservation	✓ Support research	Educational programs
✓ State	Soil conservation	✓ Conduct research	Field trips, seminars
National	✓ General conservation	Publish research	Open to the public
	Prairie conservation		Membership
	Restoration		
	Landscape design		

National Council of State Garden Clubs, Inc., Operation Wildflower
P. O. Box 860
Pocasset, MA 02559   (617)563-3629

Brief description: A nonprofit organization of local clubs that work with highway departments to beautify roadsides.

Publications: Columbine (monthly)

Regional	Purpose:	Research Programs	Public Programs
City	Water conservation	Support research	✓ Educational programs
State	Soil conservation	Conduct research	✓ Field trips, seminars
✓ National	✓ General conservation	✓ Publish research	✓ Open to the public
	Prairie conservation		Membership
	Restoration		
	✓ Landscape design		

Nature Conservancy, The
Massachusetts/Rhode Island Field Office, 294 Washington Street, Room 740
Boston, MA 02108   (617)423-2545

Brief description: A nonprofit conservation organization devoted to preservation
of natural diversity through land acquisition.

Publications: The Nature Conservancy News (monthly); Chapter Newsletter

Regional	Purpose:	Research Programs	Public Programs
City	Water conservation	✓ Support research	Educational programs
✓ State	Soil conservation	Conduct research	✓ Field trips, seminars
National	✓ General conservation	Publish research	✓ Open to the public
	Prairie conservation		✓ Membership
	Restoration		
	Landscape design		

New England Botanical Club, Inc., Harvard University
22 Divinity Avenue
Cambridge, MA 02138

Brief description: A nonprofit club which promotes the study of the flora of New
England; also maintains an herbarium and library.

Publications: Rhodora

Regional	Purpose:	Research Programs	Public Programs
City	Water conservation	✓ Support research	Educational programs
✓ State	Soil conservation	Conduct research	Field trips, seminars
National	✓ General conservation	✓ Publish research	Open to the public
	Prairie conservation		✓ Membership
	Restoration		
	Landscape design		

New England Wild Flower Society
Garden in the Woods, Hemenway Road
Framingham, MA 01701   (617)237-4924

Brief description: A nonprofit society whose purpose is conservation and
propagation of native plants through education, plant displays
and seed exchanges.

Publications: Wild Flower Notes (quarterly); Newsletter (quarterly); Nursery List

Regional	Purpose:	Research Programs	Public Programs
City	Water conservation	Support research	✓ Educational programs
✓ State	Soil conservation	✓ Conduct research	✓ Field trips, seminars
National	✓ General conservation	✓ Publish research	✓ Open to the public
	Prairie conservation		✓ Membership
	Restoration		
	Landscape design		

MARYLAND

Cylburn Arboretum Associates, Inc.
4915 Greenspring Avenue
Baltimore, MD 21209   (301)367-2217

Brief description: A nonprofit educational organization devoted to preserving the existing natural beauty of Cylburn Arboretum.

Publications: Cylburn Newsletter (quarterly)

Regional	Purpose:	Research Programs	Public Programs
✓ City	Water conservation	Support research	Educational programs
State	Soil conservation	✓ Conduct research	✓ Field trips, seminars
National	✓ General conservation	Publish research	✓ Open to the public
	Prairie conservation		✓ Membership
	Restoration		
	Landscape design		

Landon School Wildflower Committee
Perkins Garden, 6106 Wilson Lane
Bethesda, MD 20817-3199   (301)320-3200

Brief description: A committee of volunteers who maintain a wildflower garden and produce 100 species of wildflowers for an annual sale.

Publications:

Regional	Purpose:	Research Programs	Public Programs
✓ City	Water conservation	Support research	Educational programs
State	Soil conservation	Conduct research	Field trips, seminars
National	✓ General conservation	Publish research	Open to the public
	Prairie conservation		✓ Membership
	Restoration		
	Landscape design		

Maryland Heritage Project, Department of Natural Resources
C3, Tawes State Office Building
Annapolis, MD 21401   (301)974-2870

Brief description: A state agency which identifies, monitors, and protects rare and endangered species.

Publications:

Regional	Purpose:	Research Programs	Public Programs
City	Water conservation	Support research	Educational programs
✓ State	Soil conservation	Conduct research	Field trips, seminars
National	✓ General conservation	Publish research	Open to the public
	Prairie conservation		Membership
	Restoration		
	Landscape design		

Maryland Native Plant Society
c/o Scaffidi, 14720 Claude Lane
Silver Spring, MD 20904   (301)236-4124

Brief description: A nonprofit society devoted to educating the public and promoting the conservation of Maryland's native plants.

Publications: Newsletter

Regional	Purpose:	Research Programs	Public Programs
City	Water conservation	Support research	Educational programs
✓ State	Soil conservation	Conduct research	✓ Field trips, seminars
National	✓ General conservation	Publish research	✓ Open to the public
	Prairie conservation		Membership
	Restoration		
	Landscape design		

Nature Conservancy, The
Maryland/Delaware Field Office, 35 Wisconsin Circle, Suite 304
Chevy Chase, MD 20815   (301)656-8673

Brief description: A nonprofit conservation organization dedicated to the preservation of natural diversity through land acquisition.

Publications: The Nature Conservancy News (monthly); Chapter Newsletter

Regional	Purpose:	Research Programs	Public Programs
City	Water conservation	Support research	Educational programs
✓ State	Soil conservation	Conduct research	Field trips, seminars
National	✓ General conservation	Publish research	Open to the public
	Prairie conservation		✓ Membership
	Restoration		
	Landscape design		

USDA Soil Conservation Service, Plant Materials Center
Bldg. 509, Barc-East
Beltsville, MD 20705   (301)344-2175

Brief description: A plant materials center that tests plants for potential use in conservation and produces foundation seed for growers.

Publications: Numerous

Regional	Purpose:	Research Programs	Public Programs
City	Water conservation	Support research	Educational programs
State	✓ Soil conservation	✓ Conduct research	Field trips, seminars
✓ National	General conservation	✓ Publish research	✓ Open to the public
	Prairie conservation		Membership
	Restoration		
	Landscape design		

MAINE

Fay Hayland Arboretum, University of Maine
202 Deering Hall
Orono, ME 04469   (207)581-2976

Brief description: A ten-acre arboretum owned and maintained by the University
of Maine.

Publications:

Regional	**Purpose:**	**Research Programs**	**Public Programs**
City	Water conservation	Support research	✓ Educational programs
✓ State	Soil conservation	✓ Conduct research	Field trips, seminars
National	✓ General conservation	✓ Publish research	Open to the public
	Prairie conservation		Membership
	Restoration		
	Landscape design		

Josselyn Botanical Society
University of Maine, Department of Botany and Plant Pathology
Orono, ME 04469

Brief description: A botanical society which explores the natural areas and
identifies the native plants of Maine.

Publications: Bulletins

Regional	**Purpose:**	**Research Programs**	**Public Programs**
City	Water conservation	Support research	✓ Educational programs
✓ State	Soil conservation	Conduct research	✓ Field trips, seminars
National	✓ General conservation	Publish research	✓ Open to the public
	Prairie conservation		Membership
	Restoration		
	Landscape design		

L. M. Nelsen Landscape
Rt. 1, Box 2220
Litchfield, ME 04350-9742   (207)268-4569

Brief description: A private firm which designs and installs landscapes with a
primary focus on native species.

Publications:

Regional	**Purpose:**	**Research Programs**	**Public Programs**
✓ City	Water conservation	Support research	Educational programs
State	Soil conservation	Conduct research	Field trips, seminars
National	General conservation	Publish research	Open to the public
	Prairie conservation		Membership
	Restoration		
	✓ Landscape design		

Maine Natural Heritage Program, The Nature Conservancy
122 Main Street, P. O. Box 338
Topsham, ME 04086   (207)729-5181

Brief description: An organization that inventories and computerizes information on rare species and natural communities in Maine.

Publications:

Regional	Purpose:	Research Programs	Public Programs
City	Water conservation	✓ Support research	Educational programs
✓ State	Soil conservation	Conduct research	Field trips, seminars
National	✓ General conservation	Publish research	Open to the public
	Prairie conservation		Membership
	Restoration		
	Landscape design		

Nature Conservancy, The
Maine Chapter, P. O. Box 122
Topsham, ME 04086   (207)729-5181

Brief description: A nonprofit organization which preserves biological diversity by protecting rare species and exemplary communities.

Publications: The Nature Conservancy News (monthly); Chapter Newsletter

Regional	Purpose:	Research Programs	Public Programs
City	Water conservation	✓ Support research	Educational programs
✓ State	Soil conservation	✓ Conduct research	✓ Field trips, seminars
National	✓ General conservation	Publish research	✓ Open to the public
	Prairie conservation		✓ Membership
	Restoration		
	Landscape design		

New England Wildflower Society, Maine Chapter
107 Nichols Street
Lewiston, ME 04240   (207)782-5238

Brief description: A state chapter of a regional organization established to promote and conserve native plants.

Publications: Chapter Newsletter

Regional	Purpose:	Research Programs	Public Programs
City	Water conservation	✓ Support research	✓ Educational programs
✓ State	Soil conservation	✓ Conduct research	✓ Field trips, seminars
National	✓ General conservation	✓ Publish research	✓ Open to the public
	Prairie conservation		✓ Membership
	Restoration		
	Landscape design		

MICHIGAN

Federated Garden Clubs of Michigan, Operation Wildflower
154 West 23rd Street
Holland, MI 49423   *(616)396-7782*

Brief description: Approximately 203 clubs working with the Department of Transportation to beautify their communities.

Publications: Through the Garden Gate; National Gardener (monthly)

Regional	Purpose:	Research Programs	Public Programs
City	Water conservation	✔ Support research	✔ Educational programs
✔ State	Soil conservation	Conduct research	✔ Field trips, seminars
National	✔ General conservation	Publish research	✔ Open to the public
	Prairie conservation		✔ Membership
	Restoration		
	✔ Landscape design		

Fernwood Botanic Garden and Center
1720 Rangeline Road
Niles, MI 49120   *(616)683-8653*

Brief description: An educational center for horticultural and natural science with 105 acres of woods, gardens and an arboretum.

Publications: Fernwood Notes (bimonthly)

Regional	Purpose:	Research Programs	Public Programs
✔ City	Water conservation	Support research	✔ Educational programs
✔ State	Soil conservation	✔ Conduct research	✔ Field trips, seminars
National	✔ General conservation	✔ Publish research	✔ Open to the public
	✔ Prairie conservation		✔ Membership
	Restoration		
	Landscape design		

Hidden Lake Gardens
Attn: Curator
Tipton, MI 49287   *(517)431-2060*

Brief description: A 670-acre arboretum with a plant conservatory, numerous plant collections and nature trails.

Publications:

Regional	Purpose:	Research Programs	Public Programs
City	Water conservation	Support research	✔ Educational programs
✔ State	Soil conservation	Conduct research	✔ Field trips, seminars
National	✔ General conservation	Publish research	✔ Open to the public
	Prairie conservation		Membership
	Restoration		
	Landscape design		

Matthaei Botanical Gardens, The University of Michigan
1800 North Dixboro Road
Ann Arbor, MI 48105   (313)763-7060

Brief description: A university botanical garden with primary missions in plant research, instruction and public education.

Publications: Bartlettia (occasional publication)

Regional	Purpose:	Research Programs	Public Programs
City	Water conservation	Support research	Educational programs
✔ State	Soil conservation	✔ Conduct research	✔ Field trips, seminars
National	✔ General conservation	Publish research	✔ Open to the public
	Prairie conservation		✔ Membership
	Restoration		
	Landscape design		

Michigan Natural Features Inventory
Mason Building, 5th floor, Box 30028
Lansing, MI 48909   (517)373-1552

Brief description: A state agency which identifies, monitors, and protects rare and endangered species.

Publications:

Regional	Purpose:	Research Programs	Public Programs
City	Water conservation	Support research	Educational programs
✔ State	Soil conservation	Conduct research	Field trips, seminars
National	✔ General conservation	Publish research	Open to the public
	Prairie conservation		Membership
	Restoration		
	Landscape design		

Nature Conservancy, The
Michigan Field Office, 2840 East Grand River, Suite 5
East Lansing, MI 48823   (517)332-1741

Brief description: A nonprofit conservation organization which works to preserve biological diversity through land acquisition.

Publications: The Nature Conservancy News (monthly); Chapter Newsletter

Regional	Purpose:	Research Programs	Public Programs
City	Water conservation	✔ Support research	Educational programs
✔ State	Soil conservation	✔ Conduct research	✔ Field trips, seminars
National	✔ General conservation	Publish research	✔ Open to the public
	Prairie conservation		✔ Membership
	Restoration		
	Landscape design		

W. J. Beal Botanical Garden, Michigan State University
412 Olds Hall
East Lansing, MI 48824-1047 (517)355-9582

Brief description: A university botanical garden which offers educational programs and meetings.

Publications:

Regional	Purpose:	Research Programs	Public Programs
City	Water conservation	Support research	✓ Educational programs
✓ State	Soil conservation	✓ Conduct research	✓ Field trips, seminars
National	✓ General conservation	✓ Publish research	✓ Open to the public
	Prairie conservation		✓ Membership
	Restoration		
	✓ Landscape design		

MINNESOTA

Eloise Butler Wildflower Garden, c/o Minneapolis Parks & Recreation
3800 Bryant Ave. South
Minneapolis, MN 55409 (612)348-5702

Brief description: A wildflower garden and bird sanctuary operated by the Minneapolis Parks Board and specializing in native woodland and prairie plants.

Publications: Fringed Gentian; Guidebook

Regional	Purpose:	Research Programs	Public Programs
✓ City	✓ Water conservation	Support research	✓ Educational programs
State	✓ Soil conservation	Conduct research	✓ Field trips, seminars
National	✓ General conservation	Publish research	✓ Open to the public
	✓ Prairie conservation		✓ Membership
	Restoration		
	Landscape design		

Federated Garden Clubs of Minnesota
HCR 1, Box 984
Hackensack, MN 56452 (218)682-2304

Brief description: A garden club working toward beautification and conservation.

Publications: Newsletter

Regional	Purpose:	Research Programs	Public Programs
City	Water conservation	Support research	Educational programs
✓ State	Soil conservation	Conduct research	✓ Field trips, seminars
✓ National	✓ General conservation	Publish research	✓ Open to the public
	Prairie conservation		✓ Membership
	Restoration		
	Landscape design		

Minnesota Department of Natural Resources
P. O. Box 6247
Rochester, MN 55903   (507)285-7432

Brief description: A state agency which manages parks, trails, waterways, minerals, forests, wildlife and fisheries.

Publications: The Volunteer; DNR Resource Review

Regional	Purpose:	Research Programs	Public Programs
City	Water conservation	Support research	Educational programs
✔ State	Soil conservation	Conduct research	Field trips, seminars
National	✔ General conservation	Publish research	Open to the public
	Prairie conservation		Membership
	Restoration		
	Landscape design		

Minnesota Landscape Arboretum
Box 39
Chanhassen, MN 55317   (612)443-2460

Brief description: An educational organization and arboretum associated with the University of Minnesota.

Publications:

Regional	Purpose:	Research Programs	Public Programs
City	Water conservation	✔ Support research	✔ Educational programs
✔ State	Soil conservation	✔ Conduct research	✔ Field trips, seminars
National	✔ General conservation	✔ Publish research	✔ Open to the public
	Prairie conservation		✔ Membership
	Restoration		
	Landscape design		

Minnesota Native Plant Society
220 Biological Sciences Center, 1445 Gortner Avenue
St. Paul, MN 55108

Brief description: A nonprofit organization interested in identification, conservation and appreciation of Minnesota's native plants.

Publications: Minnesota Plant Press

Regional	Purpose:	Research Programs	Public Programs
City	Water conservation	Support research	✔ Educational programs
✔ State	Soil conservation	Conduct research	✔ Field trips, seminars
National	General conservation	Publish research	✔ Open to the public
	✔ Prairie conservation		✔ Membership
	Restoration		
	Landscape design		

Minnesota Natural Heritage Program, Department of Natural Resources
Box 7, 500 Lafayette Road
St. Paul, MN 55155   *(612)296-3344*

Brief description: A governmental organization devoted to inventory and research on Minnesota's endangered species and native communities.

Publications:

Regional	Purpose:	Research Programs	Public Programs
City	Water conservation	✓ Support research	Educational programs
✓ State	Soil conservation	✓ Conduct research	Field trips, seminars
National	✓ General conservation	✓ Publish research	Open to the public
	Prairie conservation		Membership
	Restoration		
	Landscape design		

Nature Conservancy, The
Minnesota Field Office, 1313 5th Street SE
Minneapolis, MN 55414   *(612)379-2134*

Brief description: A nonprofit conservation organization dedicated to the preservation of natural diversity through land acquisition.

Publications: The Nature Conservancy News (monthly); Chapter Newsletter

Regional	Purpose:	Research Programs	Public Programs
City	Water conservation	Support research	Educational programs
✓ State	Soil conservation	✓ Conduct research	✓ Field trips, seminars
✓ National	✓ General conservation	Publish research	✓ Open to the public
	✓ Prairie conservation		✓ Membership
	Restoration		
	Landscape design		

Nature Conservancy, The
Midwest Heritage Task Force, 1313 5th Street SE
Minneapolis, MN 55414   *(612)379-2207*

Brief description: A nonprofit conservation organization which works to preserve natural diversity through land acquisition.

Publications:

Regional	Purpose:	Research Programs	Public Programs
City	Water conservation	Support research	Educational programs
✓ State	Soil conservation	✓ Conduct research	Field trips, seminars
✓ National	✓ General conservation	Publish research	✓ Open to the public
	Prairie conservation		✓ Membership
	Restoration		
	Landscape design		

MISSOURI

Missouri Botanical Garden
P. O. Box 299
St. Louis, MO 63166-0299   (314)577-5100

Brief description: The oldest botanical garden in the U. S. Many horticultural displays and educational programs are offered.

Publications: Bulletin; Annual of the Missouri Botanical Garden

Regional	Purpose:	Research Programs	Public Programs
✓ City	Water conservation	✓ Support research	✓ Educational programs
State	Soil conservation	✓ Conduct research	✓ Field trips, seminars
National	✓ General conservation	✓ Publish research	✓ Open to the public
	Prairie conservation		✓ Membership
	Restoration		
	✓ Landscape design		

Missouri Department of Conservation
P. O. Box 180
Jefferson City, MO 65102   (314)751-4115

Brief description: A state land management agency which owns and manages wildlife resources, forests, stream accesses and prairies.

Publications: Missouri Conservationist (monthly)

Regional	Purpose:	Research Programs	Public Programs
City	Water conservation	Support research	Educational programs
✓ State	Soil conservation	✓ Conduct research	✓ Field trips, seminars
National	✓ General conservation	Publish research	✓ Open to the public
	Prairie conservation		Membership
	Restoration		
	Landscape design		

Missouri Native Plant Society
P. O. Box 6612
Jefferson City, MO 65102-6612   (816)429-4933

Brief description: A nonprofit organization of amateur and professional botanists who are interested in conserving Missouri's flora.

Publications: Missouriensis

Regional	Purpose:	Research Programs	Public Programs
City	Water conservation	✓ Support research	Educational programs
✓ State	Soil conservation	Conduct research	✓ Field trips, seminars
National	✓ General conservation	✓ Publish research	Open to the public
	Prairie conservation		✓ Membership
	Restoration		
	Landscape design		

Missouri Prairie Foundation, The
P. O. Box 200
Columbia, MO 65205-0200

Brief description: A nonprofit organization working to protect prairies through acquisition, education, management and research.

Publications: Missouri Prairie Journal (monthly); Prairie Zephyr (monthly)

Regional	Purpose:	Research Programs	Public Programs
City	Water conservation	✔ Support research	Educational programs
✔ State	Soil conservation	Conduct research	✔ Field trips, seminars
National	General conservation	Publish research	✔ Open to the public
	✔ Prairie conservation		✔ Membership
	Restoration		
	Landscape design		

National Council of State Garden Clubs, Inc.
4401 Magnolia Avenue
St. Louis, MO 63110   (314)776-7574

Brief description: The national office, which coordinates the activities of the State Federation of Garden Clubs.

Publications: National Gardener; Columbine (monthly)

Regional	Purpose:	Research Programs	Public Programs
City	Water conservation	✔ Support research	✔ Educational programs
State	Soil conservation	Conduct research	✔ Field trips, seminars
✔ National	✔ General conservation	✔ Publish research	✔ Open to the public
	Prairie conservation		✔ Membership
	Restoration		
	✔ Landscape design		

Nature Conservancy, The
Missouri Field Office, 2800 South Brentwood Blvd.
St. Louis, MO 63144   (314)968-1105

Brief description: A nonprofit organization working towards preserving biotic diversity through land acquisition.

Publications: The Nature Conservancy News (monthly); Chapter Newsletter

Regional	Purpose:	Research Programs	Public Programs
City	Water conservation	✔ Support research	Educational programs
✔ State	Soil conservation	✔ Conduct research	✔ Field trips, seminars
National	✔ General conservation	Publish research	✔ Open to the public
	Prairie conservation		✔ Membership
	Restoration		
	Landscape design		

Ozark Beneficial Plant Project
Ozark Resources Center
Brixey, MO 65618   (413)679-4773

Brief description: A group that researches and promotes the useful plants of the Ozark Plateau, especially those suitable for local cultivation and herbal uses.

Publications: Numerous books; Index Seminum

Regional	Purpose:	Research Programs	Public Programs
City	Water conservation	Support research	✓ Educational programs
✓ State	Soil conservation	✓ Conduct research	✓ Field trips, seminars
National	✓ General conservation	✓ Publish research	Open to the public
	Prairie conservation		Membership
	Restoration		
	Landscape design		

Powell Gardens
Rt. 1, Box 90
Kingsville, MO 64061   (816)566-2600

Brief description: A 580-acre garden administered by the University of Missouri which promotes horticulture and natural resources.

Publications: Powell Garden News

Regional	Purpose:	Research Programs	Public Programs
✓ City	Water conservation	Support research	✓ Educational programs
State	Soil conservation	✓ Conduct research	✓ Field trips, seminars
National	✓ General conservation	✓ Publish research	✓ Open to the public
	Prairie conservation		✓ Membership
	Restoration		
	✓ Landscape design		

MISSISSIPPI ——————————————————————————

Crosby Arboretum, The
P. O. Box 190, 1801 Goodyear Blvd.
Picayune, MS 39466   (601)798-6961

Brief description: An 1,800-acre natural area which preserves the Pearl River drainage basin and provides education and research.

Publications: Quarterly News Journal of Crosby Arboretum

Regional	Purpose:	Research Programs	Public Programs
City	Water conservation	✓ Support research	✓ Educational programs
✓ State	Soil conservation	✓ Conduct research	✓ Field trips, seminars
National	✓ General conservation	✓ Publish research	✓ Open to the public
	Prairie conservation		✓ Membership
	Restoration		
	Landscape design		

Mississippi Native Plant Society
Travis Salley, 202 North Andrews Avenue
Cleveland, MS 38732   (601)843-2330

Brief description: A nonprofit organization which studies and promotes the conservation of native plants of Mississippi.

Publications: MNPS Newsletter

Regional	Purpose:	Research Programs	Public Programs
City	Water conservation	Support research	✓ Educational programs
✓ State	Soil conservation	Conduct research	✓ Field trips, seminars
National	✓ General conservation	Publish research	✓ Open to the public
	Prairie conservation		✓ Membership
	Restoration		
	Landscape design		

Mississippi Natural Heritage Program, Museum of Natural Science
111 North Jefferson Street
Jackson, MS 39201-2897   (601)354-7303

Brief description: An agency that identifies, preserves and inventories the state's best remaining examples of natural diversity.

Publications:

Regional	Purpose:	Research Programs	Public Programs
City	Water conservation	Support research	Educational programs
✓ State	Soil conservation	✓ Conduct research	Field trips, seminars
National	✓ General conservation	Publish research	Open to the public
	Prairie conservation		Membership
	Restoration		
	Landscape design		

USDA Soil Conservation Service, Plant Material Center
Rt. 3, Box 215A
Coffeeville, MS 38922   (601)675-2588

Brief description: A plant material center involved in testing, selecting and releasing plants for soil conservation use.

Publications:

Regional	Purpose:	Research Programs	Public Programs
City	✓ Water conservation	Support research	Educational programs
State	✓ Soil conservation	Conduct research	Field trips, seminars
✓ National	General conservation	Publish research	✓ Open to the public
	Prairie conservation		Membership
	Restoration		
	Landscape design		

MONTANA

Montana Native Plant Society
Botany Department, University of Montana
Missoula, MT 59812   (406)243-5222

Brief description: A nonprofit membership organization focused on the native
plants of Montana.

Publications: Newsletter

Regional	Purpose:	Research Programs	Public Programs
City	Water conservation	Support research	✓ Educational programs
✓ State	Soil conservation	Conduct research	✓ Field trips, seminars
National	✓ General conservation	Publish research	✓ Open to the public
	Prairie conservation		✓ Membership
	Restoration		
	Landscape design		

Montana Natural Heritage Program
State Library Building, 1515 East 6th Avenue
Helena, MT 59620   (406)444-3009

Brief description: A state-wide computer-assisted Inventory of rare plants,
animals and communities.

Publications:

Regional	Purpose:	Research Programs	Public Programs
City	Water conservation	Support research	Educational programs
✓ State	Soil conservation	✓ Conduct research	✓ Field trips, seminars
National	✓ General conservation	✓ Publish research	✓ Open to the public
	Prairie conservation		Membership
	Restoration		
	Landscape design		

Nature Conservancy, The
Montana/Wyoming Field Office, P.O. Box 258
Helena, MT 59624   (406)443-0303

Brief description: A nonprofit conservation organization dedicated to the
preservation of natural diversity through land acquisition.

Publications: The Nature Conservancy (monthly); Chapter Newsletter

Regional	Purpose:	Research Programs	Public Programs
City	Water conservation	Support research	Educational programs
✓ State	Soil conservation	Conduct research	Field trips, seminars
National	✓ General conservation	Publish research	Open to the public
	Prairie conservation		✓ Membership
	Restoration		
	Landscape design		

NORTH CAROLINA

High Point Environmental Education Center
1228 Penny Road
High Point, NC 27260   *(919)454-4214*

Brief description: A center with emphasis on outdoor programming for children; also maintains a 200-acre wildlife refuge and nature trails.

Publications: High Points of Nature Newsletter (monthly)

Regional	Purpose:	Research Programs	Public Programs
✓ City	Water conservation	Support research	✓ Educational programs
State	Soil conservation	Conduct research	✓ Field trips, seminars
National	✓ General conservation	Publish research	✓ Open to the public
	Prairie conservation		✓ Membership
	Restoration		
	Landscape design		

North Carolina Agricultural Extension Service
2016 Fanning Bridge Road
Fletcher, NC 28732-9628   *(704)684-3562*

Brief description: A state agency researching applied cultural aspects of nursery crops including some native species.

Publications:

Regional	Purpose:	Research Programs	Public Programs
City	Water conservation	Support research	✓ Educational programs
✓ State	Soil conservation	✓ Conduct research	✓ Field trips, seminars
National	✓ General conservation	✓ Publish research	✓ Open to the public
	Prairie conservation		Membership
	Restoration		
	Landscape design		

North Carolina Natural Heritage Program
Department of Natural Resources, P.O. Box 27687
Raleigh, NC 27611   *(919)733-7701*

Brief description: A state agency which monitors and protects endangered species of North Carolina.

Publications: Newsletter

Regional	Purpose:	Research Programs	Public Programs
City	Water conservation	✓ Support research	Educational programs
✓ State	Soil conservation	✓ Conduct research	Field trips, seminars
National	✓ General conservation	✓ Publish research	Open to the public
	Prairie conservation		Membership
	Restoration		
	Landscape design		

North Carolina Nature Conservancy
P. O. Box 805
Chapel Hill, NC 27514   (919)967-7007

Brief description: A field office of The Nature Conservancy committed to the preservation of natural diversity through land acquisition.

Publications: The Nature Conservancy News (monthly); Chapter Newsletter

Regional	Purpose:	Research Programs	Public Programs
City	Water conservation	✔ Support research	Educational programs
✔ State	Soil conservation	✔ Conduct research	✔ Field trips, seminars
National	✔ General conservation	Publish research	Open to the public
	Prairie conservation		✔ Membership
	Restoration		
	Landscape design		

North Carolina Wild Flower Preservation Society
Totten Garden Center, 457-A, UNC-CH North Carolina Botanical Garden
Chapel Hill, NC 27514

Brief description: A nonprofit organization interested in preserving and studying native habitats of wildflowers in North Carolina.

Publications: North Carolina Native Plant Propagation Handbook

Regional	Purpose:	Research Programs	Public Programs
City	Water conservation	Support research	✔ Educational programs
✔ State	Soil conservation	Conduct research	✔ Field trips, seminars
National	✔ General conservation	✔ Publish research	✔ Open to the public
	Prairie conservation		✔ Membership
	Restoration		
	Landscape design		

Reynolda Gardens, Wake Forest University
100 Reynolda Village
Winston-Salem, NC 27106   (919)761-5593

Brief description: The former garden of R. J. Reynolds, now owned by Wake Forest University, includes formal and wild gardens with nature trails.

Publications: Reynolda Newsletter; Calendar

Regional	Purpose:	Research Programs	Public Programs
✔ City	Water conservation	Support research	Educational programs
State	Soil conservation	Conduct research	✔ Field trips, seminars
National	✔ General conservation	Publish research	✔ Open to the public
	Prairie conservation		✔ Membership
	Restoration		
	✔ Landscape design		

Sarah Duke Gardens, H. L. Blomquist Garden of Natives
Duke University
Durham, NC 27706   (919)684-3698

Brief description: An eight-acre garden featuring Southeastern native plants in mass groupings.

Publications: Flora

Regional	Purpose:	Research Programs	Public Programs
City	Water conservation	Support research	✔ Educational programs
State	Soil conservation	Conduct research	Field trips, seminars
National	✔ General conservation	Publish research	✔ Open to the public
	Prairie conservation		✔ Membership
	Restoration		
	✔ Landscape design		

University Botanical Gardens
151 Weaver Blvd.
Asheville, NC 28804   (704)252-5190

Brief description: A botanical garden which displays native plants of the southern Appalachians in a natural setting.

Publications:

Regional	Purpose:	Research Programs	Public Programs
City	Water conservation	Support research	✔ Educational programs
✔ State	Soil conservation	Conduct research	✔ Field trips, seminars
National	✔ General conservation	Publish research	✔ Open to the public
	Prairie conservation		✔ Membership
	Restoration		
	Landscape design		

WCC Gardens
P. O. Box 120
Wilkesboro, NC 28697   (919)667-7136

Brief description: A nonprofit garden with a diverse collection of indigenous and ornamental plants.

Publications: WCC Newsletter

Regional	Purpose:	Research Programs	Public Programs
City	Water conservation	Support research	✔ Educational programs
✔ State	Soil conservation	Conduct research	✔ Field trips, seminars
National	✔ General conservation	Publish research	✔ Open to the public
	Prairie conservation		✔ Membership
	Restoration		
	Landscape design		

NORTH DAKOTA

North Dakota Natural Heritage Inventory
North Dakota Game and Fish Department, 100 North Bismarck Expressway
Bismarck, ND 58501   (701)224-9870

Brief description: A state agency which identifies, monitors, and protects rare and endangered species.

Publications:

Regional	Purpose:	Research Programs	Public Programs
City	Water conservation	Support research	Educational programs
✓ State	Soil conservation	Conduct research	Field trips, seminars
National	✓ General conservation	Publish research	Open to the public
	Prairie conservation		Membership
	Restoration		
	Landscape design		

NEBRASKA

Chadron State College Herbarium
Division of Science and Math, Chadron State College
Chadron, NE 69337   (308)432-6385

Brief description: A small college herbarium affiliated with the Great Plains Botanical Society and Claude Barr Memorial Garden.

Publications:

Regional	Purpose:	Research Programs	Public Programs
City	Water conservation	✓ Support research	✓ Educational programs
✓ State	Soil conservation	✓ Conduct research	✓ Field trips, seminars
National	General conservation	✓ Publish research	✓ Open to the public
	✓ Prairie conservation		Membership
	Restoration		
	Landscape design		

Chet Ager Nature Center and Preserve, Pioneer Park
2740 A Street
Lincoln, NE 68502   (402)471-7895

Brief description: A 56-acre center with exhibit building and three miles of trails. The preserve includes 80 acres of animal exhibits.

Publications:

Regional	Purpose:	Research Programs	Public Programs
✓ City	Water conservation	Support research	✓ Educational programs
State	Soil conservation	Conduct research	✓ Field trips, seminars
National	✓ General conservation	Publish research	✓ Open to the public
	✓ Prairie conservation		Membership
	Restoration		
	Landscape design		

Flatland Impressions
1307 L Street
Aurora, NE 68818   *(402)694-5535*

Brief description: A private firm active in native plant propagation, landscape design, habitat restoration and ecological consulting for Midwest prairies.

Publications:

Regional	Purpose:	Research Programs	Public Programs
City	Water conservation	Support research	Educational programs
✓ State	Soil conservation	Conduct research	Field trips, seminars
National	✓ General conservation	Publish research	Open to the public
	✓ Prairie conservation		Membership
	✓ Restoration		
	✓ Landscape design		

National Arbor Day Foundation
100 Arbor Avenue
Nebraska City, NE 68410   *(402)474-5655*

Brief description: A nonprofit organization promoting tree planting and proper care throughout the U. S.

Publications: Arbor Day (bimonthly)

Regional	Purpose:	Research Programs	Public Programs
City	Water conservation	Support research	✓ Educational programs
State	Soil conservation	Conduct research	Field trips, seminars
✓ National	✓ General conservation	Publish research	✓ Open to the public
	Prairie conservation		✓ Membership
	Restoration		
	Landscape design		

Nebraska Statewide Arboretum, University of Nebraska
112 Forestry Sciences Laboratory
Lincoln, NE 68583-0823   *(402)472-2971*

Brief description: A statewide affiliation of arboreta where trees, shrubs and other plants are displayed and evaluated for use in landscapes.

Publications: The "Seed"

Regional	Purpose:	Research Programs	Public Programs
✓ City	Water conservation	Support research	Educational programs
State	Soil conservation	Conduct research	Field trips, seminars
✓ National	✓ General conservation	✓ Publish research	Open to the public
	Prairie conservation		Membership
	Restoration		
	Landscape design		

Prairie/Plains Resource Institute
1307 L Street
Aurora, NE 68818   *(402)694-5535*

Brief description: A nonprofit organization dedicated to the preservation, restoration, and management of native grasslands and other unique plains habitats.

Publications: Newsletter (monthly)

Regional	Purpose:	Research Programs	Public Programs
City	✓ Water conservation	Support research	✓ Educational programs
✓ State	✓ Soil conservation	Conduct research	✓ Field trips, seminars
National	✓ General conservation	Publish research	✓ Open to the public
	✓ Prairie conservation		✓ Membership
	✓ Restoration		
	Landscape design		

Wayne State Arboretum
Wayne State College
Wayne, NE 68787   *(402)375-2200*

Brief description: An affiliate site in the Nebraska Statewide Arboretum with landscape displays, a nature center and trails.

Publications: Trail guides; checklists

Regional	Purpose:	Research Programs	Public Programs
City	Water conservation	Support research	Educational programs
✓ State	Soil conservation	Conduct research	Field trips, seminars
National	✓ General conservation	Publish research	✓ Open to the public
	Prairie conservation		Membership
	Restoration		
	Landscape design		

NEW HAMPSHIRE

Nature Conservancy, The
New Hampshire Field Office, 7 South State Street, Suite 1
Concord, N H 03301   *(603)224-5853*

Brief description: A nonprofit organization which protects rare and threatened species through land acquistion and protection.

Publications: The Nature Conservancy News (monthly); Chapter Newsletter

Regional	Purpose:	Research Programs	Public Programs
City	Water conservation	✓ Support research	Educational programs
✓ State	Soil conservation	✓ Conduct research	✓ Field trips, seminars
✓ National	✓ General conservation	✓ Publish research	✓ Open to the public
	Prairie conservation		✓ Membership
	Restoration		
	Landscape design		

New Hampshire Natural Heritage Inventory
Department of Natural Resources, P.O. Box 856
Concord, N H 03301   *(603)271-3623*

Brief description: An agency that identifies and inventories endangered species and the best remaining examples of natural diversity.

Publications:

Regional	Purpose:	Research Programs	Public Programs
City	Water conservation	Support research	Educational programs
✓ State	Soil conservation	✓ Conduct research	Field trips, seminars
National	✓ General conservation	Publish research	Open to the public
	Prairie conservation		Membership
	Restoration		
	Landscape design		

NEW JERSEY ───────────────────────────────

Cora Hartshorn Arboretum
324 Forest Drive South
Short Hills, NJ 07078   *(201)376-3587*

Brief description: An arboretum with three miles of trails through native woods and wildflowers, a museum and conference area.

Publications:

Regional	Purpose:	Research Programs	Public Programs
✓ City	Water conservation	Support research	✓ Educational programs
State	Soil conservation	Conduct research	✓ Field trips, seminars
National	✓ General conservation	Publish research	✓ Open to the public
	Prairie conservation		✓ Membership
	Restoration		
	Landscape design		

Morris County Park Commission
P. O. Box 1295
Morristown, NJ 07960-1295

Brief description: A governmental agency with 23 locations which specializes in horticulture, education, recreation and preservation.

Publications:

Regional	Purpose:	Research Programs	Public Programs
✓ City	Water conservation	Support research	✓ Educational programs
State	Soil conservation	Conduct research	✓ Field trips, seminars
National	✓ General conservation	Publish research	✓ Open to the public
	Prairie conservation		✓ Membership
	Restoration		
	Landscape design		

Nature Conservancy, The
New Jersey Field Office, 17 Fairmount Road
Pottersville, NJ 07979-9999   (201)439-3007

Brief description: A nonprofit conservation organization dedicated to the preservation of natural diversity through land acquisition.

Publications: The Nature Conservancy News (monthly); Chapter Newsletter

Regional	Purpose:	Research Programs	Public Programs
City	Water conservation	Support research	Educational programs
✓ State	Soil conservation	Conduct research	Field trips, seminars
National	✓ General conservation	Publish research	Open to the public
	Prairie conservation		Membership
	Restoration		
	Landscape design		

New Jersey Conservation Foundation
300 Mendham Road
Morristown, NJ 07960-4898   (201)539-7540

Brief description: A nonprofit foundation which promotes conservation of natural resources through open space preservation and proper management.

Publications:

Regional	Purpose:	Research Programs	Public Programs
City	Water conservation	Support research	Educational programs
✓ State	Soil conservation	Conduct research	Field trips, seminars
National	✓ General conservation	Publish research	Open to the public
	Prairie conservation		Membership
	Restoration		
	Landscape design		

New Jersey Division of Parks, John Fitch Plaza
Labor & Industry Building, Room 806, CN 404
Trenton, NJ 08625   (609)984-1339

Brief description: A division within the state's Department of Environmental Protection.

Publications:

Regional	Purpose:	Research Programs	Public Programs
City	Water conservation	Support research	Educational programs
✓ State	Soil conservation	✓ Conduct research	Field trips, seminars
National	✓ General conservation	Publish research	✓ Open to the public
	Prairie conservation		Membership
	Restoration		
	Landscape design		

New Jersey Native Plant Society
c/o Frelinghuysen Arboretum, P. O. Box 1295 R
Morristown, NJ 07960   (201)377-3956

Brief description: A nonprofit educational organization advancing knowledge and uses of New Jersey native plants.

Publications: Newsletter (bimonthly)

Regional	**Purpose:**	**Research Programs**	**Public Programs**
City	Water conservation	Support research	✓ Educational programs
✓ State	Soil conservation	Conduct research	✓ Field trips, seminars
National	✓ General conservation	Publish research	✓ Open to the public
	Prairie conservation		✓ Membership
	Restoration		
	✓ Landscape design		

New Jersey Natural Heritage Program, Office of Natural Land Management
109 West State Street
Trenton, NJ 08608   (609)984-1339

Brief description: A state agency which identifies, monitors, and protects rare and endangered species.

Publications:

Regional	**Purpose:**	**Research Programs**	**Public Programs**
City	Water conservation	Support research	Educational programs
✓ State	Soil conservation	Conduct research	Field trips, seminars
National	✓ General conservation	Publish research	Open to the public
	Prairie conservation		Membership
	Restoration		
	Landscape design		

Project SNAP
c/o Dr. Betty Knorr, 459 Easy Street
Howell, NJ 07731   (201)938-3085

Brief description: Project SNAP started in 1960 as a movement to rescue native species from destruction due to development; many clubs now participate.

Publications:

Regional	**Purpose:**	**Research Programs**	**Public Programs**
City	Water conservation	Support research	Educational programs
✓ State	Soil conservation	✓ Conduct research	Field trips, seminars
National	✓ General conservation	Publish research	Open to the public
	Prairie conservation		Membership
	Restoration		
	Landscape design		

Reeves-Reed Arboretum
165 Hobart Avenue
Summit, NJ 07901   *(201)273-8787*

Brief description: A twelve-acre arboretum of which 25 percent is formally landscaped within a natural woodland.

Publications:

Regional	Purpose:	Research Programs	Public Programs
✓ City	Water conservation	Support research	✓ Educational programs
State	Soil conservation	Conduct research	✓ Field trips, seminars
National	✓ General conservation	Publish research	✓ Open to the public
	Prairie conservation		✓ Membership
	Restoration		
	Landscape design		

Skylands Association
P. O. Box 1304
Ringwood, NJ 07456   *(201)962-9534*

Brief description: A support group at Skylands Botanic Garden and Ringwood State Park which maintains a wildflower area.

Publications: Newsletter

Regional	Purpose:	Research Programs	Public Programs
✓ City	Water conservation	Support research	✓ Educational programs
✓ State	Soil conservation	Conduct research	✓ Field trips, seminars
National	✓ General conservation	Publish research	✓ Open to the public
	Prairie conservation		✓ Membership
	Restoration		
	Landscape design		

Somerset County Park Commission, Horticultural Services Department
R. D. 2, Layton Road
Far Hills, NJ 07931   *(201)234-2677*

Brief description: A county agency which operates the Leonard Buck Garden, a 35-acre natural rock garden, and Colonial Park Arboretum.

Publications:

Regional	Purpose:	Research Programs	Public Programs
✓ City	Water conservation	Support research	✓ Educational programs
State	Soil conservation	Conduct research	✓ Field trips, seminars
National	✓ General conservation	Publish research	✓ Open to the public
	Prairie conservation		✓ Membership
	Restoration		
	✓ Landscape design		

T & M Associates
P. O. Box 828
Red Bank, NJ 07701   *(201)671-6400*

Brief description: A consulting firm with municipal engineers, site developers, land use planners, and landscape architects.

Publications:

Regional	Purpose:	Research Programs	Public Programs
✓ City	Water conservation	Support research	Educational programs
State	Soil conservation	Conduct research	Field trips, seminars
National	General conservation	Publish research	Open to the public
	Prairie conservation		Membership
	Restoration		
	✓ Landscape design		

NEW MEXICO ───────────────────────────

Native Plant Society of New Mexico
1302 Canyon Road
Alamogordo, NM 88310   *(505)434-3041*

Brief description: A nonprofit organization promoting the appreciation of native plants and the preservation of endangered species.

Publications: Newsletter

Regional	Purpose:	Research Programs	Public Programs
City	Water conservation	Support research	✓ Educational programs
✓ State	Soil conservation	Conduct research	✓ Field trips, seminars
National	✓ General conservation	Publish research	✓ Open to the public
	Prairie conservation		✓ Membership
	Restoration		
	Landscape design		

Native Plant Society of New Mexico
P. O. Box 5917
Santa Fe, NM 87502   *(505)865-4684*

Brief description: A nonprofit organization which promotes all aspects of native plants (conservation, landscaping, education, etc.).

Publications: Newsletter (bimonthly)

Regional	Purpose:	Research Programs	Public Programs
City	Water conservation	✓ Support research	✓ Educational programs
✓ State	Soil conservation	Conduct research	✓ Field trips, seminars
National	✓ General conservation	Publish research	✓ Open to the public
	Prairie conservation		✓ Membership
	Restoration		
	✓ Landscape design		

Nature Conservancy, The
New Mexico Field Office, P.O. Box 1846
Albuquerque, NM 87102   (505)242-2015

Brief description: A nonprofit conservation organization dedicated to the preservation of natural diversity through land acquisition.

Publications: The Nature Conservancy News (monthly); Chapter Newsletter

Regional	Purpose:	Research Programs	Public Programs
City	Water conservation	Support research	Educational programs
✓ State	Soil conservation	Conduct research	Field trips, seminars
National	✓ General conservation	Publish research	Open to the public
	Prairie conservation		✓ Membership
	Restoration		
	Landscape design		

New Mexico Natural Resources Department, Forestry Division
Santa Fe, NM 87503   (505)827-7853

Brief description: The resource survey section monitors endangered species, conducts surveys, and develops recovery actions for rare species.

Publications:

Regional	Purpose:	Research Programs	Public Programs
City	Water conservation	Support research	Educational programs
✓ State	Soil conservation	✓ Conduct research	Field trips, seminars
National	✓ General conservation	Publish research	Open to the public
	Prairie conservation		Membership
	Restoration		
	Landscape design		

Rio Grande Zoological Park
903 10th Street SW
Albuquerque, NM 87102   (505)843-7413

Brief description: A city-owned and operated zoo displaying exotic and native animals in naturalistic surroundings.

Publications:

Regional	Purpose:	Research Programs	Public Programs
✓ City	Water conservation	Support research	Educational programs
State	Soil conservation	Conduct research	✓ Field trips, seminars
National	✓ General conservation	Publish research	✓ Open to the public
	Prairie conservation		✓ Membership
	Restoration		
	Landscape design		

USDA Soil Conservation Service, Plant Materials Center
1036 Miller Street SW
Los Lunas, NM 87031 (505)865-4684

Brief description: A plant materials center which tests and releases trees, shrubs, forbs, and grasses for conservation purposes.

Publications:

Regional	Purpose:	Research Programs	Public Programs
City	Water conservation	Support research	Educational programs
✓ State	Soil conservation	✓ Conduct research	✓ Field trips, seminars
National	✓ General conservation	✓ Publish research	Open to the public
	Prairie conservation		Membership
	Restoration		
	Landscape design		

NEVADA

Nevada Natural Heritage Program
201 South Fall Street
Carson City, NV 89710 (702)885-4370

Brief description: A state agency which maintains a computerized database on rare and endangered species.

Publications:

Regional	Purpose:	Research Programs	Public Programs
City	Water conservation	Support research	✓ Educational programs
✓ State	Soil conservation	✓ Conduct research	✓ Field trips, seminars
National	✓ General conservation	Publish research	✓ Open to the public
	Prairie conservation		✓ Membership
	Restoration		
	Landscape design		

Northern Nevada Native Plant Society
P. O. Box 8965
Reno, NV 89507

Brief description: A nonprofit organization which promotes native plants and environmental education through meetings, field trips, etc.

Publications: Mentzelia; Newsletter

Regional	Purpose:	Research Programs	Public Programs
City	Water conservation	Support research	✓ Educational programs
✓ State	Soil conservation	Conduct research	✓ Field trips, seminars
National	✓ General conservation	Publish research	✓ Open to the public
	Prairie conservation		✓ Membership
	Restoration		
	Landscape design		

NEW YORK

Bayard Cutting Arboretum
Box 466
Oakdale, NY 11769   *(516)581-1002*

Brief description: A state park with wildflowers featured throughout the grounds, particularly along the wildflower trail.

Publications:

Regional	Purpose:	Research Programs	Public Programs
City	Water conservation	Support research	Educational programs
✓ State	Soil conservation	Conduct research	Field trips, seminars
National	✓ General conservation	Publish research	Open to the public
	Prairie conservation		Membership
	Restoration		
	Landscape design		

Cornell Plantations
1 Plantations Road, Cornell University
Ithaca, NY 14850   *(607)256-3020*

Brief description: The botanic garden, arboretum and natural areas of Cornell University; also a research facility.

Publications: Cornell Plantations Quarterly Magazine

Regional	Purpose:	Research Programs	Public Programs
✓ City	Water conservation	Support research	✓ Educational programs
State	Soil conservation	✓ Conduct research	✓ Field trips, seminars
National	✓ General conservation	✓ Publish research	✓ Open to the public
	Prairie conservation		✓ Membership
	Restoration		
	✓ Landscape design		

Federated Garden Clubs of New York State, Inc.
234 Point of Woods Drive
Albany, NY 12203   *(518)869-6311*

Brief description: An educational and service club of 15,000 members which is part of the National Council of State Garden Clubs.

Publications: News

Regional	Purpose:	Research Programs	Public Programs
City	Water conservation	✓ Support research	✓ Educational programs
✓ State	Soil conservation	Conduct research	✓ Field trips, seminars
National	✓ General conservation	Publish research	✓ Open to the public
	Prairie conservation		✓ Membership
	Restoration		
	Landscape design		

Garden Club of America, The
598 Madison Avenue
New York City, NY 10461   *(212)753-8288*

Brief description: A national club that promotes gardening among amateurs and encourages civic plantings which often include wildflowers.

Publications:

Regional	Purpose:	Research Programs	Public Programs
✓ City	Water conservation	Support research	Educational programs
State	Soil conservation	Conduct research	Field trips, seminars
National	✓ General conservation	Publish research	Open to the public
	Prairie conservation		Membership
	Restoration		
	Landscape design		

Institute of Ecosystem Studies
Box AB
Millbrook, NY 12545   *(914)677-5343*

Brief description: A research center with botanical gardens and an arboretum which is a division of the New York Botanical Garden.

Publications:

Regional	Purpose:	Research Programs	Public Programs
✓ City	Water conservation	Support research	✓ Educational programs
State	Soil conservation	✓ Conduct research	✓ Field trips, seminars
National	✓ General conservation	✓ Publish research	✓ Open to the public
	Prairie conservation		✓ Membership
	Restoration		
	Landscape design		

Mohonk Mountain House
Mohonk Lake
New Paltz, NY 12561   *(914)255-1000*

Brief description: A resort hotel with over 5,000 acres of extensive gardens and preserve areas surrounding the property.

Publications: Booklets

Regional	Purpose:	Research Programs	Public Programs
City	Water conservation	Support research	✓ Educational programs
State	Soil conservation	✓ Conduct research	✓ Field trips, seminars
National	✓ General conservation	✓ Publish research	✓ Open to the public
	Prairie conservation		✓ Membership
	Restoration		
	✓ Landscape design		

Nature Conservancy, The
Eastern New York Chapter, 1736 Western Avenue
Albany, NY 12203   (518)869-0453

Brief description: A nonprofit organization dedicated to the preservation of natural areas through land acquisition.

Publications: The Nature Conservancy News (monthly); Chapter Newsletter

Regional	Purpose:	Research Programs	Public Programs
✓ City	Water conservation	Support research	Educational programs
State	Soil conservation	Conduct research	✓ Field trips, seminars
✓ National	✓ General conservation	Publish research	✓ Open to the public
	Prairie conservation		✓ Membership
	Restoration		
	Landscape design		

Nature Conservancy, The
Lower Hudson Chapter, RFD 2, Chestnut Ridge Road
Mount Kisco, NY 10549   (914)666-5365

Brief description: A nonprofit organization which preserves unique and significant natural areas.

Publications: The Nature Conservancy News (monthly); Chapter Newsletter

Regional	Purpose:	Research Programs	Public Programs
City	Water conservation	Support research	Educational programs
✓ State	Soil conservation	✓ Conduct research	✓ Field trips, seminars
National	✓ General conservation	Publish research	✓ Open to the public
	Prairie conservation		✓ Membership
	Restoration		
	Landscape design		

Nature Conservancy, The
Central New York Chapter, P. O. Box 175
Ithaca, NY 14851   (607)273-4215

Brief description: A nonprofit conservation organization which preserves unique and significant natural areas and endangered species.

Publications: The Nature Conservancy News (monthly); Chapter Newsletter

Regional	Purpose:	Research Programs	Public Programs
City	Water conservation	✓ Support research	Educational programs
✓ State	Soil conservation	✓ Conduct research	✓ Field trips, seminars
✓ National	✓ General conservation	Publish research	✓ Open to the public
	Prairie conservation		✓ Membership
	Restoration		
	Landscape design		

New York Botanical Garden, The
200th Street and Southern Blvd.
Bronx, N Y 10458   *(212)220-8700*

Brief description: A botanical garden with many collections including a native plant garden; also sponsors symposia and classes.

Publications: Books; Newsletter (quarterly); Booklets; Brochures

Regional	Purpose:	Research Programs	Public Programs
✓ City	Water conservation	Support research	✓ Educational programs
✓ State	Soil conservation	✓ Conduct research	✓ Field trips, seminars
✓ National	✓ General conservation	✓ Publish research	✓ Open to the public
	Prairie conservation		✓ Membership
	Restoration		
	✓ Landscape design		

New York City Parks Department
The Arsenal, Room 203
New York, N Y 10021   *(212)360-8193*

Brief description: A city park department responsible for 7,000 acres of parkland.
Publications:

Regional	Purpose:	Research Programs	Public Programs
✓ City	Water conservation	Support research	✓ Educational programs
State	Soil conservation	Conduct research	✓ Field trips, seminars
National	✓ General conservation	Publish research	✓ Open to the public
	Prairie conservation		Membership
	Restoration		
	✓ Landscape design		

New York City Street Tree Consortium
3 West 29th Street, 6th Floor
New York, N Y 10001   *(212)679-4481*

Brief description: Publishers of information on street trees.
Publications: Tree Tips Fact Sheet; Tree Talk Newsletter

Regional	Purpose:	Research Programs	Public Programs
✓ City	Water conservation	Support research	✓ Educational programs
State	Soil conservation	Conduct research	✓ Field trips, seminars
National	✓ General conservation	Publish research	✓ Open to the public
	Prairie conservation		Membership
	Restoration		
	Landscape design		

New York Natural Heritage Program
Wildlife Resources Center
Delmar, NY 12054-9767   *(518)439-7488*

Brief description: A state agency which identifies, monitors, and protects rare and endangered species.

Publications:

Regional	Purpose:	Research Programs	Public Programs
City	Water conservation	Support research	Educational programs
✓ State	Soil conservation	Conduct research	Field trips, seminars
National	✓ General conservation	Publish research	Open to the public
	Prairie conservation		Membership
	Restoration		
	Landscape design		

Old Westbury Gardens, Inc.
P. O. Box 430, 71 Old Westbury Road
Old Westbury, NY 11568-0430   *(516)333-0048*

Brief description: A former estate now open to the public as a museum and formal garden; sponsors a symposium on gardening with native species.

Publications: Old Westbury Gardens News (quarterly); Old Westbury Gardens

Regional	Purpose:	Research Programs	Public Programs
✓ City	Water conservation	Support research	✓ Educational programs
✓ State	Soil conservation	Conduct research	✓ Field trips, seminars
✓ National	✓ General conservation	Publish research	✓ Open to the public
	Prairie conservation		✓ Membership
	Restoration		
	✓ Landscape design		

Syracuse Botanical Club
306 Cleveland Blvd.
Fayetteville, NY 13066   *(315)637-6555*

Brief description: A study group which primarily encourages knowledge of botany and protects endangered species.

Publications:

Regional	Purpose:	Research Programs	Public Programs
✓ City	Water conservation	Support research	✓ Educational programs
State	Soil conservation	Conduct research	✓ Field trips, seminars
National	✓ General conservation	Publish research	Open to the public
	Prairie conservation		✓ Membership
	Restoration		
	Landscape design		

Tifft Farm Nature Preserve
1200 Fuhrmann Blvd.
Buffalo, NY 14203   (716)896-5200

Brief description: A 264-acre urban nature preserve with goals of preservation of habitat, education and passive recreation.

Publications: Collections (bimonthly)

Regional	Purpose:	Research Programs	Public Programs
✓ City	Water conservation	Support research	✓ Educational programs
State	Soil conservation	✓ Conduct research	✓ Field trips, seminars
National	✓ General conservation	✓ Publish research	✓ Open to the public
	Prairie conservation		✓ Membership
	Restoration		
	Landscape design		

OHIO _____

Cox Arboretum
6733 Springboro Pike
Dayton, OH 45449   (513)434-9005

Brief description: An arboretum with numerous plant collections.

Publications: Cox Arboretum News (bimonthly)

Regional	Purpose:	Research Programs	Public Programs
City	Water conservation	Support research	✓ Educational programs
✓ State	Soil conservation	✓ Conduct research	✓ Field trips, seminars
National	✓ General conservation	✓ Publish research	✓ Open to the public
	Prairie conservation		✓ Membership
	Restoration		
	✓ Landscape design		

_____

Davey Tree Expert Co.
1500 North Mantua Street
Kent, OH 44240   (216)673-9511

Brief description: A horticultural tree service company for residential, commercial and utility markets; also researches tree diseases and pests.

Publications:

Regional	Purpose:	Research Programs	Public Programs
City	Water conservation	Support research	Educational programs
State	Soil conservation	Conduct research	Field trips, seminars
✓ National	✓ General conservation	Publish research	Open to the public
	Prairie conservation		Membership
	Restoration		
	Landscape design		

Dawes Arboretum, The
7770 Jacksontown Road SE
Newark, OH 43055 (614)323-2355

Brief description: A 950-acre arboretum which demonstrates the value of trees and offers courses in horticulture and natural history.

Publications: The Dawes Arboretum Newsletter

Regional	Purpose:	Research Programs	Public Programs
✓ City	Water conservation	Support research	✓ Educational programs
State	Soil conservation	✓ Conduct research	✓ Field trips, seminars
National	✓ General conservation	Publish research	✓ Open to the public
	Prairie conservation		✓ Membership
	Restoration		
	✓ Landscape design		

George P. Crosby Gardens
P. O. Box 7430, 5403 Elmer Drive
Toledo, OH 43615 (419)536-8365

Brief description: A city-owned garden with a cultural center for the arts; a 3.8-acre shade garden includes both native and introduced plants.

Publications:

Regional	Purpose:	Research Programs	Public Programs
✓ City	Water conservation	Support research	✓ Educational programs
State	Soil conservation	✓ Conduct research	✓ Field trips, seminars
National	✓ General conservation	Publish research	✓ Open to the public
	Prairie conservation		✓ Membership
	Restoration		
	Landscape design		

Holden Arboretum, The
9500 Sperry Road
Mentor, OH 44060 (216)946-4400

Brief description: A 2,800-acre preserve with natural woodlands and horticultural displays; also conducts research on rare plants of the Midwest.

Publications: Arboretum Leaves

Regional	Purpose:	Research Programs	Public Programs
City	Water conservation	Support research	✓ Educational programs
✓ State	Soil conservation	✓ Conduct research	✓ Field trips, seminars
National	✓ General conservation	Publish research	✓ Open to the public
	Prairie conservation		✓ Membership
	Restoration		
	Landscape design		

Nature Conservancy, The
Ohio Chapter, 1504 West First Avenue
Columbus, OH 43212   (614)486-6789

Brief description: A nonprofit organization which preserves habitats for rare
species and communities through land acquisition.

Publications: The Nature Conservancy News (monthly); Chapter Newsletter

Regional	Purpose:	Research Programs	Public Programs
City	Water conservation	✓ Support research	Educational programs
✓ State	Soil conservation	✓ Conduct research	✓ Field trips, seminars
National	✓ General conservation	✓ Publish research	✓ Open to the public
	Prairie conservation		✓ Membership
	✓ Restoration		
	Landscape design		

Ohio Native Plant Society
6 Louise Drive
Chagrin Falls, OH 44022   (216)338-6622

Brief description: A nonprofit organization dedicated to conservation of native
plants and habitats through educational programs and trips.

Publications: On the Fringe (bimonthly)

Regional	Purpose:	Research Programs	Public Programs
✓ City	Water conservation	✓ Support research	✓ Educational programs
✓ State	Soil conservation	Conduct research	✓ Field trips, seminars
National	✓ General conservation	Publish research	✓ Open to the public
	Prairie conservation		✓ Membership
	Restoration		
	Landscape design		

Ohio Natural Heritage Program, Division of Natural Areas
Fountain Square, Building F
Columbus, OH 43224   (614)265-6453

Brief description: A state program which inventories natural areas and
endangered species.

Publications: Ohio Endangered and Threatened Plants

Regional	Purpose:	Research Programs	Public Programs
City	Water conservation	Support research	Educational programs
✓ State	Soil conservation	✓ Conduct research	Field trips, seminars
National	✓ General conservation	✓ Publish research	✓ Open to the public
	Prairie conservation		Membership
	Restoration		
	Landscape design		

OKLAHOMA

Nature Conservancy, The
Oklahoma Field Office, South Boston, Suite 846
Tulsa, OK 74103   (918)585-1117

Brief description: A nonprofit conservation organization dedicated to the preservation of natural diversity through land acquisition.

Publications: The Nature Conservancy News (monthly); Chapter Newsletter

Regional	Purpose:	Research Programs	Public Programs
City	Water conservation	Support research	Educational programs
✓ State	Soil conservation	Conduct research	Field trips, seminars
National	✓ General conservation	Publish research	Open to the public
	Prairie conservation		✓ Membership
	Restoration		
	Landscape design		

Oklahoma Native Plant Society
2435 South Peoria Avenue
Tulsa, OK 74114   (918)749-6401

Brief description: A nonprofit society which offers meetings, field trips, a speaker's bureau and newsletter to further knowledge of native plants.

Publications: The Gaillardia (quarterly)

Regional	Purpose:	Research Programs	Public Programs
City	Water conservation	Support research	✓ Educational programs
✓ State	Soil conservation	✓ Conduct research	✓ Field trips, seminars
National	✓ General conservation	Publish research	✓ Open to the public
	Prairie conservation		✓ Membership
	Restoration		
	Landscape design		

Oklahoma Natural Heritage Program, Oklahoma Biological Survey
Sutton Hall, University of Oklahoma
Norman, OK 73019   (405)325-4034

Brief description: A state agency which identifies, monitors, and protects rare and endangered species.

Publications:

Regional	Purpose:	Research Programs	Public Programs
City	Water conservation	Support research	Educational programs
✓ State	Soil conservation	Conduct research	Field trips, seminars
National	✓ General conservation	Publish research	Open to the public
	Prairie conservation		Membership
	Restoration		
	Landscape design		

OREGON

Berry Botanic Garden
11505 SW Summerville Avenue
Portland, OR 97219   (503)636-4112

Brief description: A botanic garden committed to scientific, educational and
conservation efforts.

Publications: Bulletin of the Berry Botanic Garden (quarterly)

Regional	Purpose:	Research Programs	Public Programs
City	Water conservation	Support research	✓ Educational programs
✓ State	Soil conservation	✓ Conduct research	✓ Field trips, seminars
National	✓ General conservation	Publish research	✓ Open to the public
	Prairie conservation		✓ Membership
	Restoration		
	Landscape design		

Hoyt Arboretum
4000 SW Fairview Blvd.
Portland, OR 97221   (503)228-8732

Brief description: An exotic tree and shrub arboretum interplanted within a
native Oregon forest.

Publications: News from Hoyt Arboretum (monthly)

Regional	Purpose:	Research Programs	Public Programs
City	Water conservation	Support research	✓ Educational programs
✓ State	Soil conservation	Conduct research	✓ Field trips, seminars
National	✓ General conservation	Publish research	✓ Open to the public
	Prairie conservation		✓ Membership
	Restoration		
	Landscape design		

Leach Botanical Garden
6704 SE 122nd Avenue
Portland, OR 97236   (503)761-9503

Brief description: The Garden is a public facility for study of horticulture, botany,
landscape architecture and natural history of the Pacific
Northwest.

Publications: Sleepy Hollow News (monthly); Brochures

Regional	Purpose:	Research Programs	Public Programs
City	Water conservation	Support research	✓ Educational programs
✓ State	Soil conservation	Conduct research	✓ Field trips, seminars
National	✓ General conservation	Publish research	✓ Open to the public
	Prairie conservation		✓ Membership
	Restoration		
	Landscape design		

Mount Pisgah Arboretum
P. O. Box 5621, 34909 Frank Parrish Road
Eugene, OR 97405   (503)747-3817

Brief description: An arboretum with trees from all over the world; also includes
several miles of nature trails and a two-acre wildflower area.

Publications: Tree Time (quarterly)

Regional	Purpose:	Research Programs	Public Programs
✓ City	Water conservation	Support research	✓ Educational programs
State	Soil conservation	Conduct research	Field trips, seminars
National	✓ General conservation	Publish research	✓ Open to the public
	Prairie conservation		✓ Membership
	Restoration		
	Landscape design		

Native Plant Society of Oregon
393 Fulvue Drive
Eugene, OR 97405   (503)345-6241

Brief description: A nonprofit organization devoted to the study and preservation
of native plants and their habitats.

Publications: Bulletin (monthly)

Regional	Purpose:	Research Programs	Public Programs
City	Water conservation	Support research	✓ Educational programs
✓ State	Soil conservation	Conduct research	✓ Field trips, seminars
National	✓ General conservation	Publish research	✓ Open to the public
	Prairie conservation		✓ Membership
	Restoration		
	Landscape design		

Nature Conservancy, The
Oregon Field Office, 1234 NW 25th
Portland, OR 97210   (503)228-9561

Brief description: A nonprofit conservation organization dedicated to the
preservation of natural diversity through land acquisition.

Publications: The Nature Conservancy News (monthly); Chapter Newsletter

Regional	Purpose:	Research Programs	Public Programs
City	Water conservation	Support research	Educational programs
✓ State	Soil conservation	Conduct research	Field trips, seminars
National	✓ General conservation	Publish research	Open to the public
	Prairie conservation		✓ Membership
	Restoration		
	Landscape design		

Oregon Natural Heritage Database
1234 NW 25th Avenue
Portland, OR 97214   (503)228-9561

Brief description: A state agency which surveys and monitors rare and endangered species and their habitats.

Publications: Rare, Threatened and Endangered Plants and Animals of Oregon

Regional	Purpose:	Research Programs	Public Programs
City	Water conservation	Support research	Educational programs
✓ State	Soil conservation	✓ Conduct research	Field trips, seminars
✓ National	✓ General conservation	✓ Publish research	✓ Open to the public
	Prairie conservation		✓ Membership
	Restoration		
	Landscape design		

Oregon State University, Research Forests
Peavy Hall, Room 212
Corvallis, OR 97331   (503)754-4452

Brief description: A university research forest of 14,444 acres including over 100 species of native trees and shrubs of the Pacific Northwest.

Publications:

Regional	Purpose:	Research Programs	Public Programs
City	Water conservation	Support research	✓ Educational programs
✓ State	Soil conservation	✓ Conduct research	✓ Field trips, seminars
National	✓ General conservation	Publish research	✓ Open to the public
	Prairie conservation		Membership
	Restoration		
	Landscape design		

PENNSYLVANIA

Beechwood Farms Nature Preserve
Audubon Society of Western Pennsylvania, 614 Dorseyville Road
Pittsburg, PA 15238   (412)963-6100

Brief description: An environmental education and conservation organization.

Publications:

Regional	Purpose:	Research Programs	Public Programs
City	Water conservation	Support research	✓ Educational programs
✓ State	Soil conservation	✓ Conduct research	✓ Field trips, seminars
National	✓ General conservation	Publish research	✓ Open to the public
	Prairie conservation		✓ Membership
	Restoration		
	Landscape design		

Bowman Hill Wildflower Preserve
Washington Crossing Historic Park
Washington Crossing, PA 18977   *(215)862-2924*

Brief description: A wildflower preserve established in 1934 for the conservation
and preservation of Pennsylvania native plants.

Publications: Ways with Wildflowers

Regional	Purpose:	Research Programs	Public Programs
City	Water conservation	Support research	Educational programs
✓ State	Soil conservation	Conduct research	✓ Field trips, seminars
✓ National	✓ General conservation	Publish research	✓ Open to the public
	Prairie conservation		✓ Membership
	Restoration		
	Landscape design		

Brandywine Conservancy, Inc.
P. O. Box 141
Chadds Ford, PA 19317   *(215)388-7601*

Brief description: A nonprofit institution which includes a fine arts museum and
environmental management center featuring a native plant
garden.

Publications: How to Grow Native Shrubs; Landscaping with Native Plants

Regional	Purpose:	Research Programs	Public Programs
✓ City	Water conservation	✓ Support research	Educational programs
✓ State	Soil conservation	✓ Conduct research	✓ Field trips, seminars
✓ National	✓ General conservation	✓ Publish research	Open to the public
	Prairie conservation		✓ Membership
	Restoration		
	Landscape design		

Department of Environmental Resources, Bureau of Forestry
FAS P.O. Box 1467
Harrisburg, PA 17120   *(717)787-3444*

Brief description: A state agency that manages state forestland and native wild
plants.

Publications:

Regional	Purpose:	Research Programs	Public Programs
City	Water conservation	✓ Support research	Educational programs
✓ State	Soil conservation	✓ Conduct research	✓ Field trips, seminars
National	✓ General conservation	✓ Publish research	✓ Open to the public
	Prairie conservation		Membership
	Restoration		
	Landscape design		

Jenkins Arboretum
631 Berwyn Baptist Road
Devon, PA 19333   (215)647-8870

Brief description: An arboretum devoted to azaleas; also has a 350-species nature trail including 50 poisonous plants.

Publications:

Regional	Purpose:	Research Programs	Public Programs
✔ City	Water conservation	Support research	Educational programs
State	Soil conservation	Conduct research	Field trips, seminars
National	✔ General conservation	Publish research	✔ Open to the public
	Prairie conservation		Membership
	Restoration		
	Landscape design		

Longwood Gardens
Rt. 1, P. O. Box 501
Kennett Square, PA 19348-0501   (215)388-6741

Brief description: A 1,000-acre display garden with 11,000 species, also offers an extensive educational program.

Publications: Schedule of Events; Continuing Education Courses

Regional	Purpose:	Research Programs	Public Programs
City	Water conservation	Support research	✔ Educational programs
State	Soil conservation	✔ Conduct research	✔ Field trips, seminars
✔ National	✔ General conservation	Publish research	✔ Open to the public
	Prairie conservation		Membership
	Restoration		
	✔ Landscape design		

Muhlenberg Botanical Society, c/o Franklin and Marshall College
P. O. Box 3003
Lancaster, PA 17604   (717)291-3942

Brief description: A nonprofit group of 70 amateur and professional botanists who organize lectures, field trips and workshops for members.

Publications:

Regional	Purpose:	Research Programs	Public Programs
✔ City	Water conservation	Support research	Educational programs
State	Soil conservation	Conduct research	✔ Field trips, seminars
National	✔ General conservation	Publish research	✔ Open to the public
	Prairie conservation		Membership
	Restoration		
	Landscape design		

Nature Center of Charlestown
P. O. Box 82, Rt. 29 and Hollow Road
Devault, PA 19432   (215)935-9777

Brief description: A nature center with programs for students and a wildflower garden with species native to Pennsylvania.

Publications: The Oak Log (quarterly)

Regional	Purpose:	Research Programs	Public Programs
✓ City	Water conservation	Support research	✓ Educational programs
State	Soil conservation	Conduct research	✓ Field trips, seminars
National	✓ General conservation	Publish research	✓ Open to the public
	Prairie conservation		✓ Membership
	Restoration		
	Landscape design		

Nature Conservancy, The
1218 Chestnut Street, Suite 1002
Philadelphia, PA 19107   (215)925-1065

Brief description: A nonprofit conservation organization dedicated to the preservation of natural diversity through land acquisition.

Publications: The Nature Conservancy News (monthly); Chapter Newsletter

Regional	Purpose:	Research Programs	Public Programs
City	Water conservation	Support research	Educational programs
✓ State	Soil conservation	Conduct research	Field trips, seminars
National	✓ General conservation	Publish research	Open to the public
	Prairie conservation		✓ Membership
	Restoration		
	Landscape design		

Pennsylvania Natural Diversity Inventory
Western Pennsylvania Conservancy, 316 Fourth Avenue
Pittsburgh, PA 15222   (412)288-2777

Brief description: A group which collects and computerizes data on rare and endangered species, providing information to public and private land managers.

Publications:

Regional	Purpose:	Research Programs	Public Programs
City	Water conservation	✓ Support research	Educational programs
✓ State	Soil conservation	✓ Conduct research	Field trips, seminars
National	✓ General conservation	Publish research	✓ Open to the public
	Prairie conservation		✓ Membership
	Restoration		
	Landscape design		

Pennsylvania Natural Diversity Inventory-East
Department of Environmental Protection, 34 Airport Drive
Middletown, PA 17057   (717)783-1712

Brief description: A nonprofit organization which inventories and computerizes data on Pennsylvania's native species and natural communities.

Publications:

Regional	Purpose:	Research Programs	Public Programs
City	Water conservation	Support research	Educational programs
✓ State	Soil conservation	✓ Conduct research	Field trips, seminars
National	✓ General conservation	✓ Publish research	Open to the public
	Prairie conservation		Membership
	Restoration		
	Landscape design		

Pennypacker Mills, County of Montgomery
5 Haldeman Road
Schwenksville, PA 19473   (215)287-9349

Brief description: A historic house and museum set on 125 acres with walking trails throughout the property.

Publications:

Regional	Purpose:	Research Programs	Public Programs
✓ City	Water conservation	Support research	✓ Educational programs
✓ State	Soil conservation	✓ Conduct research	Field trips, seminars
National	✓ General conservation	✓ Publish research	✓ Open to the public
	Prairie conservation		Membership
	Restoration		
	✓ Landscape design		

Philadelphia Botanical Club, The
The Academy of Natural Sciences, 19th Street and the Parkway
Philadelphia, PA 19103   (215)299-1192

Brief description: A botanical club which holds monthly meetings and organizes trips to study plants in the field.

Publications:

Regional	Purpose:	Research Programs	Public Programs
City	Water conservation	Support research	Educational programs
State	Soil conservation	Conduct research	✓ Field trips, seminars
✓ National	✓ General conservation	Publish research	Open to the public
	Prairie conservation		Membership
	Restoration		
	Landscape design		

RHODE ISLAND

Blithewold Gardens and Arboretum
P. O. Box 417, Ferry Road
Bristol, RI 02809-0417   *(401)253-2707*

Brief description: A 33-acre garden with a nationally registered historic home; a ten-acre meadow is filled with grasses and wildflowers.

Publications: Quarterly

Regional	Purpose:	Research Programs	Public Programs
✓ City	Water conservation	✓ Support research	Educational programs
State	Soil conservation	Conduct research	✓ Field trips, seminars
✓ National	✓ General conservation	Publish research	Open to the public
	Prairie conservation		Membership
	Restoration		
	Landscape design		

Garden Club of Rhode Island
20 Harbor View Avenue
Bristol, RI 02809   *(401)253-9260*

Brief description: A garden club interested in conservation of wildflowers and other gardening activities.

Publications:

Regional	Purpose:	Research Programs	Public Programs
✓ City	Water conservation	Support research	Educational programs
State	Soil conservation	Conduct research	Field trips, seminars
National	✓ General conservation	Publish research	Open to the public
	Prairie conservation		✓ Membership
	Restoration		
	Landscape design		

Rhode Island Natural Heritage Program
Dept. of Environmental Management, 22 Hayes Street/Div. of Planning
Providence, RI 02908   *(401)277-2776*

Brief description: A state agency which locates and monitors rare and endangered species and their habitats.

Publications:

Regional	Purpose:	Research Programs	Public Programs
City	Water conservation	Support research	Educational programs
✓ State	Soil conservation	✓ Conduct research	✓ Field trips, seminars
National	✓ General conservation	Publish research	Open to the public
	Prairie conservation		Membership
	Restoration		
	Landscape design		

Rhode Island Wild Plant Society, Inc.
P. O. Box 534
West Kingston, RI 02892   (401)789-6405

Brief description: A conservation organization dedicated to the preservation and propagation of wild plants, especially those native to Rhode Island.

Publications: Newsletter (monthly)

Regional	Purpose:	Research Programs	Public Programs
City	Water conservation	Support research	✓ Educational programs
✓ State	Soil conservation	Conduct research	✓ Field trips, seminars
National	✓ General conservation	Publish research	✓ Open to the public
	Prairie conservation		✓ Membership
	Restoration		
	Landscape design		

SOUTH CAROLINA

Brookgreen Gardens
U.S. 17 South
Murrells Inlet, SC 29576   (803)237-4218

Brief description: A garden with collections of Southeastern native plants and other selected horticultural specimens in a formal setting.

Publications: Brookgreen Journal

Regional	Purpose:	Research Programs	Public Programs
City	Water conservation	Support research	✓ Educational programs
✓ State	Soil conservation	Conduct research	✓ Field trips, seminars
National	✓ General conservation	Publish research	✓ Open to the public
	Prairie conservation		✓ Membership
	Restoration		
	✓ Landscape design		

Nature Conservancy, The
South Carolina Chapter, P. O. Box 5475
Columbia, SC 29250   (803)256-7633

Brief description: A nonprofit organization working towards natural diversity through land acquisition.

Publications: The Nature Conservancy News (monthly); Chapter Newsletter

Regional	Purpose:	Research Programs	Public Programs
City	Water conservation	Support research	Educational programs
✓ State	Soil conservation	✓ Conduct research	✓ Field trips, seminars
National	✓ General conservation	Publish research	✓ Open to the public
	Prairie conservation		✓ Membership
	Restoration		
	Landscape design		

South Carolina Heritage Trust
South Carolina Wildlife and Marine Resources, P. O. Box 167
Columbia, SC 29202   (803)734-3893

Brief description: A unit of state government working for the preservation of natural diversity within the state.

Publications:

Regional	Purpose:	Research Programs	Public Programs
City	Water conservation	✓ Support research	Educational programs
✓ State	Soil conservation	✓ Conduct research	✓ Field trips, seminars
National	✓ General conservation	✓ Publish research	✓ Open to the public
	Prairie conservation		Membership
	Restoration		
	Landscape design		

SOUTH DAKOTA

Great Plains Garden
P. O. Box 461
Hot Springs, SD 57747-0461   (605)745-3397

Brief description: A nonprofit corporation which established a botanical garden for the Great Plains Region.

Publications:

Regional	Purpose:	Research Programs	Public Programs
City	Water conservation	Support research	Educational programs
✓ State	Soil conservation	Conduct research	Field trips, seminars
National	✓ General conservation	Publish research	✓ Open to the public
	✓ Prairie conservation		✓ Membership
	Restoration		
	Landscape design		

South Dakota Natural Heritage Database
Game, Fish and Parks Department, 445 East Capitol Avenue
Pierre, SD 57501   (605)773-4227

Brief description: A government agency that maintains a statewide inventory of rare species and natural communities.

Publications: Rare Animals and Plants of South Dakota

Regional	Purpose:	Research Programs	Public Programs
City	Water conservation	Support research	Educational programs
✓ State	Soil conservation	✓ Conduct research	Field trips, seminars
National	✓ General conservation	Publish research	Open to the public
	Prairie conservation		Membership
	Restoration		
	Landscape design		

TENNESSEE

Cheekwood Botanical Gardens
Forrest Park Drive
Nashville, TN 37205   *(615)356-3306*

Brief description: A botanical garden and fine arts museum with activities including a wildflower propagation program and annual plant sale.

Publications:

Regional	Purpose:	Research Programs	Public Programs
City	Water conservation	Support research	✓ Educational programs
✓ State	Soil conservation	✓ Conduct research	✓ Field trips, seminars
National	✓ General conservation	Publish research	✓ Open to the public
	Prairie conservation		✓ Membership
	Restoration		
	✓ Landscape design		

Dixon Gallery and Gardens, The
4339 Park Avenue
Memphis, TN 38117   *(901)761-5250*

Brief description: A museum and garden with 17 acres of woodlands, gardens landscaped in English park manner, and a new two-acre wildflower site.

Publications:

Regional	Purpose:	Research Programs	Public Programs
✓ City	Water conservation	Support research	Educational programs
State	Soil conservation	Conduct research	✓ Field trips, seminars
National	General conservation	Publish research	✓ Open to the public
	Prairie conservation		✓ Membership
	Restoration		
	Landscape design		

Lichterman Nature Center
5992 Quince Road
Memphis, TN 38119-4699   *(901)685-1566*

Brief description: A 65-acre wildlife sanctuary and public environmental education facility.

Publications:

Regional	Purpose:	Research Programs	Public Programs
✓ City	Water conservation	Support research	✓ Educational programs
State	Soil conservation	✓ Conduct research	✓ Field trips, seminars
National	✓ General conservation	Publish research	✓ Open to the public
	Prairie conservation		✓ Membership
	Restoration		
	Landscape design		

Memphis Botanic Garden
750 Cherry Road
Memphis, TN 38117-4699   *(901)685-1566*

Brief description: An 87-acre garden operated by the Memphis Park Commission. The collection includes a five-acre wildflower garden.

Publications: The Garden Appeal (monthly)

Regional	Purpose:	Research Programs	Public Programs
✓ City	Water conservation	Support research	✓ Educational programs
State	Soil conservation	Conduct research	✓ Field trips, seminars
National	General conservation	Publish research	✓ Open to the public
	Prairie conservation		✓ Membership
	Restoration		
	Landscape design		

Nature Conservancy, The
Tennessee Field Office, P. O. Box 3017
Nashville, TN 37219   *(615)242-1787*

Brief description: A nonprofit organization which preserves unique and significant natural areas and endangered species through land acquisition.

Publications: The Nature Conservancy News (monthly); Chapter Newsletter

Regional	Purpose:	Research Programs	Public Programs
City	Water conservation	✓ Support research	Educational programs
✓ State	Soil conservation	✓ Conduct research	Field trips, seminars
National	✓ General conservation	Publish research	✓ Open to the public
	Prairie conservation		✓ Membership
	Restoration		
	Landscape design		

Southern Appalachian Highlands Conservancy
P.O. Box 3356
Kingsport, TN 37664   *(615)323-3677*

Brief description: A nonprofit group dedicated to the acquisition and management of a 23,000-acre scenic/natural area.

Publications:

Regional	Purpose:	Research Programs	Public Programs
City	Water conservation	✓ Support research	Educational programs
✓ State	Soil conservation	✓ Conduct research	Field trips, seminars
National	✓ General conservation	Publish research	✓ Open to the public
	Prairie conservation		✓ Membership
	Restoration		
	Landscape design		

Tennessee Heritage Program
Tennessee Department of Conservation, 701 Broadway
Nashville, TN 37203   (615)742-6545

Brief description: A state agency which identifies, monitors, and protects rare and endangered species.

Publications:

Regional	Purpose:	Research Programs	Public Programs
City	Water conservation	Support research	Educational programs
✓ State	Soil conservation	Conduct research	Field trips, seminars
National	✓ General conservation	Publish research	Open to the public
	Prairie conservation		Membership
	Restoration		
	Landscape design		

Tennessee Native Plant Society
Department of Botany, University of Tennessee
Knoxville, TN 37996-1100   (615)974-2256

Brief description: A nonprofit group interested in Tennessee native flora; also promotes identification, propagation, landscaping and preservation.

Publications: Newsletter (monthly)

Regional	Purpose:	Research Programs	Public Programs
City	Water conservation	Support research	✓ Educational programs
✓ State	Soil conservation	Conduct research	✓ Field trips, seminars
National	✓ General conservation	Publish research	✓ Open to the public
	Prairie conservation		✓ Membership
	Restoration		
	Landscape design		

Tennessee Valley Authority, Recreation Resources
Natural Resources Bldg.
Norris, TN 37828   (615)494-9808

Brief description: A governmental agency overseeing natural resources.

Publications:

Regional	Purpose:	Research Programs	Public Programs
City	Water conservation	Support research	Educational programs
✓ State	Soil conservation	Conduct research	Field trips, seminars
National	✓ General conservation	Publish research	✓ Open to the public
	Prairie conservation		Membership
	Restoration		
	Landscape design		

Tom Pellett Landscape Designer
2310 Evelyn
Memphis, TN 38104   (901)276-1631

Brief description: A landscape designer who emphasizes native plants.
Publications:

Regional	Purpose:	Research Programs	Public Programs
✓ City	Water conservation	Support research	Educational programs
State	Soil conservation	Conduct research	Field trips, seminars
National	General conservation	Publish research	Open to the public
	Prairie conservation		Membership
	Restoration		
	✓ Landscape design		

Wildflower Society, The
c/o Goldsmith Civic Garden Center, 750 Cherry Road
Memphis, TN 38119-4699   (901)685-1010

Brief description: A nonprofit organization that maintains a four-acre woodland garden; also plans field trips and plant rescues.

Publications:

Regional	Purpose:	Research Programs	Public Programs
✓ City	Water conservation	Support research	✓ Educational programs
State	Soil conservation	Conduct research	✓ Field trips, seminars
National	✓ General conservation	Publish research	✓ Open to the public
	Prairie conservation		✓ Membership
	Restoration		
	Landscape design		

TEXAS _____

Armand Bayou Nature Center
P. O. Box 58828, 8600 Bay Area Blvd.
Houston, TX 77258   (713)474-2551

Brief description: An environmental education center and nature preserve that also has a native plant nursery.

Publications: ABNC Quarterly; Nursery Newsletter; Volunteer Newsletter

Regional	Purpose:	Research Programs	Public Programs
City	Water conservation	Support research	✓ Educational programs
✓ State	Soil conservation	✓ Conduct research	✓ Field trips, seminars
National	✓ General conservation	✓ Publish research	✓ Open to the public
	✓ Prairie conservation		✓ Membership
	Restoration		
	Landscape design		

Botanica Landscapes
4407 Avenue H
Austin, TX 78751   (512)453-5850

Brief description: A landscape design, installation and maintenance partnership specializing in native plants.

Publications:

Regional	Purpose:	Research Programs	Public Programs
✓ City	Water conservation	Support research	Educational programs
State	Soil conservation	Conduct research	Field trips, seminars
National	General conservation	Publish research	Open to the public
	Prairie conservation		Membership
	Restoration		
	✓ Landscape design		

Browning & Associates
2701 Pecos Street
Austin, TX 78703

Brief description: A consulting firm which conducts landscape evaluation and design, water conservation research and educational workshops.

Publications: Landscape Style, Irrigation Patterns and Water Use

Regional	Purpose:	Research Programs	Public Programs
✓ City	✓ Water conservation	Support research	✓ Educational programs
State	Soil conservation	✓ Conduct research	Field trips, seminars
National	✓ General conservation	✓ Publish research	Open to the public
	Prairie conservation		Membership
	Restoration		
	✓ Landscape design		

Canyon Lake Wildflower Club
Rt. 5, Box 861 E
Canyon Lake, TX 78130   (512)899-2754

Brief description: A club which worked with the Corps of Engineers and established bluebonnets on 20 acres near Canyon Dam and the adjacent park.

Publications: Yearbook

Regional	Purpose:	Research Programs	Public Programs
✓ City	Water conservation	Support research	Educational programs
✓ State	Soil conservation	Conduct research	✓ Field trips, seminars
National	✓ General conservation	Publish research	Open to the public
	Prairie conservation		✓ Membership
	Restoration		
	Landscape design		

Chihuahuan Desert Research Institute
P. O. Box 1334
Alpine, TX 79831   (915)837-8370

Brief description: A research institute which studies the Chihuahuan Desert region. Many seminars and educational activities are held.

Publications: Chihuahuan Desert Discovery (semiannual); Newsbrief (quarterly)

Regional	Purpose:	Research Programs	Public Programs
City	Water conservation	✓ Support research	✓ Educational programs
✓ State	Soil conservation	✓ Conduct research	✓ Field trips, seminars
National	✓ General conservation	✓ Publish research	✓ Open to the public
	Prairie conservation		✓ Membership
	Restoration		
	✓ Landscape design		

Corpus Christi Botanical Garden & Society
P. O. Box 81183
Corpus Christi, TX 78412   (512)993-7551

Brief description: A newly developing botanical garden formed by a non-profit organization.

Publications: Palm Prints Newsletter

Regional	Purpose:	Research Programs	Public Programs
City	Water conservation	Support research	✓ Educational programs
State	Soil conservation	✓ Conduct research	✓ Field trips, seminars
National	✓ General conservation	Publish research	✓ Open to the public
	Prairie conservation		✓ Membership
	Restoration		
	Landscape design		

Dallas Arboretum and Botanic Garden
8617 Garland Road
Dallas, TX 75218   (214)327-8263

Brief description: An arboretum with future goals of building a $50 million garden for the Southwest. Many native species will be included.

Publications:

Regional	Purpose:	Research Programs	Public Programs
✓ City	Water conservation	Support research	✓ Educational programs
✓ State	Soil conservation	✓ Conduct research	✓ Field trips, seminars
✓ National	✓ General conservation	Publish research	✓ Open to the public
	Prairie conservation		Membership
	Restoration		
	Landscape design		

Dallas Nature Center
7575 Wheatland Road
Dallas, TX 75249   *(214)296-1955*

Brief description: A nature preserve with a wide variety of environmental interests; also operates a Texas native plant nursery.

Publications: Friends of Greenhills (bimonthly)

Regional	Purpose:	Research Programs	Public Programs
✓ City	✓ Water conservation	Support research	✓ Educational programs
State	Soil conservation	✓ Conduct research	✓ Field trips, seminars
National	✓ General conservation	✓ Publish research	✓ Open to the public
	✓ Prairie conservation		✓ Membership
	Restoration		
	✓ Landscape design		

East Texas Plant Materials Center, Stephen F. Austin State University
P. O. Box 13000, SFA Station
Nacogdoches, TX 75962   *(409)569-3705*

Brief description: A plant materials center working in cooperation with Stephen F. Austin State University and 35 conservation districts to evaluate East Texas species.

Publications:

Regional	Purpose:	Research Programs	Public Programs
City	Water conservation	Support research	Educational programs
✓ State	✓ Soil conservation	Conduct research	Field trips, seminars
National	✓ General conservation	Publish research	✓ Open to the public
	Prairie conservation		Membership
	Restoration		
	Landscape design		

El Paso Native Plant Society
c/o James F. George, 6804 Tolvea
El Paso, TX 79912   *(915)541-5588*

Brief description: A nonprofit society dedicated to promoting a greater appreciation of native plants and the preservation of rare species.

Publications: Newsletter (monthly)

Regional	Purpose:	Research Programs	Public Programs
✓ City	Water conservation	Support research	✓ Educational programs
State	Soil conservation	Conduct research	✓ Field trips, seminars
National	✓ General conservation	Publish research	✓ Open to the public
	Prairie conservation		✓ Membership
	Restoration		
	✓ Landscape design		

Environmental Survey Consulting
4602 Placid Place
Austin, TX 78731   (512)458-8531

Brief description: A consulting firm which specializes in erosion control, vegetation analysis and restoration of native vegetation.

Publications: The Importance of Wild Seed - a New Harvesting Tool

Regional	Purpose:	Research Programs	Public Programs
✓ City	Water conservation	Support research	Educational programs
State	Soil conservation	✓ Conduct research	Field trips, seminars
National	✓ General conservation	✓ Publish research	Open to the public
	Prairie conservation		Membership
	Restoration		
	✓ Landscape design		

Greater Texas Landscapes, Inc.
7410 Sherwood Road
Austin, TX 78745   (512)462-2311

Brief description: A firm which designs and installs landscapes and specializes in native plants.

Publications:

Regional	Purpose:	Research Programs	Public Programs
✓ City	Water conservation	Support research	Educational programs
State	Soil conservation	✓ Conduct research	Field trips, seminars
National	General conservation	Publish research	✓ Open to the public
	Prairie conservation		Membership
	Restoration		
	✓ Landscape design		

Growing Design Landscapes
1906 Airole Way
Austin, TX 78704   (512)441-0992

Brief description: A design and installation firm with emphasis on custom design, native plants and water conservation for residences.

Publications:

Regional	Purpose:	Research Programs	Public Programs
✓ City	Water conservation	Support research	Educational programs
State	Soil conservation	Conduct research	Field trips, seminars
National	General conservation	Publish research	Open to the public
	Prairie conservation		Membership
	Restoration		
	✓ Landscape design		

Heard Natural Science Museum and Wildlife Sanctuary, Inc.
Rt. 6, Box 22
McKinney, TX 75069   (214)542-5566

Brief description: A 266-acre natural science museum and wildlife sanctuary with numerous trails through woodland, bottomland and prairie.

Publications:

Regional	Purpose:	Research Programs	Public Programs
City	Water conservation	✔ Support research	✔ Educational programs
✔ State	Soil conservation	✔ Conduct research	✔ Field trips, seminars
National	✔ General conservation	✔ Publish research	✔ Open to the public
	✔ Prairie conservation		✔ Membership
	Restoration		
	Landscape design		

Herbalgram
P. O. Box 12006
Austin, TX 78711   (512)331-4244

Brief description: A newsletter of scientific research on herbs including legal updates; published by the Herb Research Foundation.

Publications: Herbalgram (quarterly)

Regional	Purpose:	Research Programs	Public Programs
City	Water conservation	Support research	✔ Educational programs
State	Soil conservation	✔ Conduct research	Field trips, seminars
✔ National	✔ General conservation	✔ Publish research	Open to the public
	Prairie conservation		Membership
	Restoration		
	Landscape design		

Houston Arboretum and Nature Center
4501 Woodway
Houston, TX 77024   (713)681-8433

Brief description: An arboretum teaching environmental education with a focus on the natural history of Harris County, Texas.

Publications:

Regional	Purpose:	Research Programs	Public Programs
✔ City	Water conservation	Support research	✔ Educational programs
State	Soil conservation	✔ Conduct research	✔ Field trips, seminars
National	✔ General conservation	✔ Publish research	✔ Open to the public
	Prairie conservation		✔ Membership
	Restoration		
	Landscape design		

John Gleason, ASLA
2406 B Southland Drive
Austin, TX 78704   (512)462-3965

Brief description: A design and building firm specializing in Xeriscape and native landscapes; also consults in landscape architecture.

Publications:

Regional	Purpose:	Research Programs	Public Programs
✓ City	✓ Water conservation	Support research	Educational programs
State	Soil conservation	Conduct research	Field trips, seminars
National	✓ General conservation	Publish research	Open to the public
	✓ Prairie conservation		Membership
	✓ Restoration		
	✓ Landscape design		

Judge Roy Bean Visitor Center
P. O. Box 160
Langtry, TX 78871-0160   (915)291-3340

Brief description: A facility of the Texas Highway Department which is a historical museum with a garden containing plants of the Trans Pecos.

Publications:

Regional	Purpose:	Research Programs	Public Programs
✓ City	Water conservation	Support research	Educational programs
State	Soil conservation	Conduct research	Field trips, seminars
National	✓ General conservation	Publish research	✓ Open to the public
	Prairie conservation		Membership
	Restoration		
	Landscape design		

Julie Ryan & Company
917 Cristler Avenue
Dallas, TX 75223   (214)827-7009

Brief description: A landscape designer who specializes in native and adapted plants of Texas; also a photographer and author.

Publications: Landscaping with Native Texas Plants

Regional	Purpose:	Research Programs	Public Programs
City	Water conservation	Support research	Educational programs
✓ State	Soil conservation	Conduct research	Field trips, seminars
National	General conservation	Publish research	Open to the public
	Prairie conservation		Membership
	✓ Restoration		
	✓ Landscape design		

Mercer Arboretum and Botanic Gardens
22306 *Aldine-Westfield Road*
Humble, TX 77338   *(713)443-8731*

Brief description: A 214-acre arboretum emphasizing native plants and
ornamental horticulture. A wildflower area is in cultivation.

Publications:

Regional	Purpose:	Research Programs	Public Programs
✓ City	Water conservation	Support research	Educational programs
State	Soil conservation	✓ Conduct research	Field trips, seminars
National	✓ General conservation	Publish research	Open to the public
	Prairie conservation		✓ Membership
	Restoration		
	Landscape design		

Native Plant Project
P. O. Box 1433
Edinburg, TX 78540-1433

Brief description: A nonprofit organization which promotes native species for
revegetation and works to increase awareness of native plants.

Publications: The Sabal (monthly)

Regional	Purpose:	Research Programs	Public Programs
City	Water conservation	Support research	✓ Educational programs
✓ State	Soil conservation	Conduct research	✓ Field trips, seminars
National	✓ General conservation	✓ Publish research	✓ Open to the public
	Prairie conservation		✓ Membership
	Restoration		
	✓ Landscape design		

Native Plant Society of Texas
P. O. Box 23836, TWU Station
Denton, TX 76204   *(817)627-2862*

Brief description: A nonprofit organization concerned with the promotion and
utilization of native plants and habitats of Texas.

Publications: Newsletter (bimonthly)

Regional	Purpose:	Research Programs	Public Programs
City	Water conservation	Support research	✓ Educational programs
✓ State	Soil conservation	Conduct research	✓ Field trips, seminars
National	✓ General conservation	Publish research	✓ Open to the public
	Prairie conservation		✓ Membership
	Restoration		
	✓ Landscape design		

Sally Wasowski, Landscape Designer
7241 Westlake
Dallas, TX 75214   (214)327-6220

Brief description: A landscape designer who specializes in native plants.

Publications: Landscaping with Native Texas Plants

Regional	Purpose:	Research Programs	Public Programs
✓ City	Water conservation	Support research	Educational programs
✓ State	Soil conservation	Conduct research	Field trips, seminars
National	General conservation	Publish research	Open to the public
	Prairie conservation		Membership
	Restoration		
	✓ Landscape design		

San Antonio Botanical Garden
555 Funston
San Antonio, TX 78209   (512)821-5115

Brief description: A 33-acre garden with collections including native Texas plants, formal designs and an indoor facility of New World exotics.

Publications:

Regional	Purpose:	Research Programs	Public Programs
✓ City	Water conservation	Support research	Educational programs
✓ State	Soil conservation	Conduct research	✓ Field trips, seminars
National	✓ General conservation	Publish research	✓ Open to the public
	Prairie conservation		✓ Membership
	Restoration		
	Landscape design		

Sierra Landscaping, Inc.
P. O. Box 16082
Austin, TX 78761   (512)835-0312

Brief description: A landscape design and installation firm specializing in Xeriscape.

Publications:

Regional	Purpose:	Research Programs	Public Programs
✓ City	Water conservation	Support research	Educational programs
State	Soil conservation	Conduct research	Field trips, seminars
National	General conservation	Publish research	Open to the public
	Prairie conservation		Membership
	Restoration		
	✓ Landscape design		

Soil Conservation Service, USDA
Grant Bldg., Rm. 403, 611 East 6th Street
Austin, TX 78737   (512)482-5592

Brief description: An agency which provides technical assistance to land managers in protecting soil and water resources.

Publications:

Regional	Purpose:	Research Programs	Public Programs
✓ City	✓ Water conservation	Support research	✓ Educational programs
✓ State	✓ Soil conservation	Conduct research	✓ Field trips, seminars
✓ National	✓ General conservation	Publish research	✓ Open to the public
	✓ Prairie conservation		Membership
	Restoration		
	Landscape design		

South Texas Plant Materials Center, Texas A & I University
P. O. Box 218
Kingsville, TX 78363   (512)595-2388

Brief description: A plant materials center which experiments with South Texas native species in cooperation with the Kleberg Wildlife Institute.

Publications:

Regional	Purpose:	Research Programs	Public Programs
City	✓ Water conservation	Support research	Educational programs
✓ State	✓ Soil conservation	✓ Conduct research	✓ Field trips, seminars
✓ National	General conservation	Publish research	✓ Open to the public
	Prairie conservation		Membership
	Restoration		
	Landscape design		

Texas A & M Research Center
1380 A & M Circle
El Paso, TX 79907   (915)859-9111

Brief description: A federal- and state-supported scientific agricultural research center; research encompasses arid land plants.

Publications:

Regional	Purpose:	Research Programs	Public Programs
City	✓ Water conservation	Support research	Educational programs
✓ State	Soil conservation	✓ Conduct research	Field trips, seminars
National	General conservation	✓ Publish research	✓ Open to the public
	Prairie conservation		Membership
	Restoration		
	Landscape design		

Texas Agricultural Experiment Station
P. O. Box 1658
Vernon, TX 76384   (817)552-9941

Brief description: An agricultural research station which develops equipment for range seeding and brush control.

Publications: Numerous journal articles

Regional	Purpose:	Research Programs	Public Programs
City	✓ Water conservation	Support research	Educational programs
✓ State	✓ Soil conservation	✓ Conduct research	✓ Field trips, seminars
National	General conservation	✓ Publish research	✓ Open to the public
	Prairie conservation		Membership
	Restoration		
	Landscape design		

Texas Agricultural Extension Service
Extension Horticulturist, Texas A & M University
College Station, TX 77843   (409)845-7341

Brief description: An extension service which publishes information for the public about agriculture, horticulture and related fields.

Publications: Numerous journal articles

Regional	Purpose:	Research Programs	Public Programs
✓ City	Water conservation	Support research	✓ Educational programs
✓ State	Soil conservation	✓ Conduct research	✓ Field trips, seminars
National	✓ General conservation	✓ Publish research	✓ Open to the public
	Prairie conservation		Membership
	✓ Restoration		
	✓ Landscape design		

Texas Association of Cactus & Succulent Societies
c/o Ed Maddox, Box 181
Decatur, TX 76234

Brief description: A society with 300 members working to promote and conserve native cacti and succulents.

Publications: Newsletter

Regional	Purpose:	Research Programs	Public Programs
City	Water conservation	Support research	✓ Educational programs
✓ State	Soil conservation	Conduct research	✓ Field trips, seminars
National	General conservation	Publish research	✓ Open to the public
	Prairie conservation		✓ Membership
	Restoration		
	Landscape design		

Texas Department of Agriculture
P. O. Box 12847
Austin, TX 78711   *(512)463-7670*

Brief description: A state regulatory agency which publishes a sourcebook for Texas trees, shrubs and grasses.

Publications: Texas Native Plant Directory

Regional	Purpose:	Research Programs	Public Programs
City	Water conservation	Support research	✓ Educational programs
✓ State	Soil conservation	✓ Conduct research	Field trips, seminars
National	✓ General conservation	✓ Publish research	✓ Open to the public
	Prairie conservation		Membership
	Restoration		
	Landscape design		

Texas Department of Highways and Public Transportation
11th and Brazos D-18L
Austin, TX 78701   *(512)465-6301*

Brief description: A state department responsible for the landscaping of the highway system, also supports an active wildflower planting program.

Publications: Wildflower Manual

Regional	Purpose:	Research Programs	Public Programs
City	Water conservation	✓ Support research	Educational programs
✓ State	✓ Soil conservation	✓ Conduct research	✓ Field trips, seminars
National	General conservation	✓ Publish research	✓ Open to the public
	Prairie conservation		Membership
	Restoration		
	✓ Landscape design		

Texas Natural Heritage Program, Texas Parks & Wildlife Department
4200 Smith School Road
Austin, TX 78744   *(512)389-4586*

Brief description: A state agency which continually updates information on the status and location of rare species and communities.

Publications: Numerous

Regional	Purpose:	Research Programs	Public Programs
City	Water conservation	✓ Support research	Educational programs
✓ State	Soil conservation	✓ Conduct research	Field trips, seminars
National	✓ General conservation	✓ Publish research	✓ Open to the public
	Prairie conservation		Membership
	Restoration		
	Landscape design		

Texas Nature Conservancy
P. O. Box 1440, 320 Maverick Walk, Suite 200
San Antonio, TX 78295-1440   (512)224-8774

Brief description: A nonprofit conservation organization which purchases and manages natural areas for the purpose of preservation.

Publications: The Nature Conservancy News (monthly); Horizons (quarterly)

Regional	Purpose:	Research Programs	Public Programs
City	Water conservation	✓ Support research	Educational programs
✓ State	Soil conservation	✓ Conduct research	✓ Field trips, seminars
National	✓ General conservation	Publish research	Open to the public
	Prairie conservation		✓ Membership
	Restoration		
	Landscape design		

Texas Organization for Endangered Species
P. O. Box 12773
Austin, TX 78711   (409)564-7145

Brief description: An nonprofit organization devoted to protection of endangered species.

Publications: TOES Animal and Plant Lists

Regional	Purpose:	Research Programs	Public Programs
City	Water conservation	Support research	✓ Educational programs
✓ State	Soil conservation	Conduct research	✓ Field trips, seminars
National	✓ General conservation	Publish research	✓ Open to the public
	Prairie conservation		✓ Membership
	Restoration		
	Landscape design		

Travis County Extension Services
1600 B Smith Road
Austin, TX 78721   (512)473-9600

Brief description: An educational arm of the Texas A & M University System that provides public information about horticulture, etc.

Publications: Pamphlets; factsheets

Regional	Purpose:	Research Programs	Public Programs
✓ City	Water conservation	Support research	✓ Educational programs
State	Soil conservation	✓ Conduct research	✓ Field trips, seminars
National	✓ General conservation	✓ Publish research	✓ Open to the public
	Prairie conservation		Membership
	Restoration		
	Landscape design		

USDA-Soil Conservation Service
Plant Materials Center, Rt. 1, Box 155
Knox City, TX 79529   (817)658-3922

Brief description: A plant materials center working on selecting and producing superior varieties of Texas native plants.

Publications:

Regional	Purpose:	Research Programs	Public Programs
City	Water conservation	Support research	Educational programs
✓ State	Soil conservation	Conduct research	✓ Field trips, seminars
National	✓ General conservation	Publish research	✓ Open to the public
	Prairie conservation		Membership
	Restoration		
	Landscape design		

Wild Basin
P. O. Box 13455
Austin, TX 78711   (512)476-4113

Brief description: A nonprofit organization devoted to habitat preservation, education, study and management of a nature preserve.

Publications:

Regional	Purpose:	Research Programs	Public Programs
✓ City	Water conservation	Support research	✓ Educational programs
State	Soil conservation	✓ Conduct research	✓ Field trips, seminars
National	✓ General conservation	Publish research	✓ Open to the public
	Prairie conservation		✓ Membership
	Restoration		
	Landscape design		

Wildwood Enterprises
4401 Rosedale Avenue
Austin, TX 78756   (512)459-9501

Brief description: A landscape contractor who designs and installs landscapes with emphasis on native plants.

Publications:

Regional	Purpose:	Research Programs	Public Programs
✓ City	Water conservation	Support research	Educational programs
✓ State	Soil conservation	Conduct research	Field trips, seminars
National	✓ General conservation	Publish research	Open to the public
	Prairie conservation		Membership
	Restoration		
	✓ Landscape design		

Xeriscape Garden Club
2220 Barton Springs Road
Austin, TX 78704   (512)452-4850

Brief description: A nonprofit club promoting water conservation through creative native landscaping.

Publications:

Regional	Purpose:	Research Programs	Public Programs
✓ City	✓ Water conservation	Support research	✓ Educational programs
State	Soil conservation	Conduct research	✓ Field trips, seminars
National	✓ General conservation	Publish research	✓ Open to the public
	Prairie conservation		✓ Membership
	Restoration		
	✓ Landscape design		

Xeriscape Program of Austin, Resource Management Department
P. O. Box 1088
Austin, TX 78767-8818   (512)444-2300

Brief description: A city agency which promotes xeriscape (water conservation through creative landscaping).

Publications: Xeriscape publications

Regional	Purpose:	Research Programs	Public Programs
✓ City	✓ Water conservation	Support research	✓ Educational programs
State	Soil conservation	✓ Conduct research	✓ Field trips, seminars
National	✓ General conservation	✓ Publish research	✓ Open to the public
	Prairie conservation		Membership
	Restoration		
	✓ Landscape design		

UTAH

Nature Conservancy, The
Great Basin Field Office, P. O. Box 11486
Salt Lake City, UT 84147-0486   (801)521-1034

Brief description: A nonprofit organization which works to preserve biotic diversity through land preservation.

Publications: The Nature Conservancy News (monthly); Great Basin Newsletter

Regional	Purpose:	Research Programs	Public Programs
City	Water conservation	Support research	Educational programs
✓ State	Soil conservation	✓ Conduct research	✓ Field trips, seminars
National	✓ General conservation	Publish research	✓ Open to the public
	Prairie conservation		✓ Membership
	Restoration		
	Landscape design		

Nature Conservancy, The
Utah Public Lands Coordinator, 2225 South Hwy 88-91
Wellsville, UT 84339   (801)752-4154

Brief description: A nonprofit organization dedicated to identifying, protecting and maintaining biological diversity through land acquisition.

Publications:

Regional	Purpose:	Research Programs	Public Programs
City	Water conservation	Support research	Educational programs
✓ State	Soil conservation	Conduct research	Field trips, seminars
✓ National	✓ General conservation	Publish research	Open to the public
	Prairie conservation		✓ Membership
	Restoration		
	Landscape design		

State Arboretum of Utah, University of Utah
Building 436
Salt Lake City, UT 84112   (801)581-5322

Brief description: A university-affiliated arboretum on a 1,500-acre campus including a 45-acre botanical garden and conservatory.

Publications: The Cultivator (quarterly)

Regional	Purpose:	Research Programs	Public Programs
✓ City	Water conservation	✓ Support research	✓ Educational programs
✓ State	Soil conservation	✓ Conduct research	✓ Field trips, seminars
National	✓ General conservation	✓ Publish research	✓ Open to the public
	Prairie conservation		✓ Membership
	Restoration		
	✓ Landscape design		

Utah Botanical Gardens
1817 North Main
Farmington, UT 84025   (801)451-3204

Brief description: A botanical garden working with Utah State University Experiment & Research Station and Davis County Extension Office.

Publications: Green Thumb Connection

Regional	Purpose:	Research Programs	Public Programs
City	Water conservation	Support research	✓ Educational programs
✓ State	Soil conservation	✓ Conduct research	Field trips, seminars
National	✓ General conservation	✓ Publish research	✓ Open to the public
	Prairie conservation		✓ Membership
	Restoration		
	✓ Landscape design		

Utah Native Plant Society, c/o State Arboretum of Utah
Building 436, University of Utah
Salt Lake City, UT 84112   (801)581-5322

Brief description: A nonprofit organization studying and promoting the conservation of Utah's native plants.

Publications: The Sego Lily

Regional	Purpose:	Research Programs	Public Programs
✓ City	Water conservation	Support research	✓ Educational programs
✓ State	Soil conservation	Conduct research	✓ Field trips, seminars
National	✓ General conservation	Publish research	✓ Open to the public
	Prairie conservation		✓ Membership
	Restoration		
	✓ Landscape design		

VIRGINIA

American Horticultural Society
P. O. Box 0105
Mt. Vernon, V A 22301   (703)768-5700

Brief description: A nonprofit society promoting horticulture with benefits including educational meetings, a magazine and seed exchanges.

Publications: American Horticulturist (monthly)

Regional	Purpose:	Research Programs	Public Programs
City	Water conservation	Support research	✓ Educational programs
State	Soil conservation	Conduct research	✓ Field trips, seminars
✓ National	✓ General conservation	Publish research	✓ Open to the public
	Prairie conservation		✓ Membership
	Restoration		
	Landscape design		

Maymont Foundation
1700 Hampton Street
Richmond, V A 23220   (804)358-7166

Brief description: A nonprofit foundation which operates Maymont Park, an estate with gardens, a nature center and children's farmhouse.

Publications:

Regional	Purpose:	Research Programs	Public Programs
✓ City	Water conservation	Support research	✓ Educational programs
✓ State	Soil conservation	Conduct research	✓ Field trips, seminars
National	✓ General conservation	Publish research	✓ Open to the public
	Prairie conservation		✓ Membership
	Restoration		
	Landscape design		

Nature Conservancy, The
1800 North Kent Street, Suite 800
Arlington, VA 22209   (703)841-5300

Brief description: The headquaters of a national conservation organization committed to the preservation of natural diversity by protecting natural areas.

Publications: The Nature Conservancy News (monthly)

Regional	Purpose:	Research Programs	Public Programs
City	Water conservation	Support research	Educational programs
✓ State	Soil conservation	✓ Conduct research	Field trips, seminars
✓ National	✓ General conservation	Publish research	Open to the public
	Prairie conservation		✓ Membership
	✓ Restoration		
	Landscape design		

Nature Conservancy, The
Virginia Chapter, 619 East High Street, Suite 2
Charlottesville, VA 22901   (804)295-6106

Brief description: A nonprofit organization committed to preserving habitat for rare and endangered species and communities.

Publications: The Nature Conservancy News (monthly); Chapter Newsletter

Regional	Purpose:	Research Programs	Public Programs
City	Water conservation	✓ Support research	Educational programs
✓ State	Soil conservation	✓ Conduct research	✓ Field trips, seminars
✓ National	✓ General conservation	Publish research	✓ Open to the public
	Prairie conservation		✓ Membership
	Restoration		
	Landscape design		

Prince William Wildflower Society
P. O. Box 83
Manassas, VA 22110   (703)368-9803

Brief description: A chapter of the Virginia Wildflower Preservation Society that primarily educates through meetings and a newsletter.

Publications: Wild News

Regional	Purpose:	Research Programs	Public Programs
✓ City	Water conservation	Support research	✓ Educational programs
✓ State	Soil conservation	Conduct research	✓ Field trips, seminars
✓ National	✓ General conservation	Publish research	✓ Open to the public
	Prairie conservation		✓ Membership
	Restoration		
	Landscape design		

Virginia Federation of Garden Clubs, Inc.
7512 Mayland Drive
Richmond, VA 23229   *(804)741-4966*

Brief description: A federation of 431 clubs with 10,275 members who work to conserve natural resources and plant wildflowers.

Publications: Old Dominion Gardener

Regional	Purpose:	Research Programs	Public Programs
City	Water conservation	Support research	✓ Educational programs
State	Soil conservation	Conduct research	✓ Field trips, seminars
National	✓ General conservation	Publish research	Open to the public
	Prairie conservation		✓ Membership
	Restoration		
	Landscape design		

Virginia Native Plant Society
P. O. Box 844
Annandale, VA 22003   *(703)356-7425*

Brief description: A nonprofit society promoting Virginia's wild plants through local programs carried out by six chapters across the state.

Publications: VWPS Bulletin (quarterly)

Regional	Purpose:	Research Programs	Public Programs
✓ City	Water conservation	Support research	✓ Educational programs
✓ State	Soil conservation	Conduct research	✓ Field trips, seminars
National	✓ General conservation	Publish research	✓ Open to the public
	Prairie conservation		✓ Membership
	Restoration		
	✓ Landscape design		

Virginia Natural Heritage Program, Department of Conservation
1100 Washington Building
Richmond, VA 23219   *(804)225-4855*

Brief description: A state agency which inventories and sets priorities for preservation of rare plants and animals.

Publications:

Regional	Purpose:	Research Programs	Public Programs
City	Water conservation	✓ Support research	Educational programs
✓ State	Soil conservation	✓ Conduct research	Field trips, seminars
National	✓ General conservation	Publish research	✓ Open to the public
	Prairie conservation		Membership
	Restoration		
	Landscape design		

Virginia Wildflower Preservation Society, Piedmont Chapter
Box 336
The Plains, VA 22171

Brief description: A chapter of the Virginia Wildflower Preservation Society with the aim of unifying statewide conservation efforts.

Publications: Piedmont Press

Regional	Purpose:	Research Programs	Public Programs
City	Water conservation	Support research	✓ Educational programs
✓ State	Soil conservation	Conduct research	✓ Field trips, seminars
National	✓ General conservation	Publish research	Open to the public
	Prairie conservation		✓ Membership
	Restoration		
	Landscape design		

Virginia Wildflower Preservation Society, Potowmack Chapter
P. O. Box 161
McLean, VA 22101   (703)256-3157

Brief description: A nonprofit society promoting wild plants in Fairfax and Arlington counties and the cities of Alexandria, Fairfax and Falls Church.

Publications: Potowmack News (bimonthly)

Regional	Purpose:	Research Programs	Public Programs
✓ City	Water conservation	Support research	✓ Educational programs
State	Soil conservation	Conduct research	✓ Field trips, seminars
National	✓ General conservation	Publish research	Open to the public
	Prairie conservation		✓ Membership
	Restoration		
	Landscape design		

Virginia Wildflower Preservation Society, John Clayton Chapter
P. O. Box 677
Yorktown, VA 23690   (804)229-8162

Brief description: A regional chapter of the Virginia Wildflower Preservation Society with 100 members in four cities and five counties.

Publications: Clayton Quarterly

Regional	Purpose:	Research Programs	Public Programs
✓ City	Water conservation	Support research	✓ Educational programs
State	Soil conservation	Conduct research	✓ Field trips, seminars
National	✓ General conservation	Publish research	✓ Open to the public
	Prairie conservation		✓ Membership
	Restoration		
	Landscape design		

Virginia Wildflower Preservation Society, Blue Ridge Chapter
Rt. 2, Box 73
Boones Mill, VA 24065   (703)334-5783

Brief description: A regional chapter of the Virginia Wildflower Preservation
Society offering educational programs and field trips.

Publications: Newsletter

Regional	Purpose:	Research Programs	Public Programs
City	Water conservation	Support research	✓ Educational programs
✓ State	Soil conservation	✓ Conduct research	✓ Field trips, seminars
National	✓ General conservation	Publish research	✓ Open to the public
	Prairie conservation		✓ Membership
	Restoration		
	Landscape design		

Woodlawn Plantation and Pope Leighey House
P. O. Box 37
Mount Vernon, VA 22121-0037   (703)557-5492

Brief description: The house was designed by Frank Lloyd Wright and
landscaped with native species. It is a repository for native
plants.

Publications:

Regional	Purpose:	Research Programs	Public Programs
✓ City	Water conservation	Support research	Educational programs
✓ State	Soil conservation	Conduct research	Field trips, seminars
✓ National	✓ General conservation	Publish research	✓ Open to the public
	Prairie conservation		Membership
	Restoration		
	Landscape design		

VERMONT

Nature Conservancy, The
Vermont Field Office, 138 Main Street
Montpelier, VT 05602   (802)229-4425

Brief description: A nonprofit conservation organization dedicated to the
preservation of natural diversity through land acquisition.

Publications: The Nature Conservancy News (monthly); Chapter Newsletter

Regional	Purpose:	Research Programs	Public Programs
City	Water conservation	Support research	Educational programs
✓ State	Soil conservation	Conduct research	Field trips, seminars
National	✓ General conservation	Publish research	Open to the public
	Prairie conservation		✓ Membership
	Restoration		
	Landscape design		

Vermont Natural Heritage Program, Agency of Natural Resources
103 South Main Street
Waterbury, VT 05676   (802)244-8711

Brief description: A state agency which manages the database on rare species and natural communities in Vermont.

Publications:

Regional	Purpose:	Research Programs	Public Programs
City	Water conservation	✓ Support research	Educational programs
✓ State	Soil conservation	Conduct research	Field trips, seminars
National	✓ General conservation	Publish research	Open to the public
	Prairie conservation		Membership
	Restoration		
	Landscape design		

WASHINGTON

Finch Arboretum, Spokane Parks and Recreation Department
North 809 Washington
Spokane, WA 99201   (509)456-4381

Brief description: A 65-acre arboretum with collections including inland Northwest native trees and shrubs, with a nature trail throughout.

Publications:

Regional	Purpose:	Research Programs	Public Programs
✓ City	Water conservation	Support research	✓ Educational programs
✓ State	Soil conservation	Conduct research	Field trips, seminars
National	✓ General conservation	Publish research	✓ Open to the public
	Prairie conservation		Membership
	Restoration		
	✓ Landscape design		

Metropolitan Park District of Tacoma
North Division Grounds Maintenance, 5400 North Pearl, #3
Tacoma, WA 98407   (206)591-5328

Brief description: An agency that operates parks and recreational areas for Tacoma.; also helps maintain the Northwest Native Garden in Point Defiance Park.

Publications:

Regional	Purpose:	Research Programs	Public Programs
✓ City	Water conservation	Support research	Educational programs
State	Soil conservation	Conduct research	Field trips, seminars
National	✓ General conservation	Publish research	✓ Open to the public
	Prairie conservation		Membership
	Restoration		
	Landscape design		

Nature Conservancy, The
Washington/Alaska Field Office, 1601 Second Aveune, Suite 910
Seattle, WA 98101   (206)624-9623

Brief description: A nonprofit conservation organization dedicated to the preservation of natural diversity through land acquisition.

Publications: The Nature Conservancy News (monthly); Chapter Newsletter

Regional	Purpose:	Research Programs	Public Programs
City	Water conservation	Support research	Educational programs
✔ State	Soil conservation	Conduct research	Field trips, seminars
National	✔ General conservation	Publish research	Open to the public
	Prairie conservation		✔ Membership
	Restoration		
	Landscape design		

Operation Wildflower, National Council of State Garden Clubs
1416 170th Place Northeast
Bellevue, WA 98008   (206)747-0268

Brief description: A nonprofit club working with the Department of Transportation to plant wildflowers along the roadsides.

Publications:

Regional	Purpose:	Research Programs	Public Programs
City	Water conservation	Support research	Educational programs
✔ State	✔ Soil conservation	✔ Conduct research	Field trips, seminars
National	✔ General conservation	✔ Publish research	Open to the public
	✔ Prairie conservation		Membership
	Restoration		
	Landscape design		

Washington Native Plant Society
University of Washington, Department of Botany, KB-15
Seattle, WA 98195

Brief description: A nonprofit organization which studies and promotes native plants in Washington and the adjacent Pacific Northwest.

Publications: Douglasia (quarterly)

Regional	Purpose:	Research Programs	Public Programs
City	Water conservation	✔ Support research	✔ Educational programs
✔ State	Soil conservation	✔ Conduct research	✔ Field trips, seminars
National	✔ General conservation	✔ Publish research	✔ Open to the public
	Prairie conservation		✔ Membership
	Restoration		
	Landscape design		

Washington Natural Heritage Program, Department of Natural Resources
Mail Stop: EX-13
Olympia, WA 98504   (206)753-2449

Brief description: A state agency which manages a database on rare species and communities; also manages statewide preserve system.

Publications: Endangered Species List

Regional	**Purpose:**	**Research Programs**	**Public Programs**
City	Water conservation	Support research	Educational programs
✓ State	Soil conservation	✓ Conduct research	Field trips, seminars
National	✓ General conservation	Publish research	✓ Open to the public
	Prairie conservation		Membership
	Restoration		
	Landscape design		

Washington Park Arboretum
Center for Urban Horticulture, University of Washington, GF-15
Seattle, WA 98105   (206)543-8800

Brief description: An arboretum with over 5,000 species of woody plants on a 200-acre site.

Publications:

Regional	**Purpose:**	**Research Programs**	**Public Programs**
City	Water conservation	Support research	✓ Educational programs
✓ State	Soil conservation	✓ Conduct research	✓ Field trips, seminars
National	✓ General conservation	Publish research	✓ Open to the public
	Prairie conservation		Membership
	Restoration		
	Landscape design		

WISCONSIN

Applied Ecological Services
Rt. 1, Box 130, N673 Mill Road
Juda, WI 53550   (608)897-8547

Brief description: An environmental consulting firm specializing in ecological research, reclamation and natural areas management.

Publications:

Regional	**Purpose:**	**Research Programs**	**Public Programs**
City	Water conservation	✓ Support research	Educational programs
State	Soil conservation	✓ Conduct research	Field trips, seminars
✓ National	✓ General conservation	✓ Publish research	✓ Open to the public
	Prairie conservation		Membership
	Restoration		
	✓ Landscape design		

Boerner Botanical Gardens, Milwaukee County Department of Parks
5879 South 92nd Street
Hales Corners, WI 53130-2299   (414)425-1130

Brief description: An educational and cultural resource garden with many displays of native plants of the natural terrain of Wisconsin.

Publications:

Regional	Purpose:	Research Programs	Public Programs
✓ City	Water conservation	Support research	✓ Educational programs
State	Soil conservation	✓ Conduct research	✓ Field trips, seminars
National	✓ General conservation	✓ Publish research	✓ Open to the public
	Prairie conservation		✓ Membership
	Restoration		
	Landscape design		

Botanical Club of Wisconsin
c/o Theodore S. Cochrane, 449 Jean Street
Madison, WI 53703   (608)262-2792

Brief description: A club interested in botany in general, especially the study and appreciation of native flora.

Publications: Quarterly Botanical Club Bulletin

Regional	Purpose:	Research Programs	Public Programs
City	Water conservation	Support research	✓ Educational programs
✓ State	Soil conservation	Conduct research	✓ Field trips, seminars
National	✓ General conservation	Publish research	✓ Open to the public
	Prairie conservation		✓ Membership
	Restoration		
	Landscape design		

Chiwaukee Prairie Preservation Fund, Inc.
P. O. Box 1288
Kenosha, WI 53141

Brief description: A nonprofit local group which is raising money to purchase valuable habitats for preservation.

Publications:

Regional	Purpose:	Research Programs	Public Programs
✓ City	Water conservation	Support research	Educational programs
State	Soil conservation	Conduct research	✓ Field trips, seminars
National	✓ General conservation	Publish research	✓ Open to the public
	✓ Prairie conservation		✓ Membership
	Restoration		
	Landscape design		

Citizen's Natural Resources Association of Wisconsin
1240 South 11th Avenue
Wausau, WI 54401   (715)845-9318

Brief description: A nonprofit environmental organization committed to protecting natural ecosystems and working to naturalize roadsides.

Publications:

Regional	Purpose:	Research Programs	Public Programs
✓ City	Water conservation	Support research	Educational programs
State	Soil conservation	Conduct research	Field trips, seminars
National	✓ General conservation	Publish research	Open to the public
	Prairie conservation		Membership
	Restoration		
	Landscape design		

International Crane Foundation
E11376 Shady Lane Road
Baraboo, WI 53913-9778   (608)356-9462

Brief description: An international center for the study and preservation of cranes; also involved in habitat conservation and restoration.

Publications: ICF Bugle (monthly)

Regional	Purpose:	Research Programs	Public Programs
City	Water conservation	Support research	✓ Educational programs
State	Soil conservation	✓ Conduct research	✓ Field trips, seminars
✓ National	✓ General conservation	✓ Publish research	✓ Open to the public
	✓ Prairie conservation		✓ Membership
	Restoration		
	Landscape design		

Nature Conservancy, The
Wisconsin Chapter, 1045 East Dayton Street, Rm. 209
Madison, WI 53703   (608)251-8140

Brief description: The Wisconsin Chapter is part of an international membership organization committed to preservation of natural areas.

Publications: The Nature Conservancy News (monthly); Chapter Newsletter

Regional	Purpose:	Research Programs	Public Programs
City	Water conservation	Support research	Educational programs
✓ State	Soil conservation	✓ Conduct research	✓ Field trips, seminars
National	✓ General conservation	Publish research	✓ Open to the public
	Prairie conservation		✓ Membership
	Restoration		
	Landscape design		

Riveredge Nature Center
Box 26
Newburg, WI 53060   *(414)931-8095*

Brief description: An environmental education agency for schools and
communities. Also, committed to natural areas preservation.

Publications: Landscaping the Natural Way

Regional	**Purpose:**	**Research Programs**	**Public Programs**
City	Water conservation	Support research	✓ Educational programs
✓ State	Soil conservation	✓ Conduct research	✓ Field trips, seminars
National	✓ General conservation	Publish research	✓ Open to the public
	Prairie conservation		✓ Membership
	Restoration		
	Landscape design		

University of Wisconsin Arboretum
1207 Seminole Highway
Madison, WI 53711   *(608)263-7888*

Brief description: An arboretum specializing in restoration of biological
communities native to Wisconsin.

Publications: Restoration and Management Notes (quarterly)

Regional	**Purpose:**	**Research Programs**	**Public Programs**
City	Water conservation	✓ Support research	✓ Educational programs
State	Soil conservation	✓ Conduct research	✓ Field trips, seminars
✓ National	✓ General conservation	✓ Publish research	✓ Open to the public
	Prairie conservation		✓ Membership
	Restoration		
	Landscape design		

Wehr Nature Center
9701 West College Avenue
Franklin, WI 53132   *(414)421-5345*

Brief description: An environmental education center with 200 acres of
woodlands, prairie and wetlands, and a four-mile interpretive
trail.

Publications:

Regional	**Purpose:**	**Research Programs**	**Public Programs**
✓ City	Water conservation	Support research	✓ Educational programs
State	Soil conservation	Conduct research	✓ Field trips, seminars
National	✓ General conservation	Publish research	✓ Open to the public
	Prairie conservation		Membership
	Restoration		
	Landscape design		

Wisconsin Natural Heritage Program, Dept. of Natural Resources
101 South Webster Street, Box 7921
Madison, WI 53707   (608)266-0924

Brief description: A state agency which identifies, monitors, and protects rare and endangered species.

Publications:

Regional	Purpose:	Research Programs	Public Programs
City	Water conservation	Support research	Educational programs
✓ State	Soil conservation	Conduct research	Field trips, seminars
National	✓ General conservation	Publish research	Open to the public
	Prairie conservation		Membership
	Restoration		
	Landscape design		

WEST VIRGINA

Nature Conservancy, The
West Virginia Field Office, 922 Quarrier Street, Suite 414
Charleston, WV 25301   (304)345-4350

Brief description: A nonprofit conservation organization dedicated to the preservation of natural diversity through land acquisition.

Publications: The Nature Conservancy News (monthly); Chapter Newsletter

Regional	Purpose:	Research Programs	Public Programs
City	Water conservation	Support research	Educational programs
✓ State	Soil conservation	Conduct research	Field trips, seminars
National	✓ General conservation	Publish research	Open to the public
	Prairie conservation		✓ Membership
	Restoration		
	Landscape design		

West Virginia Natural Heritage Program
Department of Natural Resources, P.O. Box 67, Ward Road
Elkins, WV 26241   (304)636-1767

Brief description: A part of the state Department of Natural Resources which inventories and monitors rare species and communities.

Publications:

Regional	Purpose:	Research Programs	Public Programs
City	Water conservation	Support research	Educational programs
✓ State	Soil conservation	✓ Conduct research	Field trips, seminars
National	✓ General conservation	Publish research	Open to the public
	Prairie conservation		Membership
	Restoration		
	Landscape design		

WYOMING

Wyoming Natural Heritage Program
Department of Environmental Quality, 122 West 25th Street, 3rd Floor
Cheyenne, WY 82002   (307)777-7756

Brief description: A state office which regulates all mining; also monitors rare and endangered species.

Publications:

Regional	Purpose:	Research Programs	Public Programs
City	Water conservation	Support research	Educational programs
✓ State	Soil conservation	Conduct research	Field trips, seminars
National	✓ General conservation	Publish research	✓ Open to the public
	Prairie conservation		Membership
	Restoration		
	Landscape design		

Lilium michiganense

SOURCES OF WILDFLOWER SEED AND NATIVE PLANTS

PLEASE NOTE: This list is computer sorted by two-letter
state postal abbreviation; e.g., PA for Pennsylvania.

ALASKA

Baldwin Seed Co. of Alaska
Box 3127
Kenai, AK 99611
(907)262-2285

Percentage of the business in native species: 90

Type of business:	Primary plant focus:	Wildflower seed offered:	Propagation methods:
Retail	Trees	Regional Seed Mixes	✓ Propagate Plants
✓ Wholesale	Shrubs	Custom Mixes	Collect Wild Plants
✓ Mail Order	Grasses	✓ Individual Species Seed	✓ Collect Wild Seed
Price List/Catalog	✓ Wildflowers	Contract Grow Seed	

ALABAMA

Bill Dodd's Rare Plants
P.O. Drawer 377
Semmes, AL 36575

Percentage of the business in native species: 95

Type of business:	Primary plant focus:	Wildflower seed offered:	Propagation methods:
✓ Retail	✓ Trees	Regional Seed Mixes	✓ Propagate Plants
Wholesale	✓ Shrubs	Custom Mixes	Collect Wild Plants
✓ Mail Order	Grasses	Individual Species Seed	✓ Collect Wild Seed
Price List/Catalog	Wildflowers	Contract Grow Seed	

International Forest Seed Co.
P.O. Box 290
Odenville, AL 35120
(800)633-4506

Percentage of the business in native species: 100

Type of business:	Primary plant focus:	Wildflower seed offered:	Propagation methods:
Retail	✓ Trees	Regional Seed Mixes	✓ Propagate Plants
✓ Wholesale	Shrubs	Custom Mixes	Collect Wild Plants
Mail Order	Grasses	Individual Species Seed	Collect Wild Seed
Price List/Catalog	Wildflowers	Contract Grow Seed	

Tom Dodd Nurseries, Inc.
P.O. Drawer 45
Semmes, AL 36575
(205)649-1960

Percentage of the business in native species: 20

Type of business:	Primary plant focus:	Wildflower seed offered:	Propagation methods:
Retail	✓ Trees	Regional Seed Mixes	✓ Propagate Plants
✓ Wholesale	✓ Shrubs	Custom Mixes	Collect Wild Plants
Mail Order	Grasses	Individual Species Seed	Collect Wild Seed
Price List/Catalog	Wildflowers	Contract Grow Seed	

ARKANSAS

Holland Wildflower Farm
Rt. 2, Box 7
Elkins, AR 72727
(501)643-2240

Percentage of the business in native species: 80

Type of business:	Primary plant focus:	Wildflower seed offered:	Propagation methods:
✓ Retail	Trees	✓ Regional Seed Mixes	✓ Propagate Plants
✓ Wholesale	Shrubs	✓ Custom Mixes	✓ Collect Wild Plants
✓ Mail Order	Grasses	✓ Individual Species Seed	✓ Collect Wild Seed
Price List/Catalog	✓ Wildflowers	Contract Grow Seed	

Izard Ozark Natives
P.O. Box 454
Mountain View, AR 72560
(501)368-7439

Percentage of the business in native species: 95

Type of business:	Primary plant focus:	Wildflower seed offered:	Propagation methods:
✓ Retail	✓ Trees	Regional Seed Mixes	✓ Propagate Plants
Wholesale	✓ Shrubs	Custom Mixes	Collect Wild Plants
✓ Mail Order	Grasses	✓ Individual Species Seed	✓ Collect Wild Seed
Price List/Catalog	✓ Wildflowers	Contract Grow Seed	

ARIZONA

Cactus World
2955 E. Chula Vista Drive
Tucson, AZ 85716
(602)795-6028

Percentage of the business in native species: 100

Type of business:	Primary plant focus:	Wildflower seed offered:	Propagation methods:
Retail	Trees	Regional Seed Mixes	Propagate Plants
✓Wholesale	Shrubs	Custom Mixes	Collect Wild Plants
✓Mail Order	Grasses	Individual Species Seed	Collect Wild Seed
Price List/Catalog	Wildflowers	Contract Grow Seed	

Desert Enterprises
P. O. Box 23
Morristown, AZ 85342
(602)388-2448

Percentage of the business in native species: 100

Type of business:	Primary plant focus:	Wildflower seed offered:	Propagation methods:
Retail	✓Trees	Regional Seed Mixes	Propagate Plants
✓Wholesale	✓Shrubs	✓Custom Mixes	Collect Wild Plants
Mail Order	Grasses	✓Individual Species Seed	✓Collect Wild Seed
Price List/Catalog	✓Wildflowers	Contract Grow Seed	

Desert Tree Farm
2744 East Utopia Road
Phoenix, AZ 85024
(602)992-0402

Percentage of the business in native species: 40

Type of business:	Primary plant focus:	Wildflower seed offered:	Propagation methods:
✓Retail	✓Trees	Regional Seed Mixes	✓Propagate Plants
✓Wholesale	✓Shrubs	Custom Mixes	Collect Wild Plants
Mail Order	Grasses	Individual Species Seed	Collect Wild Seed
Price List/Catalog	✓Wildflowers	Contract Grow Seed	

Hubbs Brothers Seed Company, Inc.
1522 North 35th Street
Phoenix, AZ 85008
(602)267-8132

Percentage of the business in native species: 99

Type of business:	Primary plant focus:	Wildflower seed offered:	Propagation methods:
Retail	✓ Trees	✓ Regional Seed Mixes	Propagate Plants
✓ Wholesale	✓ Shrubs	✓ Custom Mixes	✓ Collect Wild Plants
Mail Order	✓ Grasses	✓ Individual Species Seed	✓ Collect Wild Seed
Price List/Catalog	✓ Wildflowers	✓ Contract Grow Seed	

JMG Inc. / Desert Products Nursery
2854 East Grant Road
Tucson, AZ 85712
(602)881-1448

Percentage of the business in native species: 100

Type of business:	Primary plant focus:	Wildflower seed offered:	Propagation methods:
✓ Retail	✓ Trees	Regional Seed Mixes	✓ Propagate Plants
✓ Wholesale	✓ Shrubs	Custom Mixes	✓ Collect Wild Plants
✓ Mail Order	Grasses	Individual Species Seed	Collect Wild Seed
Price List/Catalog	✓ Wildflowers	Contract Grow Seed	

Lone Mountain Nurseries, Inc.
3709 East Southern Avenue
Phoenix, AZ 85040
(602)437-8897

Percentage of the business in native species: 40

Type of business:	Primary plant focus:	Wildflower seed offered:	Propagation methods:
Retail	✓ Trees	Regional Seed Mixes	✓ Propagate Plants
✓ Wholesale	✓ Shrubs	Custom Mixes	✓ Collect Wild Plants
Mail Order	Grasses	Individual Species Seed	Collect Wild Seed
Price List/Catalog	Wildflowers	Contract Grow Seed	

Mountain States Wholesale Nursery
P. O. Box 33982
Phoenix, AZ 85067
(602)247-8507

Percentage of the business in native species: 50

Type of business:	Primary plant focus:	Wildflower seed offered:	Propagation methods:
Retail	✓ Trees	Regional Seed Mixes	Propagate Plants
✓ Wholesale	✓ Shrubs	Custom Mixes	Collect Wild Plants
Mail Order	✓ Grasses	Individual Species Seed	✓ Collect Wild Seed
Price List/Catalog	✓ Wildflowers	Contract Grow Seed	

Southwestern Native Seeds
Box 50503
Tucson, AZ 85703

Percentage of the business in native species: 100

Type of business:	Primary plant focus:	Wildflower seed offered:	Propagation methods:
✓ Retail	✓ Trees	Regional Seed Mixes	Propagate Plants
Wholesale	✓ Shrubs	Custom Mixes	Collect Wild Plants
✓ Mail Order	Grasses	✓ Individual Species Seed	✓ Collect Wild Seed
Price List/Catalog	✓ Wildflowers	Contract Grow Seed	

Starr Nursery
50 East Blacklidge
Tucson, AZ 85705
(602)628-8773

Percentage of the business in native species: 30

Type of business:	Primary plant focus:	Wildflower seed offered:	Propagation methods:
✓ Retail	Trees	Regional Seed Mixes	✓ Propagate Plants
✓ Wholesale	✓ Shrubs	Custom Mixes	Collect Wild Plants
Mail Order	Grasses	Individual Species Seed	Collect Wild Seed
Price List/Catalog	Wildflowers	Contract Grow Seed	

Wild Seed
P. O. Box 27751
Tempe, AZ 85282
(602)968-9751

Percentage of the business in native species: 95

Type of business:	Primary plant focus:	Wildflower seed offered:	Propagation methods:
Retail	✓ Trees	✓ Regional Seed Mixes	✓ Propagate Plants
✓ Wholesale	✓ Shrubs	✓ Custom Mixes	Collect Wild Plants
Mail Order	✓ Grasses	✓ Individual Species Seed	✓ Collect Wild Seed
Price List/Catalog	✓ Wildflowers	✓ Contract Grow Seed	

CALIFORNIA

Alpine Plants
P. O. Box 245
Tahoe Vista, CA 95732-0245
(916)546-5518

Percentage of the business in native species: 75

Type of business:	Primary plant focus:	Wildflower seed offered:	Propagation methods:
✓ Retail	Trees	✓ Regional Seed Mixes	✓ Propagate Plants
✓ Wholesale	✓ Shrubs	✓ Custom Mixes	Collect Wild Plants
✓ Mail Order	Grasses	✓ Individual Species Seed	✓ Collect Wild Seed
Price List/Catalog	✓ Wildflowers	Contract Grow Seed	

Anderson Valley Nursery
P. O. Box 504, 18151 Mountain View Road
Boonville, CA 95415
(707)895-3853

Percentage of the business in native species: 20

Type of business:	Primary plant focus:	Wildflower seed offered:	Propagation methods:
✓ Retail	✓ Trees	Regional Seed Mixes	✓ Propagate Plants
✓ Wholesale	✓ Shrubs	Custom Mixes	✓ Collect Wild Plants
✓ Mail Order	Grasses	Individual Species Seed	Collect Wild Seed
Price List/Catalog	Wildflowers	Contract Grow Seed	

Berkeley Horticultural Nursery
1310 McGee Avenue
Berkeley, CA 94703-1098
(415)526-4704

Percentage of the business in native species: 15

Type of business:	Primary plant focus:	Wildflower seed offered:	Propagation methods:
✓Retail	✓Trees	✓Regional Seed Mixes	Propagate Plants
Wholesale	✓Shrubs	Custom Mixes	Collect Wild Plants
Mail Order	Grasses	✓Individual Species Seed	Collect Wild Seed
Price List/Catalog	✓Wildflowers	Contract Grow Seed	

Blue Oak Nursery
2731 Mountain Oak Lane
Rescue, CA 95672
(916)677-2111

Percentage of the business in native species: 75

Type of business:	Primary plant focus:	Wildflower seed offered:	Propagation methods:
✓Retail	✓Trees	Regional Seed Mixes	✓Propagate Plants
✓Wholesale	✓Shrubs	Custom Mixes	Collect Wild Plants
✓Mail Order	Grasses	Individual Species Seed	Collect Wild Seed
Price List/Catalog	Wildflowers	Contract Grow Seed	

C. H. Baccus
900 Boynton Avenue
San Jose, CA 95117
(408)244-2923

Percentage of the business in native species: 100

Type of business:	Primary plant focus:	Wildflower seed offered:	Propagation methods:
✓Retail	Trees	Regional Seed Mixes	✓Propagate Plants
✓Wholesale	Shrubs	Custom Mixes	Collect Wild Plants
✓Mail Order	Grasses	Individual Species Seed	Collect Wild Seed
Price List/Catalog	✓Wildflowers	Contract Grow Seed	

Calaveras Nursery
1622 Hwy 12
Valley Springs, CA 95252
(209)772-1823

Percentage of the business in native species: 75

Type of business:	Primary plant focus:	Wildflower seed offered:	Propagation methods:
Retail	✓ Trees	Regional Seed Mixes	✓ Propagate Plants
✓ Wholesale	Shrubs	Custom Mixes	Collect Wild Plants
Mail Order	Grasses	Individual Species Seed	Collect Wild Seed
Price List/Catalog	Wildflowers	Contract Grow Seed	

California Flora Nursery
P. O. Box 3
Fulton, CA 95439
(707)528-8813

Percentage of the business in native species: 50

Type of business:	Primary plant focus:	Wildflower seed offered:	Propagation methods:
✓ Retail	✓ Trees	Regional Seed Mixes	✓ Propagate Plants
✓ Wholesale	✓ Shrubs	Custom Mixes	Collect Wild Plants
Mail Order	✓ Grasses	Individual Species Seed	Collect Wild Seed
Price List/Catalog	Wildflowers	Contract Grow Seed	

Carter Seed
475 Mar Vista Drive
Vista, CA 92083
(619)724-5931

Percentage of the business in native species: 20

Type of business:	Primary plant focus:	Wildflower seed offered:	Propagation methods:
✓ Retail	✓ Trees	✓ Regional Seed Mixes	Propagate Plants
✓ Wholesale	✓ Shrubs	Custom Mixes	Collect Wild Plants
✓ Mail Order	✓ Grasses	✓ Individual Species Seed	Collect Wild Seed
Price List/Catalog	✓ Wildflowers	Contract Grow Seed	

Christensen Nursery Co.
16000 Sanborn Road
Saratoga, CA 95070
(408)741-5471

Percentage of the business in native species: 20

Type of business:	Primary plant focus:	Wildflower seed offered:	Propagation methods:
✓ Retail	✓ Trees	Regional Seed Mixes	✓ Propagate Plants
✓ Wholesale	✓ Shrubs	Custom Mixes	Collect Wild Plants
Mail Order	Grasses	Individual Species Seed	Collect Wild Seed
Price List/Catalog	Wildflowers	Contract Grow Seed	

Circuit Rider Productions
9619 Old Redwood Hwy.
Windsor, CA 95492
(707)838-6641

Percentage of the business in native species: 95

Type of business:	Primary plant focus:	Wildflower seed offered:	Propagation methods:
Retail	✓ Trees	Regional Seed Mixes	✓ Propagate Plants
✓ Wholesale	✓ Shrubs	Custom Mixes	Collect Wild Plants
Mail Order	Grasses	Individual Species Seed	✓ Collect Wild Seed
Price List/Catalog	Wildflowers	✓ Contract Grow Seed	

Clotilde Merlo Forest Tree Nursery / Louisiana-Pacific Corporation
1508 Crannell Road
Trinidad, CA 95570
(707)677-0911

Percentage of the business in native species: 95

Type of business:	Primary plant focus:	Wildflower seed offered:	Propagation methods:
Retail	✓ Trees	Regional Seed Mixes	✓ Propagate Plants
✓ Wholesale	Shrubs	Custom Mixes	Collect Wild Plants
Mail Order	Grasses	Individual Species Seed	Collect Wild Seed
Price List/Catalog	Wildflowers	Contract Grow Seed	

Clyde Robin Seed Co., Inc.
25670 Nickel Place
Hayward, CA 94545-3222
(415)785-9425

Percentage of the business in native species: 70

Type of business:	Primary plant focus:	Wildflower seed offered:	Propagation methods:
✓Retail	Trees	✓Regional Seed Mixes	✓Propagate Plants
✓Wholesale	Shrubs	✓Custom Mixes	Collect Wild Plants
✓Mail Order	Grasses	✓Individual Species Seed	✓Collect Wild Seed
Price List/Catalog	✓Wildflowers	✓Contract Grow Seed	

Dal Leite
77 Willow Avenue
Walnut Creek, CA 94595
(415)939-4911

Percentage of the business in native species: 100

Type of business:	Primary plant focus:	Wildflower seed offered:	Propagation methods:
✓Retail	✓Trees	Regional Seed Mixes	✓Propagate Plants
Wholesale	✓Shrubs	Custom Mixes	Collect Wild Plants
Mail Order	Grasses	Individual Species Seed	Collect Wild Seed
Price List/Catalog	✓Wildflowers	Contract Grow Seed	

DAWN / Design Associates Working with Nature
1442A Walnut Street, Box 101
Berkeley, CA 94709
(415)644-1315

Percentage of the business in native species: 100

Type of business:	Primary plant focus:	Wildflower seed offered:	Propagation methods:
Retail	✓Trees	Regional Seed Mixes	✓Propagate Plants
✓Wholesale	✓Shrubs	Custom Mixes	Collect Wild Plants
Mail Order	✓Grasses	✓Individual Species Seed	✓Collect Wild Seed
Price List/Catalog	✓Wildflowers	✓Contract Grow Seed	

Environmental Seed Producers, Inc.
P. O. Box 5904
El Monte, CA 91734
(818)442-3330

Percentage of the business in native species: 60

Type of business:	Primary plant focus:	Wildflower seed offered:	Propagation methods:
Retail	Trees	✓Regional Seed Mixes	✓Propagate Plants
✓Wholesale	Shrubs	✓Custom Mixes	Collect Wild Plants
Mail Order	Grasses	✓Individual Species Seed	✓Collect Wild Seed
Price List/Catalog	✓Wildflowers	✓Contract Grow Seed	

Greener'n Ever Tree Farm
P. O. Box 222435
Carmel, CA 93924
(408)659-3196

Percentage of the business in native species: 75

Type of business:	Primary plant focus:	Wildflower seed offered:	Propagation methods:
✓Retail	✓Trees	Regional Seed Mixes	✓Propagate Plants
✓Wholesale	Shrubs	Custom Mixes	Collect Wild Plants
✓Mail Order	Grasses	Individual Species Seed	Collect Wild Seed
Price List/Catalog	Wildflowers	Contract Grow Seed	

Hardscrabble Seed Co.
Rt. 2, Box 255
Springville, CA 93265
(209)539-3593

Percentage of the business in native species: 100

Type of business:	Primary plant focus:	Wildflower seed offered:	Propagation methods:
✓Retail	✓Trees	Regional Seed Mixes	Propagate Plants
✓Wholesale	Shrubs	Custom Mixes	Collect Wild Plants
✓Mail Order	Grasses	Individual Species Seed	✓Collect Wild Seed
Price List/Catalog	Wildflowers	Contract Grow Seed	

J. L. Hudson, Seedsman
P. O. Box 105B
Redwood City, CA 94064

Percentage of the business in native species: 30

Type of business:	Primary plant focus:	Wildflower seed offered:	Propagation methods:
✓ Retail	✓ Trees	Regional Seed Mixes	✓ Propagate Plants
Wholesale	✓ Shrubs	Custom Mixes	✓ Collect Wild Plants
✓ Mail Order	Grasses	✓ Individual Species Seed	✓ Collect Wild Seed
✓ Price List/Catalog	✓ Wildflowers	Contract Grow Seed	

Larner Seeds
P. O. Box 407
Bolinas, CA 94924
(415)868-9407

Percentage of the business in native species: 90

Type of business:	Primary plant focus:	Wildflower seed offered:	Propagation methods:
✓ Retail	✓ Trees	✓ Regional Seed Mixes	✓ Propagate Plants
✓ Wholesale	✓ Shrubs	✓ Custom Mixes	Collect Wild Plants
✓ Mail Order	✓ Grasses	✓ Individual Species Seed	✓ Collect Wild Seed
Price List/Catalog	✓ Wildflowers	Contract Grow Seed	

Las Pilitas Nursery
Star Route Box 23X, Las Pilitas Road
Santa Margarita, CA 93453
(805)438-5992

Percentage of the business in native species: 100

Type of business:	Primary plant focus:	Wildflower seed offered:	Propagation methods:
✓ Retail	✓ Trees	Regional Seed Mixes	✓ Propagate Plants
✓ Wholesale	✓ Shrubs	Custom Mixes	Collect Wild Plants
✓ Mail Order	Grasses	✓ Individual Species Seed	Collect Wild Seed
Price List/Catalog	✓ Wildflowers	Contract Grow Seed	

Living Desert, The
P. O. Box 1775, 47900 Portola
Palm Desert, CA 92261
(619)346-5694

Percentage of the business in native species: 97

Type of business:	Primary plant focus:	Wildflower seed offered:	Propagation methods:
✓Retail	✓Trees	✓Regional Seed Mixes	✓Propagate Plants
Wholesale	✓Shrubs	Custom Mixes	✓Collect Wild Plants
Mail Order	✓Grasses	Individual Species Seed	✓Collect Wild Seed
Price List/Catalog	✓Wildflowers	Contract Grow Seed	

Mistletoe Sales
P. O. Box 1275
Carpinteria, CA 93013
(805)684-0436

Percentage of the business in native species: 10

Type of business:	Primary plant focus:	Wildflower seed offered:	Propagation methods:
Retail	✓Trees	Regional Seed Mixes	✓Propagate Plants
✓Wholesale	✓Shrubs	Custom Mixes	Collect Wild Plants
Mail Order	Grasses	Individual Species Seed	✓Collect Wild Seed
Price List/Catalog	Wildflowers	Contract Grow Seed	

Mockingbird Nurseries, Inc.
1670 Jackson Street
Riverside, CA 92504
(714)780-3571

Percentage of the business in native species: 90

Type of business:	Primary plant focus:	Wildflower seed offered:	Propagation methods:
Retail	✓Trees	Regional Seed Mixes	✓Propagate Plants
✓Wholesale	✓Shrubs	Custom Mixes	Collect Wild Plants
Mail Order	Grasses	Individual Species Seed	Collect Wild Seed
Price List/Catalog	Wildflowers	Contract Grow Seed	

Moon Mountain Wildflowers
P. O. Box 34
Morro Bay, CA 93442
(805)772-2473

Percentage of the business in native species: 100

Type of business:	Primary plant focus:	Wildflower seed offered:	Propagation methods:
✓Retail	Trees	✓Regional Seed Mixes	✓Propagate Plants
✓Wholesale	Shrubs	✓Custom Mixes	Collect Wild Plants
✓Mail Order	Grasses	✓Individual Species Seed	Collect Wild Seed
Price List/Catalog	✓Wildflowers	Contract Grow Seed	

Native Sons Wholesale Nursery
379 West El Campo Road
Arroyo Grande, CA 93420
(805)481-5996

Percentage of the business in native species: 60

Type of business:	Primary plant focus:	Wildflower seed offered:	Propagation methods:
Retail	✓Trees	Regional Seed Mixes	✓Propagate Plants
✓Wholesale	✓Shrubs	Custom Mixes	Collect Wild Plants
Mail Order	Grasses	Individual Species Seed	Collect Wild Seed
Price List/Catalog	Wildflowers	✓Contract Grow Seed	

Plant Man Yes, The
1017 2nd Street
Santa Rosa, CA 95405
(707)525-0186

Percentage of the business in native species: 75

Type of business:	Primary plant focus:	Wildflower seed offered:	Propagation methods:
✓Retail	✓Trees	✓Regional Seed Mixes	✓Propagate Plants
✓Wholesale	✓Shrubs	✓Custom Mixes	Collect Wild Plants
✓Mail Order	✓Grasses	✓Individual Species Seed	Collect Wild Seed
Price List/Catalog	✓Wildflowers	✓Contract Grow Seed	

Plus Trees
639 7th Street
Imperial Beach, CA 92032
(619)423-8003

Percentage of the business in native species: 75

Type of business:	Primary plant focus:	Wildflower seed offered:	Propagation methods:
✓Retail	✓Trees	Regional Seed Mixes	✓Propagate Plants
✓Wholesale	✓Shrubs	Custom Mixes	Collect Wild Plants
Mail Order	Grasses	Individual Species Seed	Collect Wild Seed
Price List/Catalog	Wildflowers	Contract Grow Seed	

Redwood City Seed Co.
P. O. Box 361
Redwood City, CA 94064
(415)325-SEED

Percentage of the business in native species: 10

Type of business:	Primary plant focus:	Wildflower seed offered:	Propagation methods:
✓Retail	Trees	Regional Seed Mixes	✓Propagate Plants
✓Wholesale	Shrubs	Custom Mixes	Collect Wild Plants
✓Mail Order	✓Grasses	✓Individual Species Seed	✓Collect Wild Seed
Price List/Catalog	✓Wildflowers	Contract Grow Seed	

S & S Seeds
P. O. Box 1275
Carpenteria, CA 93013
(805)684-0436

Percentage of the business in native species: 80

Type of business:	Primary plant focus:	Wildflower seed offered:	Propagation methods:
Retail	✓Trees	✓Regional Seed Mixes	✓Propagate Plants
✓Wholesale	✓Shrubs	✓Custom Mixes	Collect Wild Plants
Mail Order	✓Grasses	✓Individual Species Seed	✓Collect Wild Seed
✓Price List/Catalog	✓Wildflowers	✓Contract Grow Seed	

San Simeon Nursery
HCR 33 Villa Creek Road
Cavucos, CA 93430
(805)995-2466

Percentage of the business in native species: 50

Type of business:	Primary plant focus:	Wildflower seed offered:	Propagation methods:
Retail	✔Trees	Regional Seed Mixes	✔Propagate Plants
✔Wholesale	✔Shrubs	Custom Mixes	✔Collect Wild Plants
Mail Order	Grasses	Individual Species Seed	✔Collect Wild Seed
Price List/Catalog	✔Wildflowers	Contract Grow Seed	

Saratoga Horticultural Foundation
15185 Murphy Avenue
San Martin, CA 95046
(408)779-3303

Percentage of the business in native species: 25

Type of business:	Primary plant focus:	Wildflower seed offered:	Propagation methods:
Retail	✔Trees	Regional Seed Mixes	✔Propagate Plants
✔Wholesale	✔Shrubs	Custom Mixes	✔Collect Wild Plants
Mail Order	Grasses	Individual Species Seed	Collect Wild Seed
Price List/Catalog	✔Wildflowers	Contract Grow Seed	

Skylark Wholesale Nursery
6735 Sonoma Hwy.
Santa Rosa, CA 95405
(707)539-1565

Percentage of the business in native species: 40

Type of business:	Primary plant focus:	Wildflower seed offered:	Propagation methods:
Retail	✔Trees	Regional Seed Mixes	✔Propagate Plants
✔Wholesale	✔Shrubs	Custom Mixes	✔Collect Wild Plants
Mail Order	Grasses	Individual Species Seed	Collect Wild Seed
Price List/Catalog	✔Wildflowers	Contract Grow Seed	

Taylor's Herb Garden, Inc.
1535 Lone Oak Road
Vista, CA 92084
(619)727-3485

Percentage of the business in native species: 60

Type of business:	Primary plant focus:	Wildflower seed offered:	Propagation methods:
✓Retail	Trees	Regional Seed Mixes	Propagate Plants
✓Wholesale	Shrubs	Custom Mixes	Collect Wild Plants
✓Mail Order	Grasses	✓Individual Species Seed	Collect Wild Seed
Price List/Catalog	✓Wildflowers	Contract Grow Seed	

Theodore Payne Foundation
10459 Tuxford Street
Sun Valley, CA 91352
(818)768-1802

Percentage of the business in native species: 100

Type of business:	Primary plant focus:	Wildflower seed offered:	Propagation methods:
✓Retail	✓Trees	✓Regional Seed Mixes	✓Propagate Plants
Wholesale	✓Shrubs	✓Custom Mixes	Collect Wild Plants
Mail Order	✓Grasses	✓Individual Species Seed	✓Collect Wild Seed
Price List/Catalog	✓Wildflowers	✓Contract Grow Seed	

Tree of Life Nursery
P. O. Box 738
San Juan Capistrano, CA 92693
(714)728-0685

Percentage of the business in native species: 100

Type of business:	Primary plant focus:	Wildflower seed offered:	Propagation methods:
Retail	✓Trees	✓Regional Seed Mixes	✓Propagate Plants
✓Wholesale	✓Shrubs	✓Custom Mixes	Collect Wild Plants
Mail Order	✓Grasses	Individual Species Seed	✓Collect Wild Seed
Price List/Catalog	✓Wildflowers	✓Contract Grow Seed	

Twin Peaks Seeds
1814 Dean Street
Eureka, CA 95501
(707)442-6142

Percentage of the business in native species: 100

Type of business:	Primary plant focus:	Wildflower seed offered:	Propagation methods:
✓Retail	Trees	Regional Seed Mixes	Propagate Plants
Wholesale	Shrubs	Custom Mixes	Collect Wild Plants
✓Mail Order	Grasses	✓Individual Species Seed	✓Collect Wild Seed
Price List/Catalog	✓Wildflowers	Contract Grow Seed	

Weber Native Plant Nursery
237 Seeman Drive
Encinitas, CA 92024
(619)753-1661

Percentage of the business in native species: 99

Type of business:	Primary plant focus:	Wildflower seed offered:	Propagation methods:
✓Retail	✓Trees	Regional Seed Mixes	✓Propagate Plants
✓Wholesale	✓Shrubs	Custom Mixes	Collect Wild Plants
Mail Order	Grasses	Individual Species Seed	Collect Wild Seed
Price List/Catalog	Wildflowers	Contract Grow Seed	

Wildflowers International, Inc.
918 B Enterprise Way
Napa, CA 94558
(707)253-0570

Percentage of the business in native species: 60

Type of business:	Primary plant focus:	Wildflower seed offered:	Propagation methods:
Retail	Trees	✓Regional Seed Mixes	Propagate Plants
✓Wholesale	Shrubs	✓Custom Mixes	Collect Wild Plants
Mail Order	Grasses	✓Individual Species Seed	Collect Wild Seed
Price List/Catalog	✓Wildflowers	✓Contract Grow Seed	

Wildwood Farm
10300 Sonoma Hwy
Kenwood, CA 95452
(707)833-1161

Percentage of the business in native species: 75

Type of business:	Primary plant focus:	Wildflower seed offered:	Propagation methods:
✓Retail	✓Trees	Regional Seed Mixes	✓Propagate Plants
✓Wholesale	✓Shrubs	Custom Mixes	Collect Wild Plants
✓Mail Order	✓Grasses	Individual Species Seed	Collect Wild Seed
Price List/Catalog	✓Wildflowers	Contract Grow Seed	

Wildwood Nursery
3975 Emerald Ave
LaVerne, CA 91750
(714)593-4093

Percentage of the business in native species: 85

Type of business:	Primary plant focus:	Wildflower seed offered:	Propagation methods:
✓Retail	Trees	Regional Seed Mixes	✓Propagate Plants
✓Wholesale	Shrubs	✓Custom Mixes	Collect Wild Plants
✓Mail Order	Grasses	✓Individual Species Seed	✓Collect Wild Seed
✓Price List/Catalog	Wildflowers	Contract Grow Seed	

Yerba Buena Nursery
19500 Skyline Blvd.
Woodside, CA 94062
(415)851-1668

Percentage of the business in native species: 80

Type of business:	Primary plant focus:	Wildflower seed offered:	Propagation methods:
✓Retail	✓Trees	Regional Seed Mixes	✓Propagate Plants
Wholesale	✓Shrubs	Custom Mixes	✓Collect Wild Plants
Mail Order	✓Grasses	Individual Species Seed	✓Collect Wild Seed
Price List/Catalog	✓Wildflowers	Contract Grow Seed	

COLORADO

Applewood Seed Co.
5380 Vivian Street
Arvada, CO 80002
(303)431-6283

Percentage of the business in native species: 60

Type of business:	Primary plant focus:	Wildflower seed offered:	Propagation methods:
Retail	Trees	✓Regional Seed Mixes	✓Propagate Plants
✓Wholesale	Shrubs	✓Custom Mixes	Collect Wild Plants
✓Mail Order	Grasses	✓Individual Species Seed	✓Collect Wild Seed
Price List/Catalog	✓Wildflowers	✓Contract Grow Seed	

Arkansas Valley Seed Co.
Box 270
Rock Ford, CO 81067
(303)254-7469

Percentage of the business in native species: 20

Type of business:	Primary plant focus:	Wildflower seed offered:	Propagation methods:
✓Retail	Trees	✓Regional Seed Mixes	Propagate Plants
✓Wholesale	Shrubs	✓Custom Mixes	Collect Wild Plants
✓Mail Order	✓Grasses	✓Individual Species Seed	Collect Wild Seed
Price List/Catalog	✓Wildflowers	✓Contract Grow Seed	

Carhart Feed & Seed
3rd & Guymon, P. O. Box 55
Dove Creek CO 81324
(303)677-2233

Percentage of the business in native species: 20

Type of business:	Primary plant focus:	Wildflower seed offered:	Propagation methods:
✓Retail	Trees	Regional Seed Mixes	Propagate Plants
✓Wholesale	Shrubs	Custom Mixes	Collect Wild Plants
✓Mail Order	✓Grasses	Individual Species Seed	Collect Wild Seed
Price List/Catalog	Wildflowers	Contract Grow Seed	

Dean Swift Seed Co.
P. O. Box B
Jaroso, CO 81138-0028
(303)672-3739

Percentage of the business in native species: 100

Type of business:	Primary plant focus:	Wildflower seed offered:	Propagation methods:
Retail	✓ Trees	Regional Seed Mixes	Propagate Plants
✓ Wholesale	Shrubs	Custom Mixes	Collect Wild Plants
✓ Mail Order	✓ Grasses	✓ Individual Species Seed	✓ Collect Wild Seed
Price List/Catalog	✓ Wildflowers	✓ Contract Grow Seed	

Highland Nurseries, Inc.
5002 West 20 Street
Greeley, CO 80634
(303)330-4445

Percentage of the business in native species: 20

Type of business:	Primary plant focus:	Wildflower seed offered:	Propagation methods:
✓ Retail	✓ Trees	Regional Seed Mixes	Propagate Plants
Wholesale	✓ Shrubs	Custom Mixes	Collect Wild Plants
Mail Order	Grasses	Individual Species Seed	Collect Wild Seed
Price List/Catalog	Wildflowers	Contract Grow Seed	

Little Valley Wholesale Nursery
13022 East 136th Avenue
Brighton, CO 80601
(303)659-6708

Percentage of the business in native species: 30

Type of business:	Primary plant focus:	Wildflower seed offered:	Propagation methods:
✓ Retail	✓ Trees	Regional Seed Mixes	✓ Propagate Plants
✓ Wholesale	✓ Shrubs	Custom Mixes	Collect Wild Plants
Mail Order	Grasses	Individual Species Seed	✓ Collect Wild Seed
Price List/Catalog	✓ Wildflowers	Contract Grow Seed	

Neils Lunceford, Inc.
Box 102
Dillon, CO 80435
(303)468-0340

Percentage of the business in native species: 75

Type of business:	Primary plant focus:	Wildflower seed offered:	Propagation methods:
✓ Retail	✓ Trees	✓ Regional Seed Mixes	✓ Propagate Plants
✓ Wholesale	✓ Shrubs	✓ Custom Mixes	✓ Collect Wild Plants
✓ Mail Order	✓ Grasses	✓ Individual Species Seed	✓ Collect Wild Seed
Price List/Catalog	✓ Wildflowers	✓ Contract Grow Seed	

Schlichenmayer's Old Farm Nursery
5550 Indiana Street
Golden, CO 80403
(303)278-0754

Percentage of the business in native species: 30

Type of business:	Primary plant focus:	Wildflower seed offered:	Propagation methods:
✓ Retail	✓ Trees	Regional Seed Mixes	✓ Propagate Plants
✓ Wholesale	✓ Shrubs	Custom Mixes	Collect Wild Plants
✓ Mail Order	Grasses	Individual Species Seed	Collect Wild Seed
Price List/Catalog	✓ Wildflowers	Contract Grow Seed	

CONNECTICUT

Sunny Border Nurseries, Inc.
1709 Kensington Road
Kensington, CT 06037
(203)828-0321

Percentage of the business in native species: 25

Type of business:	Primary plant focus:	Wildflower seed offered:	Propagation methods:
Retail	Trees	Regional Seed Mixes	✓ Propagate Plants
✓ Wholesale	Shrubs	Custom Mixes	Collect Wild Plants
Mail Order	Grasses	Individual Species Seed	Collect Wild Seed
Price List/Catalog	✓ Wildflowers	Contract Grow Seed	

FLORIDA

Bullbay Creek Farm
Rt. 2, Box 381
Tallahassee, FL 32301
(904)878-6688

Percentage of the business in native species: 90

Type of business:	Primary plant focus:	Wildflower seed offered:	Propagation methods:
Retail	✓ Trees	Regional Seed Mixes	✓ Propagate Plants
✓ Wholesale	✓ Shrubs	Custom Mixes	Collect Wild Plants
Mail Order	Grasses	Individual Species Seed	✓ Collect Wild Seed
Price List/Catalog	✓ Wildflowers	✓ Contract Grow Seed	

Farnsworth Farms Nursery
7080 Hypoluxo Farms Road
Lake Worth, FL 33463
(305)965-2657

Percentage of the business in native species: 70

Type of business:	Primary plant focus:	Wildflower seed offered:	Propagation methods:
✓ Retail	✓ Trees	Regional Seed Mixes	✓ Propagate Plants
✓ Wholesale	✓ Shrubs	Custom Mixes	✓ Collect Wild Plants
Mail Order	Grasses	Individual Species Seed	Collect Wild Seed
Price List/Catalog	Wildflowers	Contract Grow Seed	

Florida Keys Native Nursery, Inc.
102 Mohawk Street
Tavernier, FL 33070
(305)852-2636

Percentage of the business in native species: 100

Type of business:	Primary plant focus:	Wildflower seed offered:	Propagation methods:
Retail	✓ Trees	✓ Regional Seed Mixes	✓ Propagate Plants
✓ Wholesale	✓ Shrubs	Custom Mixes	✓ Collect Wild Plants
✓ Mail Order	✓ Grasses	✓ Individual Species Seed	✓ Collect Wild Seed
Price List/Catalog	✓ Wildflowers	✓ Contract Grow Seed	

Gann's Tropical Greenery
22140 SW 152nd Avenue
Goulds, FL 33170
(305)248-5529

Percentage of the business in native species: 85

Type of business:	Primary plant focus:	Wildflower seed offered:	Propagation methods:
✓ Retail	✓ Trees	Regional Seed Mixes	✓ Propagate Plants
✓ Wholesale	✓ Shrubs	✓ Custom Mixes	Collect Wild Plants
Mail Order	✓ Grasses	✓ Individual Species Seed	✓ Collect Wild Seed
Price List/Catalog	✓ Wildflowers	✓ Contract Grow Seed	

Green Images
8100 Curry Ford Road
Orlando, FL 32822
(305)282-1469

Percentage of the business in native species: 90

Type of business:	Primary plant focus:	Wildflower seed offered:	Propagation methods:
✓ Retail	✓ Trees	Regional Seed Mixes	✓ Propagate Plants
✓ Wholesale	✓ Shrubs	✓ Custom Mixes	✓ Collect Wild Plants
Mail Order	✓ Grasses	✓ Individual Species Seed	✓ Collect Wild Seed
Price List/Catalog	✓ Wildflowers	✓ Contract Grow Seed	

Herren Nursery / Florida Division of Forestry
1801 S.R. 70 West
Lake Placid, FL 33852
(813)465-0024

Percentage of the business in native species: 80

Type of business:	Primary plant focus:	Wildflower seed offered:	Propagation methods:
Retail	✓ Trees	Regional Seed Mixes	✓ Propagate Plants
Wholesale	Shrubs	Custom Mixes	Collect Wild Plants
Mail Order	Grasses	Individual Species Seed	Collect Wild Seed
Price List/Catalog	Wildflowers	Contract Grow Seed	

Horticultural Systems, Inc.
P.O. Box 70
Parrish, FL 34219
(813)776-1760

Percentage of the business in native species: 100

Type of business:	Primary plant focus:	Wildflower seed offered:	Propagation methods:
✓ Retail	Trees	Regional Seed Mixes	✓ Propagate Plants
✓ Wholesale	Shrubs	Custom Mixes	✓ Collect Wild Plants
Mail Order	✓ Grasses	✓ Individual Species Seed	✓ Collect Wild Seed
Price List/Catalog	✓ Wildflowers	✓ Contract Grow Seed	

Liner Farm, Inc., The
P. O. Box 1369
St. Cloud, FL 32770-1369
(800)330-1484

Percentage of the business in native species: 15

Type of business:	Primary plant focus:	Wildflower seed offered:	Propagation methods:
Retail	✓ Trees	Regional Seed Mixes	✓ Propagate Plants
✓ Wholesale	✓ Shrubs	Custom Mixes	✓ Collect Wild Plants
✓ Mail Order	Grasses	Individual Species Seed	Collect Wild Seed
Price List/Catalog	✓ Wildflowers	Contract Grow Seed	

Native Nurseries
1661 Centerville Road
Tallahassee, FL 32308
(904)386-8882

Percentage of the business in native species: 80

Type of business:	Primary plant focus:	Wildflower seed offered:	Propagation methods:
✓ Retail	✓ Trees	✓ Regional Seed Mixes	Propagate Plants
Wholesale	✓ Shrubs	✓ Custom Mixes	Collect Wild Plants
Mail Order	Grasses	✓ Individual Species Seed	Collect Wild Seed
Price List/Catalog	✓ Wildflowers	Contract Grow Seed	

Native Tree Nursery, Inc.
17250 SW 232nd Street
Goulds, FL 33170
(305)247-4499

Percentage of the business in native species: 98

Type of business:	Primary plant focus:	Wildflower seed offered:	Propagation methods:
✓ Retail	✓ Trees	Regional Seed Mixes	✓ Propagate Plants
✓ Wholesale	Shrubs	Custom Mixes	✓ Collect Wild Plants
Mail Order	Grasses	Individual Species Seed	Collect Wild Seed
Price List/Catalog	Wildflowers	Contract Grow Seed	

Plants for Tomorrow
16361 Norris Road
Loxahatchee, FL 33470-9430
(305)790-1422

Percentage of the business in native species: 75

Type of business:	Primary plant focus:	Wildflower seed offered:	Propagation methods:
Retail	✓ Trees	Regional Seed Mixes	✓ Propagate Plants
✓ Wholesale	✓ Shrubs	Custom Mixes	✓ Collect Wild Plants
✓ Mail Order	Grasses	Individual Species Seed	Collect Wild Seed
Price List/Catalog	Wildflowers	Contract Grow Seed	

Salter Tree Farm
Rt. 2, Box 1332
Madison, FL 32340
(904)973-6312

Percentage of the business in native species: 95

Type of business:	Primary plant focus:	Wildflower seed offered:	Propagation methods:
✓ Retail	✓ Trees	Regional Seed Mixes	✓ Propagate Plants
✓ Wholesale	✓ Shrubs	Custom Mixes	Collect Wild Plants
✓ Mail Order	Grasses	Individual Species Seed	Collect Wild Seed
Price List/Catalog	Wildflowers	Contract Grow Seed	

Sanibel-Captiva Conservation Foundation
P. O. Drawer S, 3333 Sanibel Captiva Road
Sanibel, FL 33957
(813)472-1932

Percentage of the business in native species: 100

Type of business:	Primary plant focus:	Wildflower seed offered:	Propagation methods:
✓ Retail	✓ Trees	Regional Seed Mixes	✓ Propagate Plants
✓ Wholesale	✓ Shrubs	Custom Mixes	✓ Collect Wild Plants
Mail Order	Grasses	Individual Species Seed	Collect Wild Seed
Price List/Catalog	Wildflowers	Contract Grow Seed	

Tree Gallery, The
8855 116 Terrace South
Boynton Beach, FL 33437
(305)734-4416

Percentage of the business in native species: 100

Type of business:	Primary plant focus:	Wildflower seed offered:	Propagation methods:
✓ Retail	✓ Trees	Regional Seed Mixes	✓ Propagate Plants
✓ Wholesale	✓ Shrubs	Custom Mixes	✓ Collect Wild Plants
Mail Order	Grasses	Individual Species Seed	Collect Wild Seed
Price List/Catalog	Wildflowers	Contract Grow Seed	

Tropical Plant Locators
Box 1000
Delray Beach, FL 33447-1000
(305)278-6004

Percentage of the business in native species: 50

Type of business:	Primary plant focus:	Wildflower seed offered:	Propagation methods:
Retail	✓ Trees	✓ Regional Seed Mixes	✓ Propagate Plants
✓ Wholesale	✓ Shrubs	✓ Custom Mixes	✓ Collect Wild Plants
Mail Order	Grasses	✓ Individual Species Seed	Collect Wild Seed
Price List/Catalog	✓ Wildflowers	✓ Contract Grow Seed	

GEORGIA

Cedar Lane Farms
3790 Sandy Creed Road
Madison, GA 30650
(404)342-2626

Percentage of the business in native species: 65

Type of business:	Primary plant focus:	Wildflower seed offered:	Propagation methods:
Retail	✓ Trees	Regional Seed Mixes	✓ Propagate Plants
✓ Wholesale	✓ Shrubs	Custom Mixes	Collect Wild Plants
Mail Order	Grasses	Individual Species Seed	Collect Wild Seed
Price List/Catalog	✓ Wildflowers	✓ Contract Grow Seed	

Goodness Grows
P. O. Box 576, 156 South Woodlawn Drive
Crawford, GA 30630-0576
(404)743-5055

Percentage of the business in native species: 50

Type of business:	Primary plant focus:	Wildflower seed offered:	Propagation methods:
✓ Retail	Trees	Regional Seed Mixes	✓ Propagate Plants
✓ Wholesale	Shrubs	Custom Mixes	Collect Wild Plants
Mail Order	✓ Grasses	Individual Species Seed	✓ Collect Wild Seed
Price List/Catalog	✓ Wildflowers	Contract Grow Seed	

Piccadilly Farm
1971 Whippoorwill Road
Bishop, GA 30621
(404)769-6516

Percentage of the business in native species: 10

Type of business:	Primary plant focus:	Wildflower seed offered:	Propagation methods:
✓ Retail	Trees	Regional Seed Mixes	✓ Propagate Plants
✓ Wholesale	Shrubs	Custom Mixes	Collect Wild Plants
✓ Mail Order	✓ Grasses	Individual Species Seed	Collect Wild Seed
Price List/Catalog	✓ Wildflowers	Contract Grow Seed	

Southern Seed Co.
P. O. Box 287
Baldwin, GA 30511
(404)778-4542

Percentage of the business in native species: 100

Type of business:	Primary plant focus:	Wildflower seed offered:	Propagation methods:
Retail	✓ Trees	Regional Seed Mixes	Propagate Plants
✓ Wholesale	Shrubs	Custom Mixes	Collect Wild Plants
Mail Order	Grasses	Individual Species Seed	Collect Wild Seed
Price List/Catalog	Wildflowers	Contract Grow Seed	

Transplant Nursery
Parkertown Road
Lavonia, GA 30553
(404)356-8947

Percentage of the business in native species: 50

Type of business:	Primary plant focus:	Wildflower seed offered:	Propagation methods:
✓ Retail	Trees	Regional Seed Mixes	✓ Propagate Plants
✓ Wholesale	✓ Shrubs	Custom Mixes	Collect Wild Plants
✓ Mail Order	Grasses	Individual Species Seed	Collect Wild Seed
Price List/Catalog	Wildflowers	Contract Grow Seed	

Twisted Oaks Nursery
P. O. Box 818
Waynesboro, GA 30830
(404)554-3040

Percentage of the business in native species: 15

Type of business:	Primary plant focus:	Wildflower seed offered:	Propagation methods:
Retail	Trees	Regional Seed Mixes	✓ Propagate Plants
✓ Wholesale	✓ Shrubs	Custom Mixes	Collect Wild Plants
Mail Order	Grasses	Individual Species Seed	Collect Wild Seed
Price List/Catalog	Wildflowers	Contract Grow Seed	

IOWA

Cascade Forestry Service
RR 1
Cascade, IA 52033
(319)852-3042

Percentage of the business in native species: 80

Type of business:	Primary plant focus:	Wildflower seed offered:	Propagation methods:
✓ Retail	✓ Trees	Regional Seed Mixes	Propagate Plants
✓ Wholesale	Shrubs	Custom Mixes	Collect Wild Plants
✓ Mail Order	Grasses	Individual Species Seed	Collect Wild Seed
Price List/Catalog	Wildflowers	Contract Grow Seed	

Smith Nursery Co.
Box 515
Charles City, IA 50616
(515)228-3239

Percentage of the business in native species: 30

Type of business:	Primary plant focus:	Wildflower seed offered:	Propagation methods:
✓ Retail	✓ Trees	Regional Seed Mixes	✓ Propagate Plants
✓ Wholesale	✓ Shrubs	Custom Mixes	Collect Wild Plants
✓ Mail Order	Grasses	Individual Species Seed	Collect Wild Seed
Price List/Catalog	Wildflowers	Contract Grow Seed	

Wildflowers From Nature's Way
RR 1, Box 62
Woodburn, IA 50275

Percentage of the business in native species: 100

Type of business:	Primary plant focus:	Wildflower seed offered:	Propagation methods:
✓ Retail	Trees	✓ Regional Seed Mixes	✓ Propagate Plants
Wholesale	Shrubs	Custom Mixes	Collect Wild Plants
✓ Mail Order	✓ Grasses	✓ Individual Species Seed	✓ Collect Wild Seed
Price List/Catalog	✓ Wildflowers	Contract Grow Seed	

IDAHO

Fantasy Farms Nursery
Box 157
Peck, ID 83545
(208)486-6841

Percentage of the business in native species: 60

Type of business:	Primary plant focus:	Wildflower seed offered:	Propagation methods:
Retail	✓ Trees	Regional Seed Mixes	✓ Propagate Plants
✓ Wholesale	Shrubs	Custom Mixes	Collect Wild Plants
Mail Order	Grasses	Individual Species Seed	Collect Wild Seed
Price List/Catalog	Wildflowers	Contract Grow Seed	

High Altitude Gardens
P. O. Box 4238, 220 Lewis #8
Ketchum, ID 83340
(208)726-3221

Percentage of the business in native species: 50

Type of business:	Primary plant focus:	Wildflower seed offered:	Propagation methods:
✓ Retail	Trees	✓ Regional Seed Mixes	✓ Propagate Plants
✓ Wholesale	Shrubs	✓ Custom Mixes	✓ Collect Wild Plants
✓ Mail Order	✓ Grasses	✓ Individual Species Seed	✓ Collect Wild Seed
Price List/Catalog	✓ Wildflowers	✓ Contract Grow Seed	

Native Seed Foundation
Star Route
Moyie Springs, ID 83845
(208)267-7938

Percentage of the business in native species: 95

Type of business:	Primary plant focus:	Wildflower seed offered:	Propagation methods:
Retail	✓ Trees	Regional Seed Mixes	✓ Propagate Plants
✓ Wholesale	✓ Shrubs	Custom Mixes	✓ Collect Wild Plants
✓ Mail Order	Grasses	Individual Species Seed	✓ Collect Wild Seed
Price List/Catalog	Wildflowers	Contract Grow Seed	

Northplan Seed Producers
P. O. Box 9107
Moscow, ID 83843
(208)882-8040

Percentage of the business in native species: 75

Type of business:	Primary plant focus:	Wildflower seed offered:	Propagation methods:
Retail	✔Trees	✔Regional Seed Mixes	✔Propagate Plants
✔Wholesale	✔Shrubs	✔Custom Mixes	Collect Wild Plants
✔Mail Order	✔Grasses	Individual Species Seed	✔Collect Wild Seed
Price List/Catalog	✔Wildflowers	Contract Grow Seed	

Winterfeld Ranch Seed
P. O. Box 97
Swan Valley, ID 83449
(208)483-3683

Percentage of the business in native species: 20

Type of business:	Primary plant focus:	Wildflower seed offered:	Propagation methods:
Retail	Trees	Regional Seed Mixes	✔Propagate Plants
✔Wholesale	Shrubs	Custom Mixes	✔Collect Wild Plants
Mail Order	✔Grasses	✔Individual Species Seed	✔Collect Wild Seed
Price List/Catalog	✔Wildflowers	Contract Grow Seed	

ILLINOIS

Country Road Greenhouses, Inc.
RR 1, Box 74
Malta, IL 60150
(815)825-2305

Percentage of the business in native species: 65

Type of business:	Primary plant focus:	Wildflower seed offered:	Propagation methods:
✔Retail	Trees	Regional Seed Mixes	✔Propagate Plants
✔Wholesale	Shrubs	Custom Mixes	Collect Wild Plants
✔Mail Order	✔Grasses	Individual Species Seed	✔Collect Wild Seed
Price List/Catalog	✔Wildflowers	Contract Grow Seed	

Iversons Perennial Gardens
Box 2787 RFD
Long Grove, IL 60047
(312)359-3500

Percentage of the business in native species: 13

Type of business:	Primary plant focus:	Wildflower seed offered:	Propagation methods:
Retail	Trees	Regional Seed Mixes	Propagate Plants
✓ Wholesale	Shrubs	Custom Mixes	Collect Wild Plants
Mail Order	Grasses	Individual Species Seed	Collect Wild Seed
Price List/Catalog	✓ Wildflowers	Contract Grow Seed	

Kathy Clinebell
RR 2, Box 176
Wyoming, IL 61491
(309)286-7356

Percentage of the business in native species: 100

Type of business:	Primary plant focus:	Wildflower seed offered:	Propagation methods:
Retail	Trees	✓ Regional Seed Mixes	✓ Propagate Plants
✓ Wholesale	Shrubs	✓ Custom Mixes	Collect Wild Plants
✓ Mail Order	Grasses	✓ Individual Species Seed	✓ Collect Wild Seed
Price List/Catalog	✓ Wildflowers	✓ Contract Grow Seed	

Lafayette Home Nursery, Inc.
#1 Nursery Lane
Lafayette, IL 61449
(309)995-3311

Percentage of the business in native species: 80

Type of business:	Primary plant focus:	Wildflower seed offered:	Propagation methods:
✓ Retail	Trees	✓ Regional Seed Mixes	✓ Propagate Plants
✓ Wholesale	Shrubs	✓ Custom Mixes	Collect Wild Plants
Mail Order	✓ Grasses	✓ Individual Species Seed	✓ Collect Wild Seed
Price List/Catalog	✓ Wildflowers	✓ Contract Grow Seed	

Midwest Wildflowers
Box 64
Rockton, IL 61072
(815)624-7040

Percentage of the business in native species: 75

Type of business:	Primary plant focus:	Wildflower seed offered:	Propagation methods:
Retail	Trees	Regional Seed Mixes	✓ Propagate Plants
Wholesale	Shrubs	Custom Mixes	Collect Wild Plants
✓ Mail Order	Grasses	✓ Individual Species Seed	✓ Collect Wild Seed
Price List/Catalog	✓ Wildflowers	Contract Grow Seed	

Natural Garden, The
3BW443 Hwy 64
St. Charles, IL 60174
(312)584-0150

Percentage of the business in native species: 20

Type of business:	Primary plant focus:	Wildflower seed offered:	Propagation methods:
✓ Retail	Trees	✓ Regional Seed Mixes	✓ Propagate Plants
✓ Wholesale	Shrubs	✓ Custom Mixes	Collect Wild Plants
✓ Mail Order	✓ Grasses	✓ Individual Species Seed	✓ Collect Wild Seed
Price List/Catalog	✓ Wildflowers	✓ Contract Grow Seed	

Wildflower Source, The
Box 312
Fox Lake, IL 60020
(312)740-9796

Percentage of the business in native species: 100

Type of business:	Primary plant focus:	Wildflower seed offered:	Propagation methods:
✓ Retail	Trees	Regional Seed Mixes	✓ Propagate Plants
Wholesale	Shrubs	Custom Mixes	Collect Wild Plants
✓ Mail Order	Grasses	Individual Species Seed	Collect Wild Seed
Price List/Catalog	✓ Wildflowers	✓ Contract Grow Seed	

Windrift Prairie Shop and Nursery
RD 2
Oregon, IL 61061
(805)732-6890

Percentage of the business in native species: 100

Type of business:	Primary plant focus:	Wildflower seed offered:	Propagation methods:
✓Retail	Trees	Regional Seed Mixes	✓Propagate Plants
Wholesale	Shrubs	✓Custom Mixes	Collect Wild Plants
✓Mail Order	✓Grasses	✓Individual Species Seed	✓Collect Wild Seed
Price List/Catalog	✓Wildflowers	Contract Grow Seed	

KANSAS

Sharp Bros. Seed Co.
P. O. Box 140
Healy, KS 67850
(316)398-2231

Percentage of the business in native species: 50

Type of business:	Primary plant focus:	Wildflower seed offered:	Propagation methods:
✓Retail	Trees	✓Regional Seed Mixes	✓Propagate Plants
✓Wholesale	Shrubs	✓Custom Mixes	Collect Wild Plants
✓Mail Order	✓Grasses	✓Individual Species Seed	✓Collect Wild Seed
Price List/Catalog	✓Wildflowers	✓Contract Grow Seed	

LOUISIANA

Louisiana Nature and Science Center
11000 Lake Forest Blvd.
New Orleans, LA 70127-2816
(504)246-5672

Percentage of the business in native species: 90

Type of business:	Primary plant focus:	Wildflower seed offered:	Propagation methods:
✓Retail	Trees	✓Regional Seed Mixes	✓Propagate Plants
Wholesale	Shrubs	✓Custom Mixes	Collect Wild Plants
✓Mail Order	Grasses	✓Individual Species Seed	✓Collect Wild Seed
Price List/Catalog	✓Wildflowers	Contract Grow Seed	

Natives Nurseries
P. O. Box 2355 / Rt. 5, Box 229A
Covington, LA 70434
(504)892-5424

Percentage of the business in native species: 65

Type of business:	Primary plant focus:	Wildflower seed offered:	Propagation methods:
✓ Retail	✓ Trees	Regional Seed Mixes	✓ Propagate Plants
✓ Wholesale	✓ Shrubs	Custom Mixes	Collect Wild Plants
Mail Order	Grasses	Individual Species Seed	Collect Wild Seed
Price List/Catalog	✓ Wildflowers	Contract Grow Seed	

Prairie Basse Native Plants
Rt. 2, Box 491 F
Carencro, LA 70520
(318)896-9187

Percentage of the business in native species: 100

Type of business:	Primary plant focus:	Wildflower seed offered:	Propagation methods:
✓ Retail	✓ Trees	Regional Seed Mixes	✓ Propagate Plants
Wholesale	✓ Shrubs	Custom Mixes	Collect Wild Plants
Mail Order	Grasses	Individual Species Seed	✓ Collect Wild Seed
✓ Price List/Catalog	Wildflowers	Contract Grow Seed	

MASSACHUSETTS

F. W. Schumacher Co., Inc.
36 Spring Hill Road
Sandwich, MA 02563-1023
(617)888-0659

Percentage of the business in native species: 70

Type of business:	Primary plant focus:	Wildflower seed offered:	Propagation methods:
Retail	✓ Trees	Regional Seed Mixes	Propagate Plants
✓ Wholesale	✓ Shrubs	Custom Mixes	Collect Wild Plants
Mail Order	Grasses	Individual Species Seed	Collect Wild Seed
Price List/Catalog	Wildflowers	Contract Grow Seed	

Lexington Gardens
93 Hancock St.
Lexington, MA 02173
(617)862-7000

Percentage of the business in native species: 10

Type of business:	Primary plant focus:	Wildflower seed offered:	Propagation methods:
✓Retail	✓Trees	Regional Seed Mixes	✓Propagate Plants
Wholesale	✓Shrubs	Custom Mixes	Collect Wild Plants
Mail Order	Grasses	Individual Species Seed	Collect Wild Seed
Price List/Catalog	✓Wildflowers	Contract Grow Seed	

Tripple Brook Farm
37 Middle Road
Southampton, MA 01073
(413)527-4626

Percentage of the business in native species: 20

Type of business:	Primary plant focus:	Wildflower seed offered:	Propagation methods:
✓Retail	✓Trees	Regional Seed Mixes	✓Propagate Plants
Wholesale	✓Shrubs	Custom Mixes	✓Collect Wild Plants
✓Mail Order	✓Grasses	Individual Species Seed	Collect Wild Seed
✓Price List/Catalog	✓Wildflowers	Contract Grow Seed	

MARYLAND

Bluemount Nurseries, Inc.
2103 Blue Mount Road
Monkton, MD 21111
(301)329-6226

Percentage of the business in native species: 10

Type of business:	Primary plant focus:	Wildflower seed offered:	Propagation methods:
Retail	Trees	Regional Seed Mixes	✓Propagate Plants
✓Wholesale	Shrubs	Custom Mixes	✓Collect Wild Plants
Mail Order	✓Grasses	Individual Species Seed	✓Collect Wild Seed
Price List/Catalog	✓Wildflowers	Contract Grow Seed	

Environmental Concern, Inc.
210 West Chew Avenue, P. O. Box P
St. Michaels, MD 21663
(301)745-9620

Percentage of the business in native species: 75

Type of business:	Primary plant focus:	Wildflower seed offered:	Propagation methods:
✓ Retail	✓ Trees	Regional Seed Mixes	✓ Propagate Plants
✓ Wholesale	✓ Shrubs	Custom Mixes	Collect Wild Plants
✓ Mail Order	✓ Grasses	✓ Individual Species Seed	✓ Collect Wild Seed
Price List/Catalog	✓ Wildflowers	✓ Contract Grow Seed	

Kurt Bluemel, Inc.
2543 Hess Road / Nur @ 2740 Greene Lane, Baldwin
Fallston MD 21047
(301)557-7229

Percentage of the business in native species: 5

Type of business:	Primary plant focus:	Wildflower seed offered:	Propagation methods:
✓ Retail	Trees	Regional Seed Mixes	✓ Propagate Plants
✓ Wholesale	Shrubs	Custom Mixes	Collect Wild Plants
✓ Mail Order	✓ Grasses	Individual Species Seed	Collect Wild Seed
Price List/Catalog	✓ Wildflowers	Contract Grow Seed	

Mother Nature's Nursery
10214 Little Rock Lane
Frederick, MD 21701
(301)898-3859

Percentage of the business in native species: 95

Type of business:	Primary plant focus:	Wildflower seed offered:	Propagation methods:
Retail	Trees	Regional Seed Mixes	✓ Propagate Plants
✓ Wholesale	✓ Shrubs	Custom Mixes	✓ Collect Wild Plants
Mail Order	Grasses	Individual Species Seed	✓ Collect Wild Seed
Price List/Catalog	✓ Wildflowers	Contract Grow Seed	

Native Seeds, Inc.
14590 Triadelphia Mill Road
Dayton, MD 21036
(301)596-9818

Percentage of the business in native species: 80

Type of business:	Primary plant focus:	Wildflower seed offered:	Propagation methods:
✓ Retail	Trees	✓ Regional Seed Mixes	✓ Propagate Plants
✓ Wholesale	Shrubs	✓ Custom Mixes	✓ Collect Wild Plants
✓ Mail Order	Grasses	✓ Individual Species Seed	✓ Collect Wild Seed
Price List/Catalog	✓ Wildflowers	✓ Contract Grow Seed	

MAINE

Western Maine Nurseries, Inc.
One Evergreen Drive
Fryeburg, ME 04037
(207)935-2161

Percentage of the business in native species: 30

Type of business:	Primary plant focus:	Wildflower seed offered:	Propagation methods:
Retail	✓ Trees	Regional Seed Mixes	Propagate Plants
✓ Wholesale	Shrubs	Custom Mixes	Collect Wild Plants
Mail Order	Grasses	Individual Species Seed	✓ Collect Wild Seed
Price List/Catalog	Wildflowers	Contract Grow Seed	

MICHIGAN

Armintrout's Nursery
1156 Lincoln Road
Allegan, MI 49010
(616)673-6627

Percentage of the business in native species: 50

Type of business:	Primary plant focus:	Wildflower seed offered:	Propagation methods:
Retail	✓ Trees	Regional Seed Mixes	✓ Propagate Plants
✓ Wholesale	Shrubs	Custom Mixes	Collect Wild Plants
Mail Order	Grasses	Individual Species Seed	Collect Wild Seed
Price List/Catalog	Wildflowers	Contract Grow Seed	

Far North Gardens
16785 Harrison
Livonia, MI 48154
(313)422-0747

Percentage of the business in native species: 40

Type of business:	Primary plant focus:	Wildflower seed offered:	Propagation methods:
✓ Retail	Trees	✓ Regional Seed Mixes	✓ Propagate Plants
Wholesale	Shrubs	Custom Mixes	Collect Wild Plants
✓ Mail Order	Grasses	✓ Individual Species Seed	Collect Wild Seed
Price List/Catalog	✓ Wildflowers	Contract Grow Seed	

International Growers Exchange
P. O. Box 52248
Livonia, MI 48152-0248
(313)422-0747

Percentage of the business in native species: 15

Type of business:	Primary plant focus:	Wildflower seed offered:	Propagation methods:
Retail	✓ Trees	✓ Regional Seed Mixes	Propagate Plants
✓ Wholesale	✓ Shrubs	Custom Mixes	Collect Wild Plants
✓ Mail Order	Grasses	✓ Individual Species Seed	Collect Wild Seed
Price List/Catalog	✓ Wildflowers	Contract Grow Seed	

Van Pines, Inc.
7550 144th Avenue
West Olive, MI 49460
(616)399-1620

Percentage of the business in native species: 40

Type of business:	Primary plant focus:	Wildflower seed offered:	Propagation methods:
Retail	✓ Trees	Regional Seed Mixes	✓ Propagate Plants
✓ Wholesale	✓ Shrubs	Custom Mixes	Collect Wild Plants
✓ Mail Order	✓ Grasses	Individual Species Seed	✓ Collect Wild Seed
Price List/Catalog	Wildflowers	Contract Grow Seed	

MINNESOTA

Prairie Moon Nursery
Rt. 3, Box 163
Winona, MN 55987
(507)452-5231

Percentage of the business in native species: 100

Type of business:	Primary plant focus:	Wildflower seed offered:	Propagation methods:
✓ Retail	Trees	✓ Regional Seed Mixes	✓ Propagate Plants
✓ Wholesale	Shrubs	✓ Custom Mixes	Collect Wild Plants
✓ Mail Order	✓ Grasses	✓ Individual Species Seed	✓ Collect Wild Seed
Price List/Catalog	✓ Wildflowers	✓ Contract Grow Seed	

Prairie Restorations, Inc.
P. O. Box 327
Princeton, MN 55371
(612)389-4342

Percentage of the business in native species: 90

Type of business:	Primary plant focus:	Wildflower seed offered:	Propagation methods:
✓ Retail	✓ Trees	✓ Regional Seed Mixes	✓ Propagate Plants
✓ Wholesale	✓ Shrubs	✓ Custom Mixes	Collect Wild Plants
✓ Mail Order	✓ Grasses	✓ Individual Species Seed	✓ Collect Wild Seed
Price List/Catalog	✓ Wildflowers	Contract Grow Seed	

Regent Gardens
2460 Regent Avenue North
Golden Valley, MN 55422
(612)588-2598

Percentage of the business in native species: 80

Type of business:	Primary plant focus:	Wildflower seed offered:	Propagation methods:
✓ Retail	Trees	Regional Seed Mixes	✓ Propagate Plants
Wholesale	Shrubs	Custom Mixes	Collect Wild Plants
Mail Order	Grasses	Individual Species Seed	Collect Wild Seed
Price List/Catalog	✓ Wildflowers	Contract Grow Seed	

Rice Creek Gardens
1315 66th Avenue NE
Minneapolis, MN 55432
(612)574-1197

Percentage of the business in native species: 18

Type of business:	Primary plant focus:	Wildflower seed offered:	Propagation methods:
✓ Retail	Trees	Regional Seed Mixes	✓ Propagate Plants
✓ Wholesale	Shrubs	Custom Mixes	Collect Wild Plants
✓ Mail Order	Grasses	Individual Species Seed	Collect Wild Seed
Price List/Catalog	✓ Wildflowers	Contract Grow Seed	

Shady Acres Nursery
7777 Hwy 212
Chaska, MN 55318
(612)466-3391

Percentage of the business in native species: 35

Type of business:	Primary plant focus:	Wildflower seed offered:	Propagation methods:
✓ Retail	Trees	Regional Seed Mixes	✓ Propagate Plants
✓ Wholesale	Shrubs	Custom Mixes	Collect Wild Plants
Mail Order	Grasses	Individual Species Seed	Collect Wild Seed
Price List/Catalog	Wildflowers	Contract Grow Seed	

Willow Lake Farm
c/o Tony Thompson, Box 128
Windom, MN 56101
(507)831-3483

Percentage of the business in native species: 100

Type of business:	Primary plant focus:	Wildflower seed offered:	Propagation methods:
Retail	Trees	✓ Regional Seed Mixes	✓ Propagate Plants
✓ Wholesale	Shrubs	✓ Custom Mixes	Collect Wild Plants
✓ Mail Order	✓ Grasses	✓ Individual Species Seed	Collect Wild Seed
Price List/Catalog	✓ Wildflowers	✓ Contract Grow Seed	

MISSOURI

Hi-Mountain Farm
Rt. 2, Box 293
Galena, MO 65656
(417)538-4574

Percentage of the business in native species: 99

Type of business:	Primary plant focus:	Wildflower seed offered:	Propagation methods:
Retail	Trees	Regional Seed Mixes	✓Propagate Plants
✓Wholesale	Shrubs	Custom Mixes	✓Collect Wild Plants
✓Mail Order	Grasses	Individual Species Seed	Collect Wild Seed
Price List/Catalog	✓Wildflowers	Contract Grow Seed	

Missouri Wildflowers Nursery
Rt. 2, Box 373
Jefferson City, MO 65101-9805
(314)496-3492

Percentage of the business in native species: 100

Type of business:	Primary plant focus:	Wildflower seed offered:	Propagation methods:
✓Retail	Trees	Regional Seed Mixes	✓Propagate Plants
✓Wholesale	Shrubs	Custom Mixes	Collect Wild Plants
✓Mail Order	Grasses	✓Individual Species Seed	✓Collect Wild Seed
Price List/Catalog	✓Wildflowers	Contract Grow Seed	

Sharp Bros. Seed Co. of Missouri
Rt. 4, Box 665
Clinton, MO 64735
(816)885-8521

Percentage of the business in native species: 70

Type of business:	Primary plant focus:	Wildflower seed offered:	Propagation methods:
✓Retail	Trees	✓Regional Seed Mixes	✓Propagate Plants
✓Wholesale	✓Shrubs	Custom Mixes	Collect Wild Plants
✓Mail Order	✓Grasses	Individual Species Seed	✓Collect Wild Seed
Price List/Catalog	✓Wildflowers	Contract Grow Seed	

MISSISSIPPI

Homochitto Outdoors
Box 630
Meadville, MS 39653
(601)384-2915

Percentage of the business in native species: 88

Type of business:	Primary plant focus:	Wildflower seed offered:	Propagation methods:
✓ Retail	Trees	✓ Regional Seed Mixes	Propagate Plants
✓ Wholesale	Shrubs	Custom Mixes	Collect Wild Plants
✓ Mail Order	Grasses	Individual Species Seed	Collect Wild Seed
Price List/Catalog	✓ Wildflowers	Contract Grow Seed	

MONTANA

Lawyer Nursery, Inc.
950 Hwy 200 West
Plains, MT 59859
(406)826-3881

Percentage of the business in native species: 50

Type of business:	Primary plant focus:	Wildflower seed offered:	Propagation methods:
Retail	✓ Trees	✓ Regional Seed Mixes	✓ Propagate Plants
✓ Wholesale	✓ Shrubs	Custom Mixes	Collect Wild Plants
✓ Mail Order	Grasses	Individual Species Seed	Collect Wild Seed
Price List/Catalog	✓ Wildflowers	Contract Grow Seed	

Valley Nursery
Box 4845
Helena, MT 59604
(406)442-8460

Percentage of the business in native species: 25

Type of business:	Primary plant focus:	Wildflower seed offered:	Propagation methods:
✓ Retail	✓ Trees	Regional Seed Mixes	✓ Propagate Plants
✓ Wholesale	✓ Shrubs	Custom Mixes	✓ Collect Wild Plants
✓ Mail Order	✓ Grasses	Individual Species Seed	✓ Collect Wild Seed
Price List/Catalog	✓ Wildflowers	✓ Contract Grow Seed	

NORTH CAROLINA

Gardens of the Blue Ridge
P. O. Box 10
Pineola, NC 28662
(704)733-2417

Percentage of the business in native species: 100

Type of business:	Primary plant focus:	Wildflower seed offered:	Propagation methods:
✓Retail	Trees	Regional Seed Mixes	Propagate Plants
✓ Wholesale	✓Shrubs	Custom Mixes	✓Collect Wild Plants
✓Mail Order	Grasses	Individual Species Seed	Collect Wild Seed
Price List/Catalog	✓Wildflowers	Contract Grow Seed	

Griffey's Nursery
1670 Hwy 25-70
Marshall, NC 28753
(704)656-2334

Percentage of the business in native species: 100

Type of business:	Primary plant focus:	Wildflower seed offered:	Propagation methods:
✓Retail	Trees	Regional Seed Mixes	Propagate Plants
✓ Wholesale	✓Shrubs	Custom Mixes	✓Collect Wild Plants
✓Mail Order	Grasses	Individual Species Seed	Collect Wild Seed
Price List/Catalog	✓Wildflowers	Contract Grow Seed	

Holbrook Farm & Nursery
Rt. 2, Box 223B
Fletcher, NC 28732
(704)891-7790

Percentage of the business in native species: 20

Type of business:	Primary plant focus:	Wildflower seed offered:	Propagation methods:
✓Retail	✓Trees	Regional Seed Mixes	✓Propagate Plants
Wholesale	✓Shrubs	Custom Mixes	Collect Wild Plants
✓Mail Order	Grasses	Individual Species Seed	Collect Wild Seed
Price List/Catalog	✓Wildflowers	Contract Grow Seed	

Montrose Nursery
P. O. Box 957
Hillsborough, NC 27278-0957
(919)732-7787

Percentage of the business in native species: 30

Type of business:	Primary plant focus:	Wildflower seed offered:	Propagation methods:
✓Retail	Trees	Regional Seed Mixes	✓Propagate Plants
Wholesale	Shrubs	Custom Mixes	Collect Wild Plants
✓Mail Order	Grasses	Individual Species Seed	Collect Wild Seed
Price List/Catalog	✓Wildflowers	Contract Grow Seed	

Niche Gardens
Rt. 1, Box 290
Chapel Hill, NC 27514
(919)967-0078

Percentage of the business in native species: 90

Type of business:	Primary plant focus:	Wildflower seed offered:	Propagation methods:
✓Retail	Trees	Regional Seed Mixes	✓Propagate Plants
✓Wholesale	Shrubs	Custom Mixes	Collect Wild Plants
✓Mail Order	Grasses	Individual Species Seed	Collect Wild Seed
Price List/Catalog	✓Wildflowers	Contract Grow Seed	

Passiflora Wildflowers
Rt. 1, Box 190A
Germantown, NC 27019
(919)591-5816

Percentage of the business in native species: 70

Type of business:	Primary plant focus:	Wildflower seed offered:	Propagation methods:
✓Retail	Trees	✓Regional Seed Mixes	✓Propagate Plants
Wholesale	Shrubs	✓Custom Mixes	Collect Wild Plants
✓Mail Order	Grasses	✓Individual Species Seed	✓Collect Wild Seed
Price List/Catalog	✓Wildflowers	Contract Grow Seed	

We-Du Nurseries
Rt. 5, Box 724
Marion, NC 28752
(704)738-8300

Percentage of the business in native species: 60

Type of business:	Primary plant focus:	Wildflower seed offered:	Propagation methods:
✓Retail	Trees	Regional Seed Mixes	✓Propagate Plants
Wholesale	Shrubs	Custom Mixes	Collect Wild Plants
✓Mail Order	Grasses	Individual Species Seed	✓Collect Wild Seed
Price List/Catalog	✓Wildflowers	Contract Grow Seed	

NORTH DAKOTA

Lincoln-Oakes Nurseries
Box 1601
Bismarck, ND 58501
(701)223-8575

Percentage of the business in native species: 35

Type of business:	Primary plant focus:	Wildflower seed offered:	Propagation methods:
Retail	✓Trees	Regional Seed Mixes	✓Propagate Plants
✓Wholesale	✓Shrubs	Custom Mixes	Collect Wild Plants
Mail Order	✓Grasses	Individual Species Seed	Collect Wild Seed
Price List/Catalog	Wildflowers	Contract Grow Seed	

NEBRASKA

Bluebird Nursery, Inc.
Box 460, 515 Linden Street
Clarkson, NE 68629
(402)892-3457

Percentage of the business in native species: 30

Type of business:	Primary plant focus:	Wildflower seed offered:	Propagation methods:
✓Retail	✓Trees	Regional Seed Mixes	✓Propagate Plants
✓Wholesale	✓Shrubs	Custom Mixes	Collect Wild Plants
✓Mail Order	✓Grasses	✓Individual Species Seed	✓Collect Wild Seed
Price List/Catalog	✓Wildflowers	✓Contract Grow Seed	

Horizon Seeds, Inc.
Box 81823
Lincoln, NE 68501
(402)475-1232

Percentage of the business in native species: 50

Type of business:	Primary plant focus:	Wildflower seed offered:	Propagation methods:
✓Retail	Trees	Regional Seed Mixes	Propagate Plants
✓Wholesale	Shrubs	✓Custom Mixes	Collect Wild Plants
Mail Order	✓Grasses	✓Individual Species Seed	Collect Wild Seed
Price List/Catalog	✓Wildflowers	✓Contract Grow Seed	

Stock Seed Farms, Inc.
RR 1, Box 112
Murdock, NE 68407
(402)867-3771

Percentage of the business in native species: 80

Type of business:	Primary plant focus:	Wildflower seed offered:	Propagation methods:
✓Retail	Trees	Regional Seed Mixes	✓Propagate Plants
✓Wholesale	Shrubs	Custom Mixes	Collect Wild Plants
✓Mail Order	✓Grasses	✓Individual Species Seed	✓Collect Wild Seed
Price List/Catalog	✓Wildflowers	Contract Grow Seed	

NEW JERSEY

Lofts Seed, Inc.
Chimney Rock Road
Bound Brook, NJ 08805
(201)560-1590

Percentage of the business in native species: 50

Type of business:	Primary plant focus:	Wildflower seed offered:	Propagation methods:
✓Retail	Trees	✓Regional Seed Mixes	Propagate Plants
✓Wholesale	Shrubs	✓Custom Mixes	Collect Wild Plants
✓Mail Order	✓Grasses	✓Individual Species Seed	Collect Wild Seed
Price List/Catalog	✓Wildflowers	✓Contract Grow Seed	

Princeton Nurseries
P. O. Box 191
Princeton, NJ 08540
(609)924-1776

Percentage of the business in native species: 45

Type of business:	Primary plant focus:	Wildflower seed offered:	Propagation methods:
Retail	✓ Trees	Regional Seed Mixes	✓ Propagate Plants
✓ Wholesale	✓ Shrubs	Custom Mixes	Collect Wild Plants
Mail Order	Grasses	Individual Species Seed	Collect Wild Seed
Price List/Catalog	Wildflowers	Contract Grow Seed	

NEW MEXICO

Bernardo Beach Native Plant Farm
1 Sanchez Road
Veguita, NM 87062
(505)345-6248

Percentage of the business in native species: 90

Type of business:	Primary plant focus:	Wildflower seed offered:	Propagation methods:
✓ Retail	✓ Trees	Regional Seed Mixes	✓ Propagate Plants
✓ Wholesale	✓ Shrubs	✓ Custom Mixes	Collect Wild Plants
✓ Mail Order	Grasses	✓ Individual Species Seed	✓ Collect Wild Seed
Price List/Catalog	✓ Wildflowers	Contract Grow Seed	

CH & E Diebold LTD.
268 La Ladera Road
Los Lunas, NM 87031
(505)869-2517

Percentage of the business in native species: 90

Type of business:	Primary plant focus:	Wildflower seed offered:	Propagation methods:
Retail	Trees	Regional Seed Mixes	✓ Propagate Plants
✓ Wholesale	Shrubs	Custom Mixes	Collect Wild Plants
Mail Order	✓ Grasses	Individual Species Seed	Collect Wild Seed
Price List/Catalog	Wildflowers	Contract Grow Seed	

Dry Country Plants
5840 North Main
Las Cruces, NM 88001
(505)522-4434

Percentage of the business in native species: 95

Type of business:	Primary plant focus:	Wildflower seed offered:	Propagation methods:
✓Retail	Trees	✓Regional Seed Mixes	✓Propagate Plants
✓Wholesale	✓Shrubs	Custom Mixes	Collect Wild Plants
Mail Order	Grasses	✓Individual Species Seed	✓Collect Wild Seed
Price List/Catalog	✓Wildflowers	Contract Grow Seed	

Mesa Garden
P. O. Box 72
Belen, NM 87002
(505)864-3131

Percentage of the business in native species: 40

Type of business:	Primary plant focus:	Wildflower seed offered:	Propagation methods:
✓Retail	Trees	Regional Seed Mixes	✓Propagate Plants
Wholesale	Shrubs	Custom Mixes	Collect Wild Plants
✓Mail Order	Grasses	Individual Species Seed	Collect Wild Seed
Price List/Catalog	Wildflowers	Contract Grow Seed	

New Mexico Cactus Research
P. O. Box 787, 1132 F River Road
Belen, NM 87002
(505)864-4027

Percentage of the business in native species: 10

Type of business:	Primary plant focus:	Wildflower seed offered:	Propagation methods:
✓Retail	Trees	Regional Seed Mixes	✓Propagate Plants
✓Wholesale	Shrubs	Custom Mixes	Collect Wild Plants
✓Mail Order	Grasses	Individual Species Seed	✓Collect Wild Seed
Price List/Catalog	Wildflowers	Contract Grow Seed	

New Mexico Native Plant Nursery
309 West College Avenue
Silver City, NM 88061
(505)538-5201

Percentage of the business in native species: 90

Type of business:	Primary plant focus:	Wildflower seed offered:	Propagation methods:
✓Retail	✓Trees	Regional Seed Mixes	✓Propagate Plants
✓Wholesale	✓Shrubs	Custom Mixes	✓Collect Wild Plants
✓Mail Order	Grasses	Individual Species Seed	Collect Wild Seed
Price List/Catalog	✓Wildflowers	Contract Grow Seed	

Plants of the Southwest
1812 Second Street
Santa Fe, NM 87501
(505)983-1548

Percentage of the business in native species: 95

Type of business:	Primary plant focus:	Wildflower seed offered:	Propagation methods:
✓Retail	✓Trees	✓Regional Seed Mixes	✓Propagate Plants
✓Wholesale	✓Shrubs	✓Custom Mixes	Collect Wild Plants
✓Mail Order	✓Grasses	✓Individual Species Seed	✓Collect Wild Seed
Price List/Catalog	✓Wildflowers	Contract Grow Seed	

Wildland and Native Seeds Foundation
2402 Hoffman Drive, NE
Albuquerque, NM 87110
(505)298-1980

Percentage of the business in native species: 100

Type of business:	Primary plant focus:	Wildflower seed offered:	Propagation methods:
Retail	✓Trees	Regional Seed Mixes	Propagate Plants
✓Wholesale	✓Shrubs	Custom Mixes	Collect Wild Plants
Mail Order	✓Grasses	✓Individual Species Seed	✓Collect Wild Seed
Price List/Catalog	✓Wildflowers	Contract Grow Seed	

NEW YORK

Bentley Seed Co.
P. O. Box 38, Pearl Street
Cambridge, NY 12816-0038
(518)677-8808

Percentage of the business in native species: 6

Type of business:	Primary plant focus:	Wildflower seed offered:	Propagation methods:
Retail	Trees	✓Regional Seed Mixes	Propagate Plants
✓Wholesale	Shrubs	✓Custom Mixes	Collect Wild Plants
✓Mail Order	Grasses	✓Individual Species Seed	Collect Wild Seed
Price List/Catalog	✓Wildflowers	Contract Grow Seed	

Botanic Garden Seed Co., Inc.
9 Wyckoff Street
Brooklyn, NY 11201
(718)624-8839

Percentage of the business in native species: 35

Type of business:	Primary plant focus:	Wildflower seed offered:	Propagation methods:
✓Retail	Trees	✓Regional Seed Mixes	Propagate Plants
✓Wholesale	Shrubs	✓Custom Mixes	Collect Wild Plants
✓Mail Order	Grasses	✓Individual Species Seed	Collect Wild Seed
Price List/Catalog	✓Wildflowers	✓Contract Grow Seed	

Panfield Nurseries, Inc.
322 Southdown Road
Huntington, NY 11743
(516)427-0112

Percentage of the business in native species: 15

Type of business:	Primary plant focus:	Wildflower seed offered:	Propagation methods:
✓Retail	✓Trees	✓Regional Seed Mixes	✓Propagate Plants
✓Wholesale	✓Shrubs	Custom Mixes	Collect Wild Plants
Mail Order	✓Grasses	Individual Species Seed	Collect Wild Seed
Price List/Catalog	✓Wildflowers	Contract Grow Seed	

OKLAHOMA

Valley View Nursery
HC 73, Box 36
Parkhill, OK 74451
(918)456-3241

Percentage of the business in native species: 5

Type of business:	Primary plant focus:	Wildflower seed offered:	Propagation methods:
✓Retail	✓Trees	Regional Seed Mixes	✓Propagate Plants
✓Wholesale	✓Shrubs	Custom Mixes	Collect Wild Plants
✓Mail Order	Grasses	Individual Species Seed	Collect Wild Seed
Price List/Catalog	Wildflowers	Contract Grow Seed	

OREGON

Bovees Nursery, The
1737 SW Coronado Street
Portland, OR 97219-7654
(503)244-9341

Percentage of the business in native species: 10

Type of business:	Primary plant focus:	Wildflower seed offered:	Propagation methods:
✓Retail	Trees	Regional Seed Mixes	✓Propagate Plants
Wholesale	✓Shrubs	Custom Mixes	Collect Wild Plants
✓Mail Order	Grasses	Individual Species Seed	Collect Wild Seed
Price List/Catalog	Wildflowers	Contract Grow Seed	

Callahan Seeds
6045 Foley Lane
Central Point, OR 97502
(503)855-1164

Percentage of the business in native species: 90

Type of business:	Primary plant focus:	Wildflower seed offered:	Propagation methods:
✓Retail	✓Trees	Regional Seed Mixes	Propagate Plants
✓Wholesale	✓Shrubs	Custom Mixes	Collect Wild Plants
✓Mail Order	Grasses	Individual Species Seed	Collect Wild Seed
Price List/Catalog	Wildflowers	Contract Grow Seed	

Forestfarm
990 Tetherwire Road
Williams, OR 97544
(503)846-6963

Percentage of the business in native species: 25

Type of business:	Primary plant focus:	Wildflower seed offered:	Propagation methods:
✓ Retail	✓ Trees	Regional Seed Mixes	✓ Propagate Plants
✓ Wholesale	✓ Shrubs	Custom Mixes	Collect Wild Plants
✓ Mail Order	Grasses	Individual Species Seed	Collect Wild Seed
Price List/Catalog	✓ Wildflowers	Contract Grow Seed	

Lofts/Great Western Seeds
P. O. Box 387, 810 Jackson Street
Albany, OR 97321
(503)928-3100

Percentage of the business in native species:

Type of business:	Primary plant focus:	Wildflower seed offered:	Propagation methods:
Retail	Trees	✓ Regional Seed Mixes	Propagate Plants
✓ Wholesale	Shrubs	✓ Custom Mixes	Collect Wild Plants
✓ Mail Order	✓ Grasses	✓ Individual Species Seed	Collect Wild Seed
Price List/Catalog	✓ Wildflowers	✓ Contract Grow Seed	

Nature's Garden
Rt. 1, Box 488
Beaverton, OR 97007
(503)649-6772

Percentage of the business in native species: 5

Type of business:	Primary plant focus:	Wildflower seed offered:	Propagation methods:
✓ Retail	Trees	Regional Seed Mixes	✓ Propagate Plants
✓ Wholesale	Shrubs	Custom Mixes	Collect Wild Plants
✓ Mail Order	Grasses	✓ Individual Species Seed	Collect Wild Seed
Price List/Catalog	✓ Wildflowers	Contract Grow Seed	

Northwest Biological Enterprises
23351 SW Basky Dell Lane
West Linn, OR 97068
(503)638-6029

Percentage of the business in native species: 100

Type of business:	Primary plant focus:	Wildflower seed offered:	Propagation methods:
✓Retail	✓Trees	Regional Seed Mixes	✓Propagate Plants
✓Wholesale	✓Shrubs	Custom Mixes	✓Collect Wild Plants
✓Mail Order	Grasses	Individual Species Seed	✓Collect Wild Seed
Price List/Catalog	✓Wildflowers	Contract Grow Seed	

Russell Graham
4030 Eagle Crest Road, NW
Salem, OR 97304
(503)362-1135

Percentage of the business in native species: 25

Type of business:	Primary plant focus:	Wildflower seed offered:	Propagation methods:
✓Retail	Trees	Regional Seed Mixes	✓Propagate Plants
✓Wholesale	Shrubs	Custom Mixes	Collect Wild Plants
✓Mail Order	Grasses	Individual Species Seed	Collect Wild Seed
Price List/Catalog	✓Wildflowers	Contract Grow Seed	

Siskiyou Rare Plant Nursery
2825 Cummings Road
Medford, OR 97501-1524
(503)772-6846

Percentage of the business in native species: 30

Type of business:	Primary plant focus:	Wildflower seed offered:	Propagation methods:
✓Retail	Trees	Regional Seed Mixes	✓Propagate Plants
Wholesale	Shrubs	Custom Mixes	Collect Wild Plants
✓Mail Order	Grasses	Individual Species Seed	Collect Wild Seed
Price List/Catalog	✓Wildflowers	Contract Grow Seed	

Turf Seed, Inc.
P. O. Box 250
Hubbard, OR 97032
(503)981-9571

Percentage of the business in native species: 10

Type of business:	Primary plant focus:	Wildflower seed offered:	Propagation methods:
Retail	Trees	Regional Seed Mixes	Propagate Plants
✓ Wholesale	Shrubs	✓ Custom Mixes	Collect Wild Plants
Mail Order	✓ Grasses	✓ Individual Species Seed	Collect Wild Seed
Price List/Catalog	✓ Wildflowers	✓ Contract Grow Seed	

Wrights-Browning Nursery
Rt. 1, Box 1230
Bandonis, OR 97411
(503)347-9657

Percentage of the business in native species: 100

Type of business:	Primary plant focus:	Wildflower seed offered:	Propagation methods:
Retail	✓ Trees	Regional Seed Mixes	✓ Propagate Plants
✓ Wholesale	✓ Shrubs	Custom Mixes	✓ Collect Wild Plants
✓ Mail Order	Grasses	Individual Species Seed	✓ Collect Wild Seed
Price List/Catalog	✓ Wildflowers	Contract Grow Seed	

PENNSYLVANIA

Appalachian Wildflower Nursery
Rt. 1, Box 275A
Reedsville, PA 17084
(717)667-6998

Percentage of the business in native species: 50

Type of business:	Primary plant focus:	Wildflower seed offered:	Propagation methods:
✓ Retail	✓ Trees	Regional Seed Mixes	✓ Propagate Plants
Wholesale	✓ Shrubs	Custom Mixes	Collect Wild Plants
✓ Mail Order	Grasses	✓ Individual Species Seed	✓ Collect Wild Seed
Price List/Catalog	✓ Wildflowers	Contract Grow Seed	

Carino Nurseries
P. O. Box 538
Indiana, PA 15701
(412)463-3350

Percentage of the business in native species: 25

Type of business:	Primary plant focus:	Wildflower seed offered:	Propagation methods:
Retail	✓ Trees	Regional Seed Mixes	✓ Propagate Plants
✓ Wholesale	Shrubs	Custom Mixes	Collect Wild Plants
✓ Mail Order	Grasses	Individual Species Seed	Collect Wild Seed
Price List/Catalog	Wildflowers	Contract Grow Seed	

Giunta's Herb Farm
RD 1, Box 706
Honey Brook, PA 19344
(215)273-2863

Percentage of the business in native species: 30

Type of business:	Primary plant focus:	Wildflower seed offered:	Propagation methods:
✓ Retail	Trees	Regional Seed Mixes	✓ Propagate Plants
Wholesale	Shrubs	Custom Mixes	Collect Wild Plants
✓ Mail Order	Grasses	Individual Species Seed	Collect Wild Seed
Price List/Catalog	✓ Wildflowers	Contract Grow Seed	

Natural Landscapes
354 North Jennersville Road
West Grove, PA 19390
(215)869-3788

Percentage of the business in native species: 90

Type of business:	Primary plant focus:	Wildflower seed offered:	Propagation methods:
Retail	✓ Trees	Regional Seed Mixes	✓ Propagate Plants
✓ Wholesale	✓ Shrubs	Custom Mixes	Collect Wild Plants
Mail Order	Grasses	Individual Species Seed	Collect Wild Seed
Price List/Catalog	✓ Wildflowers	Contract Grow Seed	

Painted Meadows Seed Co.
P. O. Box 1865
Kingston, PA 18704
(717)283-2911

Percentage of the business in native species:

Type of business:	Primary plant focus:	Wildflower seed offered:	Propagation methods:
✓Retail	Trees	✓Regional Seed Mixes	Propagate Plants
✓Wholesale	Shrubs	✓Custom Mixes	Collect Wild Plants
✓Mail Order	Grasses	Individual Species Seed	Collect Wild Seed
Price List/Catalog	✓Wildflowers	Contract Grow Seed	

Strathmeyer Forests, Inc.
255 Zeigler Road
Dover, PA 17315
(717)292-5683

Percentage of the business in native species: 75

Type of business:	Primary plant focus:	Wildflower seed offered:	Propagation methods:
Retail	✓Trees	Regional Seed Mixes	✓Propagate Plants
✓Wholesale	Shrubs	Custom Mixes	Collect Wild Plants
✓Mail Order	Grasses	Individual Species Seed	Collect Wild Seed
Price List/Catalog	Wildflowers	Contract Grow Seed	

Vick's Wildgardens
Box 115
Gladwyne, PA 19035
(215)525-6773

Percentage of the business in native species: 50

Type of business:	Primary plant focus:	Wildflower seed offered:	Propagation methods:
✓Retail	✓Trees	Regional Seed Mixes	✓Propagate Plants
Wholesale	✓Shrubs	Custom Mixes	Collect Wild Plants
✓Mail Order	Grasses	Individual Species Seed	Collect Wild Seed
Price List/Catalog	✓Wildflowers	Contract Grow Seed	

Wildflower Patch
442RC Brookside Drive
Walnutport, PA 18088
(215)767-3195

Percentage of the business in native species: 80

Type of business:	Primary plant focus:	Wildflower seed offered:	Propagation methods:
✓Retail	Trees	✓Regional Seed Mixes	✓Propagate Plants
Wholesale	Shrubs	✓Custom Mixes	Collect Wild Plants
✓Mail Order	Grasses	✓Individual Species Seed	✓Collect Wild Seed
✓Price List/Catalog	✓Wildflowers	Contract Grow Seed	

SOUTH CAROLINA

George W. Park Seed Co., Inc.
P. O. Box 31
Greenwood, SC 29647-0001
(803)223-7333

Percentage of the business in native species: 4

Type of business:	Primary plant focus:	Wildflower seed offered:	Propagation methods:
✓Retail	Trees	✓Regional Seed Mixes	Propagate Plants
✓Wholesale	✓Shrubs	✓Custom Mixes	Collect Wild Plants
✓Mail Order	✓Grasses	✓Individual Species Seed	Collect Wild Seed
Price List/Catalog	✓Wildflowers	Contract Grow Seed	

Oak Hill Farm
204 Pressley Street
Clover, SC 29710
(803)222-4245

Percentage of the business in native species: 99

Type of business:	Primary plant focus:	Wildflower seed offered:	Propagation methods:
✓Retail	Trees	Regional Seed Mixes	✓Propagate Plants
✓Wholesale	✓Shrubs	Custom Mixes	Collect Wild Plants
✓Mail Order	Grasses	✓Individual Species Seed	Collect Wild Seed
Price List/Catalog	✓Wildflowers	Contract Grow Seed	

Woodlanders, Inc.
1128 Colleton Avenue
Aiken, SC 29801
(803)648-7522

Percentage of the business in native species: 60

Type of business:	Primary plant focus:	Wildflower seed offered:	Propagation methods:
✓ Retail	✓ Trees	Regional Seed Mixes	✓ Propagate Plants
Wholesale	✓ Shrubs	Custom Mixes	Collect Wild Plants
✓ Mail Order	Grasses	Individual Species Seed	Collect Wild Seed
Price List/Catalog	✓ Wildflowers	Contract Grow Seed	

SOUTH DAKOTA

Cenex Seed Plant
Box 964
Sioux Falls, SD 57101
(605)336-0623

Percentage of the business in native species: 5

Type of business:	Primary plant focus:	Wildflower seed offered:	Propagation methods:
Retail	Trees	Regional Seed Mixes	Propagate Plants
✓ Wholesale	Shrubs	Custom Mixes	Collect Wild Plants
Mail Order	✓ Grasses	Individual Species Seed	Collect Wild Seed
Price List/Catalog	Wildflowers	Contract Grow Seed	

Echinational Plant Products
602 Jefferson Street
Vermillion, SD 57069
(605)624-6849

Percentage of the business in native species: 100

Type of business:	Primary plant focus:	Wildflower seed offered:	Propagation methods:
Retail	Trees	Regional Seed Mixes	✓ Propagate Plants
Wholesale	Shrubs	Custom Mixes	Collect Wild Plants
✓ Mail Order	Grasses	✓ Individual Species Seed	✓ Collect Wild Seed
Price List/Catalog	✓ Wildflowers	Contract Grow Seed	

Rethke Nursery
P. O. Box 82
Milbank, SD 57252
(605)432-6073

Percentage of the business in native species: 80

Type of business:	Primary plant focus:	Wildflower seed offered:	Propagation methods:
Retail	✓Trees	Regional Seed Mixes	✓Propagate Plants
✓Wholesale	✓Shrubs	Custom Mixes	✓Collect Wild Plants
Mail Order	Grasses	Individual Species Seed	Collect Wild Seed
Price List/Catalog	Wildflowers	Contract Grow Seed	

TENNESSEE

Native Gardens
Rt. 1, Box 494 / Fisher Lane
Greenback, TN 37742
(615)856-3350

Percentage of the business in native species: 75

Type of business:	Primary plant focus:	Wildflower seed offered:	Propagation methods:
✓Retail	✓Trees	Regional Seed Mixes	✓Propagate Plants
✓Wholesale	✓Shrubs	Custom Mixes	Collect Wild Plants
✓Mail Order	Grasses	✓Individual Species Seed	✓Collect Wild Seed
Price List/Catalog	✓Wildflowers	✓Contract Grow Seed	

Natural Gardens
113 Jasper Lane
Oak Ridge, TN 37830
(615)482-6746

Percentage of the business in native species: 85

Type of business:	Primary plant focus:	Wildflower seed offered:	Propagation methods:
✓Retail	Trees	Regional Seed Mixes	✓Propagate Plants
Wholesale	Shrubs	Custom Mixes	Collect Wild Plants
✓Mail Order	Grasses	✓Individual Species Seed	✓Collect Wild Seed
Price List/Catalog	✓Wildflowers	Contract Grow Seed	

Sunlight Gardens, Inc.
Rt. 3, Box 286TX
Loudon, TN 37774
(615)986-6071

Percentage of the business in native species: 95

Type of business:	Primary plant focus:	Wildflower seed offered:	Propagation methods:
✔Retail	Trees	Regional Seed Mixes	✔Propagate Plants
✔Wholesale	Shrubs	Custom Mixes	Collect Wild Plants
✔Mail Order	Grasses	✔Individual Species Seed	✔Collect Wild Seed
Price List/Catalog	✔Wildflowers	✔Contract Grow Seed	

TEXAS

Aldridge Nursery, The
Rt. 1, Box 8
Von Ormy, TX 78073
(512)622-3491

Percentage of the business in native species: 10

Type of business:	Primary plant focus:	Wildflower seed offered:	Propagation methods:
Retail	✔Trees	Regional Seed Mixes	✔Propagate Plants
✔Wholesale	✔Shrubs	Custom Mixes	Collect Wild Plants
Mail Order	Grasses	Individual Species Seed	Collect Wild Seed
Price List/Catalog	Wildflowers	Contract Grow Seed	

Antique Rose Emporium
Rt. 5, Box 143
Brenham, TX 77833
(409)836-9051

Percentage of the business in native species: 20

Type of business:	Primary plant focus:	Wildflower seed offered:	Propagation methods:
✔Retail	✔Trees	Regional Seed Mixes	✔Propagate Plants
✔Wholesale	✔Shrubs	Custom Mixes	Collect Wild Plants
✔Mail Order	Grasses	Individual Species Seed	Collect Wild Seed
Price List/Catalog	✔Wildflowers	Contract Grow Seed	

Anton Seed Co., Inc.
P. O. Box 667
Lockhart, TX 78644
(512)398-2433

Percentage of the business in native species: 1

Type of business:	Primary plant focus:	Wildflower seed offered:	Propagation methods:
✓Retail	Trees	Regional Seed Mixes	Propagate Plants
✓Wholesale	Shrubs	Custom Mixes	Collect Wild Plants
Mail Order	✓Grasses	Individual Species Seed	Collect Wild Seed
Price List/Catalog	Wildflowers	Contract Grow Seed	

Bamert Seed Co.
Rt. 3, Box 1120
Muleshoe, TX 79347
(806)272-4787

Percentage of the business in native species: 75

Type of business:	Primary plant focus:	Wildflower seed offered:	Propagation methods:
✓Retail	Trees	Regional Seed Mixes	✓Propagate Plants
✓Wholesale	Shrubs	Custom Mixes	Collect Wild Plants
✓Mail Order	✓Grasses	Individual Species Seed	Collect Wild Seed
Price List/Catalog	Wildflowers	Contract Grow Seed	

Barton Springs Nursery
428 Sterzing Street
Austin, TX 78704
(512)474-9000

Percentage of the business in native species: 50

Type of business:	Primary plant focus:	Wildflower seed offered:	Propagation methods:
✓Retail	✓Trees	✓Regional Seed Mixes	✓Propagate Plants
✓Wholesale	✓Shrubs	Custom Mixes	✓Collect Wild Plants
Mail Order	Grasses	✓Individual Species Seed	Collect Wild Seed
Price List/Catalog	✓Wildflowers	Contract Grow Seed	

Big Tree Farm Nursery
Rt. 1, Box 627A
Sanger, TX 76266
(817)458-4373

Percentage of the business in native species: 30

Type of business:	Primary plant focus:	Wildflower seed offered:	Propagation methods:
✓ Retail	✓ Trees	✓ Regional Seed Mixes	✓ Propagate Plants
✓ Wholesale	✓ Shrubs	Custom Mixes	✓ Collect Wild Plants
Mail Order	Grasses	✓ Individual Species Seed	✓ Collect Wild Seed
Price List/Catalog	✓ Wildflowers	Contract Grow Seed	

Breed & Co.
718 West 29th Street
Austin, TX 78705
(512)474-7058

Percentage of the business in native species: 30

Type of business:	Primary plant focus:	Wildflower seed offered:	Propagation methods:
✓ Retail	Trees	✓ Regional Seed Mixes	Propagate Plants
Wholesale	Shrubs	Custom Mixes	Collect Wild Plants
Mail Order	Grasses	✓ Individual Species Seed	Collect Wild Seed
Price List/Catalog	✓ Wildflowers	Contract Grow Seed	

Browning Seed Inc.
Box 1836
Plainview, TX 79072
(806)293-5271

Percentage of the business in native species: 25

Type of business:	Primary plant focus:	Wildflower seed offered:	Propagation methods:
✓ Retail	Trees	✓ Regional Seed Mixes	✓ Propagate Plants
✓ Wholesale	✓ Shrubs	✓ Custom Mixes	✓ Collect Wild Plants
✓ Mail Order	✓ Grasses	✓ Individual Species Seed	✓ Collect Wild Seed
Price List/Catalog	✓ Wildflowers	✓ Contract Grow Seed	

Buchanan's Native Plants
111 Heights Blvd.
Houston, TX 77007
(713)861-5702

Percentage of the business in native species: 50

Type of business:	Primary plant focus:	Wildflower seed offered:	Propagation methods:
✓Retail	✓Trees	✓Regional Seed Mixes	Propagate Plants
Wholesale	✓Shrubs	Custom Mixes	Collect Wild Plants
Mail Order	Grasses	Individual Species Seed	Collect Wild Seed
Price List/Catalog	✓Wildflowers	Contract Grow Seed	

Buck's Sod & Sales, Inc.
Box 906
Sweeny, TX 77480
(409)548-3776

Percentage of the business in native species: 100

Type of business:	Primary plant focus:	Wildflower seed offered:	Propagation methods:
✓Retail	✓Trees	Regional Seed Mixes	✓Propagate Plants
✓Wholesale	Shrubs	Custom Mixes	Collect Wild Plants
Mail Order	Grasses	Individual Species Seed	Collect Wild Seed
Price List/Catalog	Wildflowers	Contract Grow Seed	

Cactus Farm
Rt. 5, Box 1610
Nacogdoches, TX 75961
(409)560-6406

Percentage of the business in native species: 50

Type of business:	Primary plant focus:	Wildflower seed offered:	Propagation methods:
Retail	Trees	Regional Seed Mixes	✓Propagate Plants
✓Wholesale	Shrubs	Custom Mixes	Collect Wild Plants
✓Mail Order	Grasses	Individual Species Seed	Collect Wild Seed
Price List/Catalog	Wildflowers	Contract Grow Seed	

Callahan's General Store
501 Bastrop Hwy.
Austin, TX 78741
(512)385-3452

Percentage of the business in native species: 10

Type of business:	Primary plant focus:	Wildflower seed offered:	Propagation methods:
✓ Retail	✓ Trees	✓ Regional Seed Mixes	Propagate Plants
✓ Wholesale	✓ Shrubs	Custom Mixes	Collect Wild Plants
Mail Order	✓ Grasses	✓ Individual Species Seed	Collect Wild Seed
Price List/Catalog	✓ Wildflowers	Contract Grow Seed	

Clayton's Garden World
P. O. Box 1336
San Marcos, TX 78667
(512)353-8125

Percentage of the business in native species: 25

Type of business:	Primary plant focus:	Wildflower seed offered:	Propagation methods:
✓ Retail	✓ Trees	✓ Regional Seed Mixes	✓ Propagate Plants
Wholesale	✓ Shrubs	✓ Custom Mixes	✓ Collect Wild Plants
Mail Order	✓ Grasses	✓ Individual Species Seed	✓ Collect Wild Seed
Price List/Catalog	✓ Wildflowers	Contract Grow Seed	

Containerized Plants
Rt. 5, Box 143
Brenham, TX 77833
(409)836-9051

Percentage of the business in native species: 20

Type of business:	Primary plant focus:	Wildflower seed offered:	Propagation methods:
Retail	✓ Trees	Regional Seed Mixes	✓ Propagate Plants
✓ Wholesale	✓ Shrubs	Custom Mixes	Collect Wild Plants
Mail Order	Grasses	Individual Species Seed	Collect Wild Seed
Price List/Catalog	Wildflowers	Contract Grow Seed	

Dallas Nature Center Nursery
7575 Wheatland Road
Dallas, TX 75249
(214)296-1955

Percentage of the business in native species: 90

Type of business:	Primary plant focus:	Wildflower seed offered:	Propagation methods:
✓ Retail	✓ Trees	✓ Regional Seed Mixes	✓ Propagate Plants
✓ Wholesale	✓ Shrubs	✓ Custom Mixes	✓ Collect Wild Plants
✓ Mail Order	✓ Grasses	✓ Individual Species Seed	✓ Collect Wild Seed
Price List/Catalog	✓ Wildflowers	Contract Grow Seed	

Days of Thyme and Roses
Route 3, Box 134C
Montgomery, TX 77356
(409)588-1799

Percentage of the business in native species: 75

Type of business:	Primary plant focus:	Wildflower seed offered:	Propagation methods:
✓ Retail	Trees	Regional Seed Mixes	✓ Propagate Plants
✓ Wholesale	✓ Shrubs	Custom Mixes	Collect Wild Plants
Mail Order	Grasses	Individual Species Seed	Collect Wild Seed
✓ Price List/Catalog	✓ Wildflowers	✓ Contract Grow Seed	

Dodd's Family Tree Nursery, Inc.
515 West Main
Fredericksburg, TX 78624
(512)997-9571

Percentage of the business in native species: 15

Type of business:	Primary plant focus:	Wildflower seed offered:	Propagation methods:
✓ Retail	✓ Trees	✓ Regional Seed Mixes	Propagate Plants
Wholesale	✓ Shrubs	Custom Mixes	Collect Wild Plants
✓ Mail Order	✓ Grasses	✓ Individual Species Seed	Collect Wild Seed
Price List/Catalog	✓ Wildflowers	✓ Contract Grow Seed	

Doremus Wholesale Nursery
Rt. 2, Box 750
Warren, TX 77664
(409)547-3536

Percentage of the business in native species: 50

Type of business:	Primary plant focus:	Wildflower seed offered:	Propagation methods:
Retail	✓Trees	Regional Seed Mixes	✓Propagate Plants
✓Wholesale	✓Shrubs	Custom Mixes	Collect Wild Plants
Mail Order	Grasses	Individual Species Seed	✓Collect Wild Seed
Price List/Catalog	Wildflowers	Contract Grow Seed	

Douglass W. King Co., Inc.
P. O. Box 200320
San Antonio, TX 78220-0320
(512)661-4191

Percentage of the business in native species: 10

Type of business:	Primary plant focus:	Wildflower seed offered:	Propagation methods:
✓Retail	Trees	✓Regional Seed Mixes	✓Propagate Plants
✓Wholesale	Shrubs	Custom Mixes	Collect Wild Plants
✓Mail Order	✓Grasses	✓Individual Species Seed	✓Collect Wild Seed
Price List/Catalog	✓Wildflowers	✓Contract Grow Seed	

Ecotones
P. O. Box L
Kirbyville, TX 75956
(409)423-4995

Percentage of the business in native species: 95

Type of business:	Primary plant focus:	Wildflower seed offered:	Propagation methods:
Retail	✓Trees	Regional Seed Mixes	✓Propagate Plants
✓Wholesale	✓Shrubs	Custom Mixes	✓Collect Wild Plants
Mail Order	✓Grasses	Individual Species Seed	✓Collect Wild Seed
Price List/Catalog	✓Wildflowers	Contract Grow Seed	

Foster-Rambie Grass Seed
326 North Second Street
Uvalde, TX 78801
(512)278-2711

Percentage of the business in native species: 20

Type of business:	Primary plant focus:	Wildflower seed offered:	Propagation methods:
✓Retail	Trees	Regional Seed Mixes	Propagate Plants
✓Wholesale	Shrubs	Custom Mixes	Collect Wild Plants
✓Mail Order	✓Grasses	Individual Species Seed	Collect Wild Seed
Price List/Catalog	Wildflowers	Contract Grow Seed	

Gardens
1818 West 35th Street
Austin, TX 78703
(512)451-5490

Percentage of the business in native species: 45

Type of business:	Primary plant focus:	Wildflower seed offered:	Propagation methods:
✓Retail	✓Trees	✓Regional Seed Mixes	✓Propagate Plants
Wholesale	✓Shrubs	Custom Mixes	Collect Wild Plants
Mail Order	✓Grasses	✓Individual Species Seed	Collect Wild Seed
Price List/Catalog	✓Wildflowers	Contract Grow Seed	

Garrison Seed & Co., Inc.
P. O. Drawer 2420
Hereford, TX 79045
(806)364-0560

Percentage of the business in native species: 15

Type of business:	Primary plant focus:	Wildflower seed offered:	Propagation methods:
✓Retail	Trees	Regional Seed Mixes	✓Propagate Plants
✓Wholesale	Shrubs	Custom Mixes	Collect Wild Plants
Mail Order	✓Grasses	Individual Species Seed	Collect Wild Seed
Price List/Catalog	Wildflowers	Contract Grow Seed	

Gone Native
Rt. 4, 2001 Broken Hills East
Midland, TX 79701
(915)686-9632

Percentage of the business in native species: 80

Type of business:	Primary plant focus:	Wildflower seed offered:	Propagation methods:
✓ Retail	✓ Trees	Regional Seed Mixes	✓ Propagate Plants
✓ Wholesale	✓ Shrubs	Custom Mixes	✓ Collect Wild Plants
Mail Order	Grasses	Individual Species Seed	Collect Wild Seed
Price List/Catalog	✓ Wildflowers	Contract Grow Seed	

Green Horizons
218 Quinlan, Suite 571
Kerrville, TX 78028
(512)257-5141

Percentage of the business in native species: 100

Type of business:	Primary plant focus:	Wildflower seed offered:	Propagation methods:
✓ Retail	Trees	✓ Regional Seed Mixes	✓ Propagate Plants
Wholesale	Shrubs	✓ Custom Mixes	Collect Wild Plants
✓ Mail Order	Grasses	✓ Individual Species Seed	✓ Collect Wild Seed
Price List/Catalog	✓ Wildflowers	Contract Grow Seed	

Green 'n Growing
P.O. Box 855
Pflugerville, TX 78660
(512)251-3262

Percentage of the business in native species:

Type of business:	Primary plant focus:	Wildflower seed offered:	Propagation methods:
✓ Retail	✓ Trees	✓ Regional Seed Mixes	✓ Propagate Plants
Wholesale	✓ Shrubs	Custom Mixes	Collect Wild Plants
Mail Order	✓ Grasses	✓ Individual Species Seed	Collect Wild Seed
Price List/Catalog	✓ Wildflowers	Contract Grow Seed	

Groundskeeper, The
10201 Research Blvd.
Austin, TX 78759
(512)346-4553

Percentage of the business in native species: 50

Type of business:	Primary plant focus:	Wildflower seed offered:	Propagation methods:
✓ Retail	✓ Trees	✓ Regional Seed Mixes	Propagate Plants
Wholesale	✓ Shrubs	✓ Custom Mixes	Collect Wild Plants
Mail Order	✓ Grasses	✓ Individual Species Seed	Collect Wild Seed
Price List/Catalog	✓ Wildflowers	Contract Grow Seed	

Gunsight Mountain Ranch & Nursery
P.O. Box 86
Tarpley, TX 78883
(512)562-3225

Percentage of the business in native species: 95

Type of business:	Primary plant focus:	Wildflower seed offered:	Propagation methods:
✓ Retail	✓ Trees	Regional Seed Mixes	✓ Propagate Plants
✓ Wholesale	✓ Shrubs	Custom Mixes	Collect Wild Plants
✓ Mail Order	Grasses	Individual Species Seed	✓ Collect Wild Seed
Price List/Catalog	Wildflowers	Contract Grow Seed	

Harpool Seed Inc.
P. O. Box 15487
Dallas, TX 75212
(214)421-7181

Percentage of the business in native species: 10

Type of business:	Primary plant focus:	Wildflower seed offered:	Propagation methods:
Retail	Trees	✓ Regional Seed Mixes	Propagate Plants
✓ Wholesale	Shrubs	✓ Custom Mixes	Collect Wild Plants
Mail Order	Grasses	✓ Individual Species Seed	Collect Wild Seed
Price List/Catalog	✓ Wildflowers	✓ Contract Grow Seed	

Harpool Seed Inc.
10220 Metropolitan Drive, Suite C
Austin, TX 78758
(512)834-9359

Percentage of the business in native species: 10

Type of business:	Primary plant focus:	Wildflower seed offered:	Propagation methods:
Retail	Trees	✓Regional Seed Mixes	Propagate Plants
✓Wholesale	Shrubs	✓Custom Mixes	Collect Wild Plants
Mail Order	Grasses	✓Individual Species Seed	Collect Wild Seed
Price List/Catalog	✓Wildflowers	✓Contract Grow Seed	

Harpool Seed Inc.
P. O. Drawer B
Denton, TX 76202
(817)387-0541

Percentage of the business in native species: 10

Type of business:	Primary plant focus:	Wildflower seed offered:	Propagation methods:
Retail	Trees	✓Regional Seed Mixes	Propagate Plants
✓Wholesale	Shrubs	✓Custom Mixes	Collect Wild Plants
Mail Order	✓Grasses	✓Individual Species Seed	Collect Wild Seed
Price List/Catalog	✓Wildflowers	✓Contract Grow Seed	

Harpool Seed Inc.
1427 Greengrass Drive
Houston, TX 77008
(713)861-4771

Percentage of the business in native species: 10

Type of business:	Primary plant focus:	Wildflower seed offered:	Propagation methods:
Retail	Trees	✓Regional Seed Mixes	Propagate Plants
✓Wholesale	Shrubs	✓Custom Mixes	Collect Wild Plants
Mail Order	Grasses	✓Individual Species Seed	Collect Wild Seed
Price List/Catalog	✓Wildflowers	✓Contract Grow Seed	

Heep's Nursery
Rt. 3, Palm Drive
Harlingen, TX 78550
(512)423-4513

Percentage of the business in native species: 80

Type of business:	Primary plant focus:	Wildflower seed offered:	Propagation methods:
✓Retail	✓Trees	Regional Seed Mixes	✓Propagate Plants
✓Wholesale	✓Shrubs	Custom Mixes	Collect Wild Plants
Mail Order	Grasses	Individual Species Seed	Collect Wild Seed
Price List/Catalog	Wildflowers	Contract Grow Seed	

Hill Country Landscape
P. O. Box 201297, 11603 Jollyville Road
Austin, TX 78720
(512)258-0093

Percentage of the business in native species: 10

Type of business:	Primary plant focus:	Wildflower seed offered:	Propagation methods:
✓Retail	✓Trees	Regional Seed Mixes	Propagate Plants
Wholesale	✓Shrubs	Custom Mixes	✓Collect Wild Plants
Mail Order	Grasses	Individual Species Seed	Collect Wild Seed
Price List/Catalog	Wildflowers	Contract Grow Seed	

Horizon Seeds Inc.
Box 886, 7 miles East on Hwy 60
Hereford, TX 79045
(806)258-7288

Percentage of the business in native species: 100

Type of business:	Primary plant focus:	Wildflower seed offered:	Propagation methods:
✓Retail	Trees	Regional Seed Mixes	✓Propagate Plants
✓Wholesale	Shrubs	✓Custom Mixes	Collect Wild Plants
✓Mail Order	✓Grasses	✓Individual Species Seed	✓Collect Wild Seed
Price List/Catalog	✓Wildflowers	Contract Grow Seed	

Imperial Growers
Rt. 2, Box 55 / County Road 4545
Winnsboro, TX 75494
(214)365-2660

Percentage of the business in native species: 10

Type of business:	Primary plant focus:	Wildflower seed offered:	Propagation methods:
✓ Retail	✓ Trees	Regional Seed Mixes	✓ Propagate Plants
✓ Wholesale	✓ Shrubs	Custom Mixes	✓ Collect Wild Plants
Mail Order	Grasses	Individual Species Seed	Collect Wild Seed
Price List/Catalog	Wildflowers	Contract Grow Seed	

J'Don Seeds International
P. O. Box 10998-533
Austin, TX 78766
(512)343-6360

Percentage of the business in native species: 95

Type of business:	Primary plant focus:	Wildflower seed offered:	Propagation methods:
✓ Retail	Trees	✓ Regional Seed Mixes	Propagate Plants
✓ Wholesale	Shrubs	✓ Custom Mixes	Collect Wild Plants
✓ Mail Order	Grasses	✓ Individual Species Seed	✓ Collect Wild Seed
Price List/Catalog	✓ Wildflowers	Contract Grow Seed	

Jenco Wholesale Nurseries
P. O. Box 513, 235 Lodge Road
Coppell, TX 75019
(214)462-0011

Percentage of the business in native species: 5

Type of business:	Primary plant focus:	Wildflower seed offered:	Propagation methods:
Retail	✓ Trees	✓ Regional Seed Mixes	✓ Propagate Plants
✓ Wholesale	✓ Shrubs	✓ Custom Mixes	✓ Collect Wild Plants
Mail Order	Grasses	✓ Individual Species Seed	Collect Wild Seed
Price List/Catalog	✓ Wildflowers	Contract Grow Seed	

Jenco Wholesale Nurseries
P. O. Box 15827, Dick Price & County Road 2051
Fort Worth, TX 76119
(817)478-5903

Percentage of the business in native species: 5

Type of business:	Primary plant focus:	Wildflower seed offered:	Propagation methods:
Retail	✓Trees	✓Regional Seed Mixes	✓Propagate Plants
✓Wholesale	✓Shrubs	✓Custom Mixes	✓Collect Wild Plants
Mail Order	Grasses	✓Individual Species Seed	Collect Wild Seed
Price List/Catalog	✓Wildflowers	Contract Grow Seed	

Jenco Wholesale Nurseries
P. O. Box 16625, 1211 Alcove Avenue
Lubbock, TX 79407
(806)799-3646

Percentage of the business in native species: 5

Type of business:	Primary plant focus:	Wildflower seed offered:	Propagation methods:
Retail	✓Trees	✓Regional Seed Mixes	✓Propagate Plants
✓Wholesale	✓Shrubs	✓Custom Mixes	✓Collect Wild Plants
Mail Order	Grasses	✓Individual Species Seed	Collect Wild Seed
Price List/Catalog	✓Wildflowers	Contract Grow Seed	

Jenco Wholesale Nurseries
P. O. Box 200755, 4601 Switch Willo Road
Austin, TX 78720-0755
(512)346-0562

Percentage of the business in native species: 5

Type of business:	Primary plant focus:	Wildflower seed offered:	Propagation methods:
Retail	✓Trees	✓Regional Seed Mixes	✓Propagate Plants
✓Wholesale	✓Shrubs	✓Custom Mixes	✓Collect Wild Plants
Mail Order	Grasses	✓Individual Species Seed	Collect Wild Seed
Price List/Catalog	✓Wildflowers	Contract Grow Seed	

Lone Star Growers
Rt. 9, Box 220 / 7960 Cagnon Road
San Antonio, TX 78227
(512)677-8020

Percentage of the business in native species: 15

Type of business:	Primary plant focus:	Wildflower seed offered:	Propagation methods:
Retail	✓ Trees	Regional Seed Mixes	✓ Propagate Plants
✓ Wholesale	✓ Shrubs	Custom Mixes	Collect Wild Plants
Mail Order	✓ Grasses	Individual Species Seed	Collect Wild Seed
✓ Price List/Catalog	Wildflowers	Contract Grow Seed	

Lorany's Garden Center
11902 Alief-Clodine Road
Houston, TX 77082
(713)530-1311

Percentage of the business in native species: 15

Type of business:	Primary plant focus:	Wildflower seed offered:	Propagation methods:
✓ Retail	✓ Trees	✓ Regional Seed Mixes	Propagate Plants
Wholesale	✓ Shrubs	Custom Mixes	✓ Collect Wild Plants
Mail Order	Grasses	✓ Individual Species Seed	Collect Wild Seed
Price List/Catalog	✓ Wildflowers	Contract Grow Seed	

Lowrey Nursery, The
2323 Sleepy Hollow Road
Conroe, TX 77385
(713)367-4076

Percentage of the business in native species: 85

Type of business:	Primary plant focus:	Wildflower seed offered:	Propagation methods:
✓ Retail	✓ Trees	✓ Regional Seed Mixes	✓ Propagate Plants
Wholesale	✓ Shrubs	Custom Mixes	✓ Collect Wild Plants
✓ Mail Order	✓ Grasses	Individual Species Seed	✓ Collect Wild Seed
Price List/Catalog	✓ Wildflowers	Contract Grow Seed	

Morgan Lane Nursery
Rt. 1, Box 812 / 812 Morgan Lane
Ingleside, TX 78362
(512)776-2167

Percentage of the business in native species: 50

Type of business:	Primary plant focus:	Wildflower seed offered:	Propagation methods:
✓ Retail	✓ Trees	Regional Seed Mixes	✓ Propagate Plants
Wholesale	✓ Shrubs	Custom Mixes	Collect Wild Plants
Mail Order	Grasses	Individual Species Seed	Collect Wild Seed
Price List/Catalog	Wildflowers	Contract Grow Seed	

Native Plants, Inc./Coyle Garden
Rt. 2, Box 326 / 11002 Bowler Road
Waller, TX 77484
(713)351-0522

Percentage of the business in native species: 30

Type of business:	Primary plant focus:	Wildflower seed offered:	Propagation methods:
Retail	✓ Trees	✓ Regional Seed Mixes	✓ Propagate Plants
✓ Wholesale	✓ Shrubs	✓ Custom Mixes	✓ Collect Wild Plants
Mail Order	✓ Grasses	Individual Species Seed	Collect Wild Seed
Price List/Catalog	✓ Wildflowers	Contract Grow Seed	

Native Plants, Inc./Coyle Garden
P. O. Box 420183
Houston, TX 77242-0183
(713)495-2627

Percentage of the business in native species: 30

Type of business:	Primary plant focus:	Wildflower seed offered:	Propagation methods:
Retail	✓ Trees	✓ Regional Seed Mixes	✓ Propagate Plants
✓ Wholesale	✓ Shrubs	✓ Custom Mixes	✓ Collect Wild Plants
✓ Mail Order	✓ Grasses	✓ Individual Species Seed	✓ Collect Wild Seed
Price List/Catalog	✓ Wildflowers	✓ Contract Grow Seed	

Native Son Plant Nursery
14226 B Hwy 71 West
Austin, TX 78738
(512)263-3205

Percentage of the business in native species: 100

Type of business:	Primary plant focus:	Wildflower seed offered:	Propagation methods:
✓Retail	✓Trees	✓Regional Seed Mixes	✓Propagate Plants
✓Wholesale	✓Shrubs	✓Custom Mixes	✓Collect Wild Plants
Mail Order	✓Grasses	✓Individual Species Seed	✓Collect Wild Seed
Price List/Catalog	✓Wildflowers	Contract Grow Seed	

Neiman Environments Nursery
Rt. 1, Box 48
Flower Mound, TX 75028
(214)539-9883

Percentage of the business in native species: 10

Type of business:	Primary plant focus:	Wildflower seed offered:	Propagation methods:
✓Retail	✓Trees	✓Regional Seed Mixes	✓Propagate Plants
Wholesale	✓Shrubs	Custom Mixes	✓Collect Wild Plants
✓Mail Order	Grasses	✓Individual Species Seed	Collect Wild Seed
Price List/Catalog	✓Wildflowers	Contract Grow Seed	

Oak Hill Native Plant Nursery
792 Oakdale Drive, Sunset Valley West
Austin, TX 78745
(512)892-0690

Percentage of the business in native species: 95

Type of business:	Primary plant focus:	Wildflower seed offered:	Propagation methods:
✓Retail	✓Trees	Regional Seed Mixes	✓Propagate Plants
✓Wholesale	✓Shrubs	Custom Mixes	✓Collect Wild Plants
Mail Order	✓Grasses	Individual Species Seed	Collect Wild Seed
Price List/Catalog	✓Wildflowers	Contract Grow Seed	

PLT Wholesale Nursery
P. O. Box 1026 / Rt. 1, Box 7J
Georgetown, TX 78627
(512)863-7386

Percentage of the business in native species: 40

Type of business:	Primary plant focus:	Wildflower seed offered:	Propagation methods:
Retail	✓ Trees	✓ Regional Seed Mixes	✓ Propagate Plants
✓ Wholesale	✓ Shrubs	Custom Mixes	✓ Collect Wild Plants
Mail Order	Grasses	Individual Species Seed	✓ Collect Wild Seed
Price List/Catalog	✓ Wildflowers	Contract Grow Seed	

Prairie Restoration
6508 Welch
Fort Worth, TX 76133
(817)292-5588

Percentage of the business in native species: 100

Type of business:	Primary plant focus:	Wildflower seed offered:	Propagation methods:
✓ Retail	Trees	Regional Seed Mixes	✓ Propagate Plants
✓ Wholesale	Shrubs	✓ Custom Mixes	Collect Wild Plants
Mail Order	Grasses	✓ Individual Species Seed	✓ Collect Wild Seed
Price List/Catalog	✓ Wildflowers	Contract Grow Seed	

Radiance Growers
Rt. 6, Box 1001
Austin, TX 78737
(512)288-4316

Percentage of the business in native species: 80

Type of business:	Primary plant focus:	Wildflower seed offered:	Propagation methods:
Retail	Trees	Regional Seed Mixes	✓ Propagate Plants
✓ Wholesale	✓ Shrubs	Custom Mixes	✓ Collect Wild Plants
Mail Order	Grasses	Individual Species Seed	Collect Wild Seed
Price List/Catalog	Wildflowers	Contract Grow Seed	

Red Barn Nursery
6507 Airport Blvd.
Austin, TX 78752
(512)452-7523

Percentage of the business in native species: 10

Type of business:	Primary plant focus:	Wildflower seed offered:	Propagation methods:
✓ Retail	✓ Trees	✓ Regional Seed Mixes	✓ Propagate Plants
✓ Wholesale	✓ Shrubs	Custom Mixes	Collect Wild Plants
Mail Order	✓ Grasses	✓ Individual Species Seed	Collect Wild Seed
Price List/Catalog	✓ Wildflowers	Contract Grow Seed	

Robinson Seed Co.
1113 Jefferson Drive
Plainview, TX 79072
(806)293-4959

Percentage of the business in native species: 100

Type of business:	Primary plant focus:	Wildflower seed offered:	Propagation methods:
✓ Retail	Trees	Regional Seed Mixes	Propagate Plants
✓ Wholesale	Shrubs	Custom Mixes	Collect Wild Plants
✓ Mail Order	✓ Grasses	Individual Species Seed	Collect Wild Seed
Price List/Catalog	Wildflowers	Contract Grow Seed	

Samadhi Farms
Rt. 2, Box 173
Bastrop, TX 78602
(512)285-2661

Percentage of the business in native species: 90

Type of business:	Primary plant focus:	Wildflower seed offered:	Propagation methods:
✓ Retail	✓ Trees	Regional Seed Mixes	✓ Propagate Plants
✓ Wholesale	✓ Shrubs	Custom Mixes	✓ Collect Wild Plants
Mail Order	Grasses	Individual Species Seed	✓ Collect Wild Seed
Price List/Catalog	✓ Wildflowers	Contract Grow Seed	

Scherz Landscape Co.
Box 60087 (Zip 76906) / 2225 Knickerbocker Road
San Angelo, TX 76904
(915)944-0511

Percentage of the business in native species: 35

Type of business:	Primary plant focus:	Wildflower seed offered:	Propagation methods:
✓ Retail	✓ Trees	Regional Seed Mixes	✓ Propagate Plants
Wholesale	✓ Shrubs	Custom Mixes	· Collect Wild Plants
Mail Order	Grasses	Individual Species Seed	✓ Collect Wild Seed
Price List/Catalog	Wildflowers	Contract Grow Seed	

Seeds & Stuff
P. O. Box 836
Willis, TX 77378
(409)856-4821

Percentage of the business in native species: 95

Type of business:	Primary plant focus:	Wildflower seed offered:	Propagation methods:
Retail	✓ Trees	Regional Seed Mixes	✓ Propagate Plants
✓ Wholesale	✓ Shrubs	Custom Mixes	Collect Wild Plants
✓ Mail Order	Grasses	Individual Species Seed	✓ Collect Wild Seed
Price List/Catalog	Wildflowers	Contract Grow Seed	

Sharp Bros. Seed Co.
Rt. 9, Box 2, Hwy 87 North / 8700 Dumas Drive
Amarillo, TX 79108
(806)383-7772

Percentage of the business in native species: 16

Type of business:	Primary plant focus:	Wildflower seed offered:	Propagation methods:
✓ Retail	Trees	Regional Seed Mixes	✓ Propagate Plants
✓ Wholesale	Shrubs	Custom Mixes	Collect Wild Plants
✓ Mail Order	✓ Grasses	Individual Species Seed	✓ Collect Wild Seed
Price List/Catalog	Wildflowers	Contract Grow Seed	

Sunbelt Trees
16008 Boss Gaston
Richmond, TX 77469
(713)277-2433

Percentage of the business in native species: 10

Type of business:	Primary plant focus:	Wildflower seed offered:	Propagation methods:
Retail	✓ Trees	Regional Seed Mixes	Propagate Plants
✓ Wholesale	Shrubs	Custom Mixes	Collect Wild Plants
Mail Order	Grasses	Individual Species Seed	Collect Wild Seed
Price List/Catalog	Wildflowers	Contract Grow Seed	

Swamp Fox Herbs
Rt. 3, Box 807
Wimberly, TX 78676

Percentage of the business in native species: 90

Type of business:	Primary plant focus:	Wildflower seed offered:	Propagation methods:
✓ Retail	Trees	✓ Regional Seed Mixes	Propagate Plants
✓ Wholesale	Shrubs	Custom Mixes	Collect Wild Plants
✓ Mail Order	Grasses	✓ Individual Species Seed	✓ Collect Wild Seed
Price List/Catalog	✓ Wildflowers	Contract Grow Seed	

Tangram Nursery
Rt. 1, Box 155
Maxwell, TX 78656
(512)396-0667

Percentage of the business in native species: 40

Type of business:	Primary plant focus:	Wildflower seed offered:	Propagation methods:
✓ Retail	✓ Trees	Regional Seed Mixes	✓ Propagate Plants
✓ Wholesale	✓ Shrubs	Custom Mixes	Collect Wild Plants
Mail Order	Grasses	Individual Species Seed	Collect Wild Seed
Price List/Catalog	✓ Wildflowers	Contract Grow Seed	

Texas Native Trees
P. O. Box 817, 1006 Glass Drive
Leander, TX 78641
(512)259-3006

Percentage of the business in native species: 90

Type of business:	Primary plant focus:	Wildflower seed offered:	Propagation methods:
Retail	✓ Trees	Regional Seed Mixes	✓ Propagate Plants
✓ Wholesale	✓ Shrubs	Custom Mixes	✓ Collect Wild Plants
Mail Order	✓ Grasses	Individual Species Seed	Collect Wild Seed
Price List/Catalog	Wildflowers	Contract Grow Seed	

Texas Trees
P. O. Box 117
Giddings, TX 78942
(409)542-2611

Percentage of the business in native species: 100

Type of business:	Primary plant focus:	Wildflower seed offered:	Propagation methods:
Retail	✓ Trees	Regional Seed Mixes	✓ Propagate Plants
✓ Wholesale	✓ Shrubs	Custom Mixes	Collect Wild Plants
Mail Order	Grasses	Individual Species Seed	Collect Wild Seed
Price List/Catalog	✓ Wildflowers	Contract Grow Seed	

Turner Seed
Rt. 1, Box 292
Breckenridge, TX 76024
(817)559-2065

Percentage of the business in native species: 85

Type of business:	Primary plant focus:	Wildflower seed offered:	Propagation methods:
✓ Retail	Trees	Regional Seed Mixes	Propagate Plants
✓ Wholesale	Shrubs	✓ Custom Mixes	Collect Wild Plants
✓ Mail Order	✓ Grasses	✓ Individual Species Seed	Collect Wild Seed
Price List/Catalog	✓ Wildflowers	Contract Grow Seed	

Wildseed
16810 Barker Springs Road, Suite 218
Houston, TX 77084
(713)578-7800

Percentage of the business in native species: 90

Type of business:	Primary plant focus:	Wildflower seed offered:	Propagation methods:
Retail	Trees	✓Regional Seed Mixes	✓Propagate Plants
✓Wholesale	Shrubs	✓Custom Mixes	✓Collect Wild Plants
✓Mail Order	✓Grasses	✓Individual Species Seed	✓Collect Wild Seed
Price List/Catalog	✓Wildflowers	✓Contract Grow Seed	

UTAH

NPI
417 Wakara Way
Salt Lake City, UT 84108
(801)582-0144

Percentage of the business in native species: 40

Type of business:	Primary plant focus:	Wildflower seed offered:	Propagation methods:
Retail	✓Trees	✓Regional Seed Mixes	✓Propagate Plants
✓Wholesale	✓Shrubs	✓Custom Mixes	Collect Wild Plants
Mail Order	✓Grasses	✓Individual Species Seed	✓Collect Wild Seed
Price List/Catalog	✓Wildflowers	✓Contract Grow Seed	

VIRGINIA

Ingleside Plantation Nurseries
P. O. Box 1038
Oak Grove, VA 22443-0838
(804)224-7111

Percentage of the business in native species: 20

Type of business:	Primary plant focus:	Wildflower seed offered:	Propagation methods:
Retail	✓Trees	Regional Seed Mixes	✓Propagate Plants
✓Wholesale	✓Shrubs	Custom Mixes	Collect Wild Plants
Mail Order	Grasses	Individual Species Seed	Collect Wild Seed
Price List/Catalog	Wildflowers	Contract Grow Seed	

Mid-Atlantic Wildflowers
S/R Box 226
Gloucester Point, VA 23062
(804)642-4602

Percentage of the business in native species: 95

Type of business:	Primary plant focus:	Wildflower seed offered:	Propagation methods:
✓Retail	Trees	Regional Seed Mixes	✓Propagate Plants
✓Wholesale	Shrubs	Custom Mixes	Collect Wild Plants
✓Mail Order	Grasses	✓Individual Species Seed	✓Collect Wild Seed
Price List/Catalog	✓Wildflowers	✓Contract Grow Seed	

Virginia Natives
Wildside, P. O. Box 18
Hume, VA 22639
(703)364-1001

Percentage of the business in native species: 99

Type of business:	Primary plant focus:	Wildflower seed offered:	Propagation methods:
✓Retail	Trees	Regional Seed Mixes	✓Propagate Plants
✓Wholesale	Shrubs	Custom Mixes	Collect Wild Plants
Mail Order	Grasses	Individual Species Seed	Collect Wild Seed
Price List/Catalog	✓Wildflowers	✓Contract Grow Seed	

VERMONT

Putney Nursery Inc.
Rt. 5, Box 265
Putney, VT 05346
(802)387-5577

Percentage of the business in native species:

Type of business:	Primary plant focus:	Wildflower seed offered:	Propagation methods:
✓Retail	✓Trees	✓Regional Seed Mixes	✓Propagate Plants
Wholesale	✓Shrubs	Custom Mixes	Collect Wild Plants
✓Mail Order	Grasses	✓Individual Species Seed	Collect Wild Seed
Price List/Catalog	✓Wildflowers	Contract Grow Seed	

Vermont Wildflower Farm
U. S. Rt. 7
Charlotte, VT 05445
(802)425-3500

Percentage of the business in native species: 95

Type of business:	Primary plant focus:	Wildflower seed offered:	Propagation methods:
✓Retail	Trees	✓Regional Seed Mixes	Propagate Plants
✓Wholesale	Shrubs	✓Custom Mixes	Collect Wild Plants
✓Mail Order	Grasses	✓Individual Species Seed	✓Collect Wild Seed
✓Price List/Catalog	✓Wildflowers	Contract Grow Seed	

WASHINGTON

Abundant Life Seed Foundation
P. O. Box 772, 1029 Lawrence
Port Townsend, WA 98368
(206)385-5660

Percentage of the business in native species: 10

Type of business:	Primary plant focus:	Wildflower seed offered:	Propagation methods:
✓Retail	✓Trees	✓Regional Seed Mixes	✓Propagate Plants
✓Wholesale	Shrubs	✓Custom Mixes	Collect Wild Plants
✓Mail Order	Grasses	✓Individual Species Seed	✓Collect Wild Seed
Price List/Catalog	✓Wildflowers	✓Contract Grow Seed	

Brown Seed Co.
P. O. Box 1792
Vancouver, WA 98668-1792
(206)892-4111

Percentage of the business in native species: 85

Type of business:	Primary plant focus:	Wildflower seed offered:	Propagation methods:
Retail	✓Trees	Regional Seed Mixes	Propagate Plants
✓Wholesale	Shrubs	Custom Mixes	Collect Wild Plants
Mail Order	Grasses	Individual Species Seed	Collect Wild Seed
Price List/Catalog	Wildflowers	Contract Grow Seed	

Daybreak Gardens
25321 NE 72 Avenue
Battle Ground, WA 98604
(206)687-5641

Percentage of the business in native species: 95

Type of business:	Primary plant focus:	Wildflower seed offered:	Propagation methods:
✓Retail	✓Trees	Regional Seed Mixes	✓Propagate Plants
✓Wholesale	✓Shrubs	Custom Mixes	Collect Wild Plants
Mail Order	Grasses	Individual Species Seed	Collect Wild Seed
Price List/Catalog	Wildflowers	Contract Grow Seed	

Foliage Gardens
2003 128th Avenue SE
Bellevue, WA 98005
(206)747-2998

Percentage of the business in native species: 30

Type of business:	Primary plant focus:	Wildflower seed offered:	Propagation methods:
Retail	Trees	Regional Seed Mixes	✓Propagate Plants
✓Wholesale	Shrubs	Custom Mixes	Collect Wild Plants
✓Mail Order	Grasses	Individual Species Seed	Collect Wild Seed
Price List/Catalog	Wildflowers	Contract Grow Seed	

Friends of the Trees
P. O. Box 1466
Chelan, WA 98816
(509)687-9714

Percentage of the business in native species: 40

Type of business:	Primary plant focus:	Wildflower seed offered:	Propagation methods:
✓Retail	✓Trees	Regional Seed Mixes	✓Propagate Plants
Wholesale	✓Shrubs	Custom Mixes	Collect Wild Plants
✓Mail Order	Grasses	✓Individual Species Seed	✓Collect Wild Seed
Price List/Catalog	✓Wildflowers	Contract Grow Seed	

Frosty Hollow Nursery
Box 53
Langley, WA 98260
(206)221-2332

Percentage of the business in native species: 70

Type of business:	Primary plant focus:	Wildflower seed offered:	Propagation methods:
✓Retail	✓Trees	Regional Seed Mixes	✓Propagate Plants
✓Wholesale	✓Shrubs	✓Custom Mixes	Collect Wild Plants
✓Mail Order	✓Grasses	✓Individual Species Seed	✓Collect Wild Seed
Price List/Catalog	✓Wildflowers	Contract Grow Seed	

J Hofert Forest Nursery
P. O. Box 88
Olympia, WA 98507

Percentage of the business in native species: 80

Type of business:	Primary plant focus:	Wildflower seed offered:	Propagation methods:
✓Retail	✓Trees	Regional Seed Mixes	✓Propagate Plants
✓Wholesale	Shrubs	Custom Mixes	Collect Wild Plants
Mail Order	Grasses	Individual Species Seed	Collect Wild Seed
Price List/Catalog	Wildflowers	Contract Grow Seed	

Julius Rosso Wholesale Nursery Co.
P. O. Box 80345, 6404 Ellis Avenue South
Seattle, WA 98108-0345
(206)763-1888

Percentage of the business in native species: 10

Type of business:	Primary plant focus:	Wildflower seed offered:	Propagation methods:
Retail	✓Trees	Regional Seed Mixes	✓Propagate Plants
✓Wholesale	✓Shrubs	Custom Mixes	✓Collect Wild Plants
Mail Order	Grasses	Individual Species Seed	Collect Wild Seed
Price List/Catalog	Wildflowers	Contract Grow Seed	

McLaughlin's Seeds
P. O. Box 550, Buttercup's Acre
Mead, WA 99021-0550
(509)466-0230

Percentage of the business in native species: 50

Type of business:	Primary plant focus:	Wildflower seed offered:	Propagation methods:
✓Retail	Trees	Regional Seed Mixes	✓Propagate Plants
✓Wholesale	Shrubs	Custom Mixes	Collect Wild Plants
✓Mail Order	Grasses	✓Individual Species Seed	✓Collect Wild Seed
Price List/Catalog	✓Wildflowers	✓Contract Grow Seed	

Plants of the Wild
P. O. Box 866
Tekoa, WA 99033
(509)284-2848

Percentage of the business in native species: 97

Type of business:	Primary plant focus:	Wildflower seed offered:	Propagation methods:
✓Retail	✓Trees	Regional Seed Mixes	✓Propagate Plants
✓Wholesale	✓Shrubs	Custom Mixes	Collect Wild Plants
✓Mail Order	Grasses	Individual Species Seed	Collect Wild Seed
Price List/Catalog	Wildflowers	✓Contract Grow Seed	

Silvaseed Company
Box 118
Roy, WA 98580
(206)843-2246

Percentage of the business in native species: 95

Type of business:	Primary plant focus:	Wildflower seed offered:	Propagation methods:
Retail	✓Trees	Regional Seed Mixes	✓Propagate Plants
✓Wholesale	Shrubs	Custom Mixes	Collect Wild Plants
Mail Order	Grasses	Individual Species Seed	Collect Wild Seed
Price List/Catalog	Wildflowers	Contract Grow Seed	

Stanwood Wholesale Nursery
3205 324th NW
Stanwood, WA 98292
(206)629-2918

Percentage of the business in native species: 25

Type of business:	Primary plant focus:	Wildflower seed offered:	Propagation methods:
Retail	✓Trees	Regional Seed Mixes	✓Propagate Plants
✓Wholesale	Shrubs	Custom Mixes	✓Collect Wild Plants
Mail Order	Grasses	Individual Species Seed	✓Collect Wild Seed
Price List/Catalog	Wildflowers	Contract Grow Seed	

WISCONSIN

Country Wetlands Nursery
South 75 - West 20755 / Field Drive
Muskego, WI 53150
(414)679-1268

Percentage of the business in native species: 95

Type of business:	Primary plant focus:	Wildflower seed offered:	Propagation methods:
✓Retail	Trees	Regional Seed Mixes	✓Propagate Plants
Wholesale	Shrubs	Custom Mixes	Collect Wild Plants
✓Mail Order	✓Grasses	✓Individual Species Seed	✓Collect Wild Seed
Price List/Catalog	✓Wildflowers	Contract Grow Seed	

Evergreen Nursery Co., Inc.
5027 County TT
Sturgeon Bay, WI 54235
(414)743-4464

Percentage of the business in native species: 20

Type of business:	Primary plant focus:	Wildflower seed offered:	Propagation methods:
Retail	✓Trees	Regional Seed Mixes	✓Propagate Plants
✓Wholesale	✓Shrubs	Custom Mixes	Collect Wild Plants
Mail Order	Grasses	Individual Species Seed	Collect Wild Seed
Price List/Catalog	Wildflowers	Contract Grow Seed	

Hauser's Superior View Farm
Rt. 1, Box 199
Bayfield, WI 54814
(715)779-5404

Percentage of the business in native species: 50

Type of business:	Primary plant focus:	Wildflower seed offered:	Propagation methods:
✓Retail	Trees	✓Regional Seed Mixes	✓Propagate Plants
✓Wholesale	Shrubs	Custom Mixes	Collect Wild Plants
✓Mail Order	Grasses	Individual Species Seed	Collect Wild Seed
Price List/Catalog	✓Wildflowers	Contract Grow Seed	

Little Valley Farm
RR 1, Box 287
Richland Center, WI 53581
(608)538-3180

Percentage of the business in native species: 100

Type of business:	Primary plant focus:	Wildflower seed offered:	Propagation methods:
✓Retail	Trees	✓Regional Seed Mixes	✓Propagate Plants
Wholesale	✓Shrubs	Custom Mixes	Collect Wild Plants
✓Mail Order	✓Grasses	✓Individual Species Seed	✓Collect Wild Seed
Price List/Catalog	✓Wildflowers	✓Contract Grow Seed	

Natural Habitat Nursery
4818 Terminal Road
McFarland, WI 53558
(608)838-3376

Percentage of the business in native species: 100

Type of business:	Primary plant focus:	Wildflower seed offered:	Propagation methods:
✓Retail	Trees	✓Regional Seed Mixes	Propagate Plants
✓Wholesale	Shrubs	✓Custom Mixes	Collect Wild Plants
✓Mail Order	✓Grasses	✓Individual Species Seed	✓Collect Wild Seed
Price List/Catalog	✓Wildflowers	Contract Grow Seed	

Prairie Nursery
P. O. Box 365
Westfield, WI 53964
(608)296-3679

Percentage of the business in native species: 100

Type of business:	Primary plant focus:	Wildflower seed offered:	Propagation methods:
✓Retail	Trees	✓Regional Seed Mixes	✓Propagate Plants
✓Wholesale	✓Shrubs	✓Custom Mixes	Collect Wild Plants
✓Mail Order	Grasses	✓Individual Species Seed	✓Collect Wild Seed
Price List/Catalog	✓Wildflowers	✓Contract Grow Seed	

Prairie Ridge Nursery / CRM Ecosystems, Inc.
9738 Overland Road
Mount Horeb, WI 53572-2832
(608)437-5245

Percentage of the business in native species: 100

Type of business:	Primary plant focus:	Wildflower seed offered:	Propagation methods:
✓Retail	Trees	✓Regional Seed Mixes	✓Propagate Plants
✓Wholesale	Shrubs	✓Custom Mixes	Collect Wild Plants
✓Mail Order	✓Grasses	✓Individual Species Seed	✓Collect Wild Seed
Price List/Catalog	✓Wildflowers	✓Contract Grow Seed	

Prairie Seed Source
P. O. Box 83
North Lake, WI 53064-0083

Percentage of the business in native species: 100

Type of business:	Primary plant focus:	Wildflower seed offered:	Propagation methods:
✓Retail	Trees	✓Regional Seed Mixes	✓Propagate Plants
Wholesale	Shrubs	✓Custom Mixes	Collect Wild Plants
✓Mail Order	✓Grasses	✓Individual Species Seed	Collect Wild Seed
Price List/Catalog	✓Wildflowers	Contract Grow Seed	

Strand Nursery Company
Rt. 3, Box 187
Osceola, WI 54020
(715)294-3779

Percentage of the business in native species: 100

Type of business:	Primary plant focus:	Wildflower seed offered:	Propagation methods:
✓Retail	Trees	Regional Seed Mixes	Propagate Plants
✓Wholesale	Shrubs	Custom Mixes	✓Collect Wild Plants
✓Mail Order	Grasses	Individual Species Seed	Collect Wild Seed
Price List/Catalog	✓Wildflowers	Contract Grow Seed	

Wehr Nature Center
9701 West College Avenue
Franklin, WI 53132
(414)425-8550

Percentage of the business in native species: 100

Type of business:	Primary plant focus:	Wildflower seed offered:	Propagation methods:
✓Retail	Trees	✓Regional Seed Mixes	Propagate Plants
Wholesale	Shrubs	Custom Mixes	Collect Wild Plants
Mail Order	Grasses	Individual Species Seed	✓Collect Wild Seed
Price List/Catalog	✓Wildflowers	Contract Grow Seed	

WYOMING

Absaroka Seed
Rt. 1, Box 97
Manderson, WY 82432
(307)568-2205

Percentage of the business in native species: 100

Type of business:	Primary plant focus:	Wildflower seed offered:	Propagation methods:
Retail	Trees	Regional Seed Mixes	✓Propagate Plants
✓Wholesale	Shrubs	Custom Mixes	Collect Wild Plants
✓Mail Order	✓Grasses	✓Individual Species Seed	✓Collect Wild Seed
Price List/Catalog	✓Wildflowers	✓Contract Grow Seed	

Mountain West Seeds
P. O. Box 1471
Cheyenne, WY 82003-1471
(307)634-6328

Percentage of the business in native species: 100

Type of business:	Primary plant focus:	Wildflower seed offered:	Propagation methods:
✓Retail	Trees	Regional Seed Mixes	Propagate Plants
Wholesale	Shrubs	Custom Mixes	Collect Wild Plants
✓Mail Order	Grasses	✓Individual Species Seed	✓Collect Wild Seed
Price List/Catalog	✓Wildflowers	Contract Grow Seed